T0384966

"As both a therapist and writer for children [...] chapters of *Reach Out to Me* compelling, moving and deeply thought-provoking. From both of those perspectives each chapter was an enlightening and fascinating picture of real-life therapy experience. The bravery and honesty of each account – from perplexed and inexperienced therapist, to (occasionally perplexed!) and experienced supervisor – reads like a gripping mini story of suspense and jeopardy, each told by thoughtful, sensitive, and strong authors. That these are real therapeutic accounts of encounters with young and very troubled clients – incorporating all the self-doubt, missteps, and soul-searching that such work entails – makes the book deeply valuable. And that so many of the stories have positive outcomes shows the urgent need for work like this. The skill, determination and creativity of the therapists and supervisors displayed in this book is inspiring. As are the clients' stories, explored so elegantly."

Julian Sedgwick, bodywork therapist and author of
Tsunami Girl; Voyages in the Underworld of Orpheus Black

"This book provides us with stories that bring together the combined depth, breadth, and aesthetic sensibilities of the wise women who seek to use their phronetic experience to make a welcoming space for children, who in the eyes of many may be seen as hard-to-reach. Their stories provide a refreshing moment to stop, listen, and join with them as they generously share their practice-based evidence. Through narrative they show the individualised and deeply relational manner in which they professionally care about the young people they meet. The book will be a valuable resource for trainee child and adolescent therapeutic practitioners, particularly those working with an integrative model. McInerny ends the volume with a thought-provoking chapter entitled 'Why can't you reach me!'. This is the key message of the book – not how do we enable hard-to-reach children to access the models of work we want to provide, but what must we do as therapists to ensure that our style of work adapts to children to enable them to connect with us and the world without being diminished."

Fiona Peacock, PhD, BACP Senior Accredited Counsellor/
Psychotherapist, Co-Lead Child and Adolescent Psychotherapeutic
Counselling programme, Faculty of Education, University of Cambridge,
Co-director Theraplay® UK

"I really enjoyed reading this book and found it profoundly moving and life-affirming how each of the children, despite complex and sometimes desperate situations, were reached. *Reach Out to Me* presents a series of heartwarming stories that demonstrate a range of approaches which successfully engage hard-to-reach young people. Whilst the book describes the therapist–client relationship within the therapeutic space, parallels can be drawn across a range of professional contexts engaging hard-to-reach young people within a significant trusting relationship. The insight which the therapists give into their own feelings as the therapeutic relationship develops makes this an immensely relatable book. As an education professional working with young people who present in many of the ways the clients in this book do, I found the reflections in the chapters particularly helpful to support my own approaches. This book is warmly recommended."

Nadine Herbert, teacher and centre lead of a specialist provision for children who are hard-to-reach

Using Art, Play, Metaphor, and Symbol with Hard-to-Reach Young Clients

This book demonstrates some of the unique ways in which therapists can help complex and vulnerable clients considered "hard-to-reach", using arts media and play.

Using a wealth of case studies, contributors describe their unique therapeutic attempts to reach clients who, for various reasons, seem unreachable. These moving therapeutic journeys are described in a phenomenological, auto-ethnographic way by the therapists themselves, as a series of "snapshot" glimpses into the therapy room. The therapists describe how combinations of art, play, metaphor, and imagination have helped them navigate the complex pathways to reach their clients. Each chapter is fully supported by the contributing therapists' own selection of theoretical ideas and analysis.

The book will help therapists consider innovate creative approaches in their work with clients who have been deemed too complex to work with in individual therapy, emphasising the importance of play and arts resources in helping them achieve this.

Aileen Webber is a Gestalt and Integrative Arts Psychotherapist who works with children and adults and also works as a supervisor and consultant to other therapists.

James Webber is an artist, musician and writer. His songs have appeared in numerous films and TV shows. He is the editor and main contributor of the print newspaper *Le Journal*, published by Overheard Le Labo.

Using Art, Play, Metaphor, and Symbol with Hard-to-Reach Young Clients

Reach Out To Me

Edited by
Aileen Webber and James Webber

LONDON AND NEW YORK

Cover image: © Getty Images

First published 2023
by Routledge
4 Park Square, Milton Park, Abingdon, Oxon OX14 4RN

and by Routledge
605 Third Avenue, New York, NY 10158

Routledge is an imprint of the Taylor & Francis Group, an informa business

British Library Cataloguing-in-Publication Data
A catalogue record for this book is available from the British Library

Library of Congress Cataloging-in-Publication Data
Publication Data
Names: Webber, Aileen, editor. | Webber, James (Editor), editor.
Title: Using art, play, metaphor, and symbol with hard-to-reach young clients: reach out to me / edited by Aileen Webber and James Webber.
Description: Abingdon, Oxon; New York, NY: Routledge, 2023.
| Includes bibliographical references and index.
| Identifiers: LCCN 2022031779 (print) | LCCN 2022031780 (ebook) | ISBN 9780367755720 (hardback) | ISBN 9780367755713 (paperback) | ISBN 9781003163015 (ebook)
Subjects: LCSH: Child psychotherapy--Case studies. | Art therapy for children--Case studies. | Play therapy--Case studies.
Classification: LCC RJ504 .U85 2023 (print) | LCC RJ504 (ebook) | DDC 618.92/8914--dc23/eng/20220824
LC record available at https://lccn.loc.gov/2022031779
LC ebook record available at https://lccn.loc.gov/2022031780

ISBN: 978-0-367-75572-0 (hbk)
ISBN: 978-0-367-75571-3 (pbk)
ISBN: 978-1-003-16301-5 (ebk)

DOI: 10.4324/9781003163015

Typeset in Bembo
by SPi Technologies India Pvt Ltd (Straive)

For the lost and unreachable
everywhere

Contents

Figures

Editors

Aileen Webber is a Gestalt and integrative arts psychotherapist (UKCP) who has been working with adults and children in private practice in Cambridge for over 20 years. She is also a qualified supervisor of arts-based therapists. She set up and managed a multidisciplinary enhanced resource within a mainstream school for children with physical, emotional and learning difficulties, and worked as an advisor and consultant for others working with children with additional needs. She is the author of various resource materials and has also written a book about transformational moments in the therapy room titled *Breakthrough Moments in Arts-Based Psychotherapy* (2017) edited by James Webber.

James Webber is an artist, musician and writer. His songs have appeared in numerous films and TV shows. He is the editor and main contributor of the print newspaper *Le Journal*, published by Overheard Le Labo. His editing credits include the book *Breakthrough Moments in Arts-Based Psychotherapy* by Aileen Webber (2017).

Contributors

Jude Adcock is an arts-based counsellor, psychotherapist, clinical supervisor, academic mentor and Doctoral researcher based near Cambridge. After studying for her Diploma in Adlerian Counselling she studied for her master's degree at the University of Cambridge before commencing Doctoral studies at The Metanoia Institute. Jude is passionate about encouraging the development of personal agency, by using the creative arts, in adults and young people who have suffered from adverse childhood experiences. She enjoys working with children, adolescents and adults. Regularly contributing to therapeutic journals, Jude loves to write and enjoys playing the violin and cello.

Angela Amos is an arts-based child therapist working in private practice in Cambridge. She has extensive experience of working as a therapist in a variety of local primary schools. She is also a qualified supervisor and supports a range of qualified and trainee arts-based therapists privately alongside providing supervision for a local charitable organisation. Previously she set up and managed a school counselling service, and has also worked as a Parent-Child therapist. She is particularly interested in Jungian Sandplay, Clay Therapy and creating therapeutic stories. She is the author of: "Can I Tell You about Multiple Sclerosis …?" An informative storybook for children. She is also a co-creator of the *Therapeutic Story StartUps* resource.

Sarah Attle works across a number of Cambridgeshire schools as a child and adolescent integrative therapist and clinical lead, providing arts- and play-based 1:1 therapy, group work, parental and teacher support, together with mental health education and training. She has also produced written resources for both children and parents. Sarah first practised as a family law solicitor and mediator for ten years, before taking time out of paid employment whilst her three children were young. Extensive involvement in local primary schools, most noticeably as a school governor for over 15 years, motivated her to retrain as a psychotherapeutic counsellor, completing a Post-Graduate Diploma and Masters at the Faculty of Education, University of Cambridge.

Elizabeth Bond worked for a year in a South African children's home with very young children before training as a musician at Oxford and the Royal College of Music.

After performing, she became a music specialist in several primary and secondary schools inspiring children to sing and play. This contributed to her later changing from teaching and embarking on child and adolescent psychotherapy Master's training using the arts, as she saw how powerful a one-to-one relationship can be in contributing to the well-being of school-age children. She has worked for three different charities as a psychotherapist alongside private work, strongly believing in the accessibility of provision and early intervention for children and adolescents. She loves her work and hopes that she will always remain playful and open to what children bring to the therapy room.

Lucy Jayne is an arts-based Child & Adolescent Psychotherapeutic Counsellor, working in schools and in private practice and has considerable experience of working with children in the care system and post adoption. Lucy is also an Equine Assisted Growth and Learning Association (EAGALA) certified Mental Health Professional (US-based training and certification) and is part of a small Equine Assisted Psychotherapy (EAP) practice. Lucy has her own horses and undertook a research study, as part of her M.Ed. degree at the University of Cambridge, based on her observations of EAP with a group of young people.

Suzanne Little has a long career working as a specialist teacher with children and young adults with profound complex needs. She has created an innovative method of using a colour tent to cut out sensory clutter and overload for students with multiple disabilities and severe cerebral visual impairment (CVI). A practice paper was published about colour tent therapy in The British Journal of Visual Impairment in 2015, which was co-authored with Professor Gordon Dutton. An audit study was co-authored with Professor Rachel Pilling a consultant ophthalmologist in 2019. Articles about Multisensory work, for children with complex needs, were published in a special needs magazine 1990–2005 and presentations about tent work given nationally and internationally. Tent therapy is being used by many specialist teachers and parents across the country alongside creating an assessment framework. Suzanne is a trustee of the CVI society, UK, which is linked to a feasibility study with Great Ormond Street in the foreseeable future.

Amy McInerny holds qualifications as a Youth Worker, a Child and Adolescent Psychotherapeutic Counsellor and a CYP-IAPT Supervisor (CWP Programme). She has enjoyed a varied career, delivering front-line services to children and young people experiencing diverse social and emotional difficulties. Her work with young cancer patients has had particular professional and personal significance. Amy currently works as a therapist, service manager, and mental health clinical lead in a charity providing holistic support to young people across Cambridgeshire and Peterborough. She is passionate about creating accessible, flexible and engaging therapeutic spaces that enable young people to explore their inner worlds creatively and safely. Amy is a strong advocate for the adolescent and young adult age range to be understood and recognised as a group with needs distinct from those of younger children and older adults and a firm proponent of the need for psychological health services, and those working within them, to adapt their thinking and practice in order to accommodate this population's unique developmental needs.

Carole Rawley is a child and adolescent psychotherapeutic counsellor working in schools and in private practice in Cambridge. She has always loved working with children and young people both as a teacher and youth worker. She did her Master's degree at Cambridge University, where her research interest was focused on bereavement, loss and change in adolescents. Carole's passion for teaching and mentoring continues alongside her clinical work. She has mentored teachers, developed and taught many parenting courses, mentors and supervises therapists. She recently had the privilege of travelling to Mongolia to help train school social workers who are working with traumatised children.

Jane Unsworth is a former youth worker and teacher, now a psychotherapeutic counsellor. She was educated at Cambridge University at Undergraduate and Master's level and has worked in various settings with children and young people over the past 30 years. She has had the privilege to know, love, and learn from many autistic people and is proud to consider herself an autism ally.

Koren Wilmer works in her own private therapeutic play and arts-based practice specialising with children and young adults with autism. Having qualified as a music therapist from the Guildhall School of Music and Drama in 1992, she worked first for the NHS in a long-stay institution for Adults with Learning Disabilities. In 1996, she opened her own private practice where she found herself working predominantly with children on the autistic spectrum, referred by their parents. To deepen her knowledge of autism and enhance her practice she undertook further postgraduate training in Asperger's Syndrome; Integrative Arts therapy and also Play Therapy. She also travelled to America with one of her clients to take part in the Son-Rise training programme (a play-based intervention which trains carers to set up and run home-based programmes to promote communication). Guided by her best teachers – the children with whom she has the privilege to work – her practice is now an eclectic mix of creative and playful techniques to support and enable communication and self-expression in a stress-free environment.

Foreword
Snapshot from the Doorstep

James Webber

I am eight years old and sat on the doorstep of our family home.

I have run away from school again.

I never know where to go except home, and yet I don't have a key so I just sit here on the step.

It's difficult to describe the feelings that have brought me here today. I didn't walk out of school in the middle of the day because I wanted to rebel. I don't want to be badly behaved, or draw attention to myself, and I certainly don't want to worry my school or my parents.

I understand it is not something I am supposed to be doing, and yet here I am, calmly watching myself do it again.

Sooner or later my mother will appear, having been contacted by the school. She will arrive on her bicycle at the house – no doubt relieved to find me on the doorstep rather than a more terrifying version of missing. She will never show any anger or judgement. Instead, she will sit down on the step beside me, and kindly and quietly ask why we are here again today.

Her kind and informal interviews on the doorstep will eventually lead me to be able to express that the problem I have with school is that they keep telling me what to write and learn about, while I long to write my own poems and stories. She will contact the school and arrange for me to be taken out of class twice a week for an hour and supervised while I write my own work.

One day, in many years to come, I will come to realise that she has helped to save my soul...

★★★

This is a book about how psychotherapy and an accompanying use of the arts can help young people find themselves and the world.

The truth is – although I couldn't have articulated it at the time – as a child I was hard to reach. I spent a large part of my childhood feeling alone in a bubble, unable to create a bridge from where I was to where the rest of the world seemed to be. How could I get to the rest of the planet from here?

It can feel difficult for any person to reach the world from their own little corner of it. We are thrust into the midst of a chaotic, random existence, and it can prove uniquely challenging to discover how we might fit in.

There is something hard to reach by definition about being a child. It can feel an impossible distance to reach oneself, let alone the grownups who tower above us and so confidently persuade us of the "correct" things to think and do.

But some children have an even harder time – whether it's from a disability or learning issue; difficulties at home – such as parental divorce, abuse or family illness, or even a pandemic. All of these events and circumstances can magnify the already vast-seeming divide between a young person and the world.

I was one of the lucky ones. I had a mother who not only refused to dismiss my existential problems but who understood enough about the world to share them. She reached me by demonstrating that I was not alone in my bubble, showing me that she had one too, and that we could visit one another from time to time.

This was many years before I became a writer, and my mother became a psychotherapist. There was always a therapeutic aspect to my art, and it was perhaps inevitable that art would end up being a critical part of her therapeutic practice. These days I seek to reach people through my work, while she uses the vehicle of art to help her clients be reached.

To be able to edit this book with my mother is a singular joy. It feels as though we now both sit on the doorstep together, each of us with the lifelong lessons we have learned (and continue to learn); both of us filled with hope that this book might be useful to therapists, clients and casual readers alike, in understanding the many ways psychotherapy and the arts can help young clients who are hard-to-reach, make the necessary connections they need to improve their lives.

Introduction

Arrival in the Land of Stories

Aileen Webber and James Webber

An existentialist might remind us that the mere fact of being human makes a person hard to reach. We are each of us trapped in our own potentially solipsistic universe, forced to take an endless leap of faith that other people have minds like ours, and share a similar phenomenological experience to us. But we can never be sure. Is it any wonder then that life can sometimes feel fraught with difficulties stemming from our uniquely human predicament – especially for a young child, whose developmental mind is still getting used to the shock of existence?

Many of the expressions that we casually use in everyday conversation capture the importance of reaching out and connecting with one another. "We tried to reach you today," the Amazon failed-delivery email tells us. We *reach* for a hand, reach for the stars, get within reach of the prize. When we are disenfranchised, we might feel lost, out of reach or "unreachable". These idioms serve to remind us how much our understanding of human relations tends to be structured around the ways in which we successfully connect with other people.

It is already the task of the psychotherapist to assist her clients in feeling reached – met, acknowledged, innocent, loved, free, "normal," independent, strong, safe, comfortable in their own skin. But when these clients are young people, the therapeutic work becomes even more challenging. Many children have not yet developed an ability to triangulate with the issues they are tackling – the human condition is a mystery that is never really solved, although we tend to get more used to its peculiarities as we grow. And when a child is additionally hard to reach in their own uniquely circumstantial ways too, it can feel almost impossible for the therapist to know how to reach them.

Stories from the Therapy Room

The stories presented in this book are of brave, dedicated psychotherapists who have refused to give up in their attempts to reach clients who might appear to be particularly hard-to-reach. These therapists were forced to think outside the box, go above and beyond their usual therapeutic approach, and recalibrate many of the methods they traditionally use with a client. They are therapists who refused to give up, and who continued to search for ways to connect and assist their clients, even when all the usual entryways to their therapeutic process were blocked. I am in awe of them all.

This book has been clamouring to be written for a long time. For over a decade it has felt as though many of the stories contained here – stories from my own experience and those of therapists I have supervised – have continued pressing themselves to be told. As a therapist, I have experienced clients who are hard to reach, many of them children. And as a supervisor, I have had the privilege of listening to tales of the most amazing courage shown by young, "hard to reach" clients, whose imaginative therapists were able to reach them through art, play, metaphor and symbol.

It only felt fair that others would get a chance to hear these stories too and have an opportunity to learn from them. So here they are. Each of the chapters in this book has been written by one of many therapists I have supervised over the past ten years. They illustrate a wide variety of reasons why an individual young client might be considered hard to reach, and a variety of ways – using art, play, metaphor and symbol – that creative psychotherapists have managed to build extraordinarily successful bridges to reach them.

The Unreachable Child

For many years, I watched my own artistic, sensitive son struggling to conform to the demands of an education system that didn't know how to accommodate him. I didn't always know how to help him either, but I could relate to his desire to remain true to himself in spite of societal demands. I too had been a vulnerable child who remained out of reach, but for very different reasons. My father died when I was 16 years old and I packaged my childhood trauma away in a box in the cellar of my unconscious, truly believing there would be no need to ever open it again. But many years later, when I was drawn to train as a psychotherapist, I came to realise for the first time that there had been an unreachable child trapped inside that box. And it wasn't too late to reach her now.

Standard "talk therapy" didn't help free the "unreachable child" within me, because my family's taboo not to speak about the trauma that had occurred remained so powerful. But I was required to attend therapy as part of my training, and after several false starts, one particularly gifted therapist found a way to reach through the wall of silence to reach her. This therapist had encouraged me to try using *the arts* in our therapy sessions. It was a revelation that finally enabled my unreachable child's story to begin to be told.

To start with, the banished child could not speak for herself. Then one day, in a particularly memorable session, an exceptionally creative therapist suggested that the silenced part of me might *spell out* her plight with an alphabet chart. I had told this therapist about children I was working with at the time, some of whom used an alphabet board to spell out what they wanted to say (as described in Chapter 12 of this book, "The Silent Voice"). Over time, my unreachable child found a way to spell out her own story, at first very slowly; but by the end of the required therapy of my training, she had learned to dance her story, paint her story, write and act out her story, *over and over again*. A story that for so many years could never be told was at last released, through the metaphor of art, dance, sand tray, drama, music and poetry.

Reached by Art

My hidden inner child had found her voice and her story was able to be told in many different ways, through differing media and approaches. It feels similarly important now that these stories of my courageous therapists and clients have a chance to be told. I hope they will come to life for readers through the case studies presented in these remarkable tales and snapshots from the therapy room.

When clients are trying to explain that they feel lost or unreachable, they will frequently be unable to use ordinary speech to communicate their difficulties. They might however be able to present a mental image of how they feel, or choose a postcard, or make a clay image, or draw or paint a picture of what they are thinking and feeling. These may include images of isolation, powerlessness, being silenced, being scared, feeling jealous, feeling lost or trapped, drowning, sinking or being caught somewhere. The idiom that a *picture paints a thousand words* comes to mind.

For example, within this book, young client Lily, declares that her "heart hurts" in Chapter 2. In Chapter 12, Samuel chooses a picture postcard of an octopus tangled up in a chain, thrashing around on huge waves to explain how he feels in his world. Armardi, in Chapter 7, does not use words at all, but rather paints stunning pictures to communicate being lost in a mire of shame. Sarah, in Chapter 1, crafts a sausage dog out of clay whose clay-legs keep collapsing and "who can't stand on her own feet." In doing so, she finds a metaphorical way to relate her experience of finding it difficult to be dependent on her mother whilst simultaneously trying to be independent from her.

Why Does a Child Become Hard to Reach?

The usual complexities of growing and developing as a child can bring all kinds of problems for a young person. These can include finding it difficult to fit into a family, into school, into society or even into their own skin. Eight key areas of experiences for a client have been described as: Physical, Spiritual, Behavioural, Sense of Self, Creative, Cognitive, Emotional and Social (Webber, 2017). Anything that changes from an area of experience (that might be experienced as positive or negative or *both*) is not part of a linear process but can present itself as part of a dynamical changing system, where one change causes multiple further changes across all the areas of experience. Any number of these areas of experience can become interwoven and affect a child's sense of self, as well as how they fit into the world around them (this includes how they *actually* fit into the world, as well as their own perceptions of how they do).

The stories presented in this book have been chosen to illustrate a wide variety of reasons why young people might be experienced as hard to reach in their therapy, and to demonstrate a variety of approaches utilised by therapists to reach them. For example, in Chapter 2, "My Heart Hurts," Lily is hard to reach as her behaviour is volatile and at times violent. Sarah behaves in a way that makes her hard to reach in Chapter 1, "A Sausage Dog Called Daisy" as she is guarded against getting close to anyone due to disruption in her early attachment to her parents. Oliver, in Chapter 3, "The Toad Croakers in the Land of Noise," has high functioning autism (previously known as Asperger's Syndrome) which makes him hard to reach, and his response to Music Therapy is consequently unique and fascinating – his therapist has to become creative and inventive in learning how she can reach him. Poppy arrives for therapy at five years old quite literally unable to use words at school in Chapter 4, "Florence Nightingale Is Just Outside the Door," and her therapist has to be uniquely creative in how they play together, in order to integrate all of her imaginary friends who act out different behaviours that Poppy doesn't have the confidence to inhabit.

In Chapter 12, "The Silent Voice," Samuel has physical and communication difficulties, and as his therapist, I have to learn new ways to enable him to use art materials in order to reach him. Martin in Chapter 9, "The Boy in the Orange Tent," has profound and multiple learning difficulties that include physical, emotional, behavioural and communication problems, and his therapist has to invent a unique way of reaching him by surrounding him in an orange tent. Mia in Chapter 10, "Lost in Lockdown," is trying to cope with being trapped at home during lockdown, when her house has recently been burgled and become a newly frightening place to be. Her therapist has to find creative ways to enable her to work through art, story and metaphor via a computer screen. Both Hattie in Chapter 8, "The Locust on The Platter," and Amardi in Chapter 7, "The Faceless Face," are hard to reach because of their feelings of shame. Their therapists have to find creative ways around this shame in order to reach them. Amardi's therapy is conducted almost entirely without words, through paintings; and Hattie is reached through metaphor, art and stories, so that she can eventually find a way to show what she cannot say in words. Charlie in Chapter 6, "The Boy Trapped in a Puffer Fish," is hard to reach because he believes his potential is limited by his circumstances. Through careful therapy he grows to realise that he has choices, and doesn't have to be forever caught and defined by his defences.

Chapter 5, "The Ripple Effect: Supervising Jane," is included to illustrate the power of using the arts in supervision. It shows how art can help a supervisor reach therapists who, through their counter-transference, may have become hard to reach themselves. Chapter 11, "Magical Horses: Equine Therapy" shows how play and metaphor involving animals can sometimes be used as a way to connect with hard-to-reach clients. Chapter 13, "Why Can't You Reach Me?" suggests some ways therapists can work creatively with hard-to-reach clients, and argues that all clients can eventually be reached, if only patient therapists can find creative and flexible ways to get there.

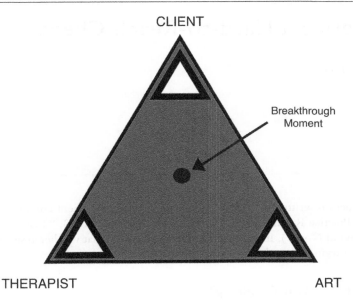

CLIENT

Breakthrough
Moment

THERAPIST   ART

Figure 0.1 The Triangular Relationship.

Adding Arts to the Therapeutic Relationship

Using the arts in therapy can be particularly powerful when working with children. Children are less likely to be able to speak about their issues directly and are generally more inclined to want to play. By incorporating art, play, metaphor and symbols into the therapeutic relationship, the traditional *dyadic* client-therapist relationship is expanded to a triangular relationship (see Figure 0.1).

Now the client and therapist don't just relate to each other during the therapy session, but also to the third entity of the art object, which is often created by the client or co-created by the therapist and client while the session takes place.

The triangle (see Figure 0.1) represents the inter-subjective matrix of the therapeutic relationship within arts-based psychotherapy. This triadic relationship is commonly used in art therapy theory (Dalley et al., 1993) and the diagram to show this visually was devised by my colleague and I, and first presented in my book *Breakthrough Moments in Arts-Based Psychotherapy* (Webber, 2017).

In this book, you will see many examples of this triangular relationship, between client-therapist-art, helping to create the bridges that allow young clients to be reached. The power of art is extraordinary. I have witnessed in my own son how healing it can be, and how liberating a vehicle of expression. And now, after over 20 years of using it in my practice, it is difficult to imagine doing therapy without it.

You will see it work its magic throughout these stories.

Meeting a Hard-to-Reach Client

Koren Wilmer

This poem is written by Koren Wilmer to an imaginary client coming to see her in her Practice Room, called The Music Box (see Chapter 3, "Toad Croakers in the Land of Noise"). It seems to capture so much of what we therapists feel when we are a trying to reach our young clients.

What Are You Thinking?

What are you thinking as you wander nonchalantly down the garden towards the Music Box?
Hands in your pockets, shoes half on and trodden down at the back.
Socks rucked, knees sporting the latest mishap in the playground.
What are you thinking?
What are you thinking as you ask me to roll you in the duvet and the carpet…
"Really tight,
Roll the ball over me.
Don't ask me about my feelings,
I don't know what I am feeling…
Perhaps I will never know.
Perhaps I don't want other people to know what's in my mind.
If you have a mind I'm not sure I want to be part of it".
OK, Ok let's just play…
Oliver sits on a trampette and allows me to surround him with percussion instruments.
He adds a bridge from the trampette to the sofa, and climbs and slides to and from his island.
He balances precariously on his wobbly bridge, enjoying his amazing agility and balancing skills.
I improvise at the piano with a sense of resigned incomprehension,
trying to forge a connection between his activity and my purpose.
What are you thinking?
How can I join you?

Chapter 1

A Sausage Dog Called Daisy

Angela Amos and Aileen Webber

Introduction

This chapter begins by discussing the use of clay in therapy with children. It continues by presenting the therapy of a ten-year-old girl, where she uses clay symbolically and metaphorically. Working therapeutically with clay through play, the use of symbols and metaphor is both finally discussed with reference to this child's therapy and relevant theoretical perspectives. The therapeutic benefits of working in a directive or a non-directive way are also discussed. Although two therapists have been involved in the writing of this chapter, only one worked with the client. The chapter has been written in the singular for ease of understanding.

What Is Symbolism and How Are Symbols Used in Therapy with Children?

In arts-based child therapy and play therapy, the child is offered a range of arts and play resources. Depending on the therapist's particular specialisms or training, a range of therapeutic approaches are on offer to the child, and generally, the therapist will work from an integrative platform. Sand tray, Jungian Sandplay, Clay Therapy, Therapeutic Story, Art, Model making, Music, Puppetry, Role Play can all be included. The child's engagement with these resources and modalities can bring them in contact with themes that can include: animals, humans, nature, mythology, religion, spirituality and fantasy.

The child will have some conscious associations with, for example, a chosen miniature object that they place in a sand tray or with an image that they have painted or made in clay. However, it can also be the child's unconscious mind that draws them to a particular object or to create a particular image. These objects or images have the potential to hold a symbolic meaning that can represent an aspect of their internal world or psyche. Souter-Anderson, when exploring Symbolism in Clay Therapy, suggests that a clay form has the potential to "make concrete something that hitherto has been unknown, unformulated or repressed" (Souter-Anderson, 2010). Jung makes a more general point that: "An image is symbolic

DOI: 10.4324/9781003163015-1

when it implies something more than its obvious and immediate meaning. It has a wider 'unconscious' aspect that is never precisely defined or fully explained" (Jung, 1964).

Often a symbol arises out of a confused mind or psyche. In order to try and make sense of the confusion, the psyche makes or selects an image, which holds the archetypal potential to illuminate the confusion and holds the key to solving it. Turner explains that the archetypal object or image that is chosen can be that which can hold "the qualities that the conscious position currently lacks, does not see, or fails to identify with" (Turner, 2005, p. 33).

Thus through the play or image making, the child has the opportunity to discover new strengths or resources that can help make sense of their internal puzzle. As Souter-Anderson asks, when reflecting on the clay image: "what is the psyche trying to bring into consciousness? That which is known can be worked with. That which is unknown remains hidden, depriving the client/maker of the opportunity of further self-development." (Souter-Anderson, 2010).

Additionally, the symbol can "hold unconscious unwanted feelings" as Winnicott suggests (Webber, 2017). In this instance, the image or symbol can be "embodied" with feelings giving it the potential to be a scapegoat for unwanted feelings or a talisman for a potential transformation.

As Kalff states "Symbols speak for the inner, energy laden pictures, of the innate potentials of the human being which, when they are manifested, always influence the development of man" (Kalff, 1980).

The Therapist's Role in the Symbolic Process

A therapist's role in the symbolic process is a significant one. Kalff when commenting on Sandplay therapy describes the role of the therapist as one that offers a "free and protected space" (Kalff, 1980). I feel that this can equally apply to all arts-based therapy. This "free and protected space" involves the therapist offering complete acceptance to the child, experiencing both pain and joy alongside them. The therapist needs to carefully manage the boundaries and protect the therapeutic space in such a way that the child feels free to express themselves – knowing that they are accepted and not alone. The therapist holds this safe space sensitively allowing enough time and space for the symbolic process to unfold.

Using an "observant attitude" (Turner, 2005), the therapist makes sense of, holds, and endures the child's work, holding the many possible meanings loosely. It is important for the therapist to have a curiosity and an on-going and developing knowledge of the potential symbolic meaning in the objects and images their client is drawn to. This is not about rushing to their nearest symbols dictionary to find a concrete interpretation but more about developing an on-going interest for the many possible meanings. This understanding runs alongside an understanding of the child's life history, their presenting problems and the felt sense the therapist has with the child and towards the object or image produced. When working with clay or other art forms, the therapist watches carefully how the image is made and is equally interested in the process of creation and in the image that is produced.

In some arts-based therapy, for example in Jungian Sandplay, the therapist remains entirely in metaphor. This can be very important as to make something conscious that sits unconsciously with the child too soon, may disturb the psyche's ability to heal itself. Within the metaphor of the story or play, the therapist using the "mirror neuron" network, will reflect back to the client the power and depth of their work and make what is happening in the tray a reality. (Stagg, 2020).

The environment facilitated by the therapist is very significant when working with the hard-to-reach child, as it can help to soften any tendency a child may have to become overly self-protective. The boundaries are held closely by the therapist and provide containment to the child and their therapeutic work. With effective attunement, mirroring and holding from the therapist, a child can work through internal struggles without ever coming out of the safety of the metaphor if they so wish; a safety that some more verbal therapies may struggle to offer. Whether or not a therapist works in or out of metaphor is an interesting question to explore, and we will pick this question up later on in this chapter. I present here a client example of the use of clay and story as a way to access and make sense of difficult feelings when working with a hard-to-reach client.

My Client Sarah

Sarah is a ten-year-old girl who has been referred for arts-based therapy by the school where I am currently based. The school staff are increasingly concerned as Sarah's attendance is falling rapidly. When she does arrive at school, Sarah appears to be experiencing extreme anxiety, she clings to her mum and screams hysterically. Once staff have physically separated Sarah from her mother, she takes a long time to calm down. Shutting off from any attempts by staff to calm her, she curls up on the floor in a ball and rocks and is unable to communicate with anyone. In class, Sarah's teacher describes her as "distracted" and says she finds it difficult to concentrate on her work. At playtime, she can often be seen pacing either in the playground or by the front entrance of the school. Any attempts to discuss and explore the situation are just ignored by Sarah. She seems unable to find the words to shed any light on her difficulties.

Sarah's mum and dad divorced several years ago. She is the only child. She lives predominantly with her mum, having occasional contact with her dad, who has a new wife and family. Sarah has a close relationship with her mum, choosing to spend time with her over her friends. Mum explains: "It's always been just me and Sarah, we haven't needed anyone else." Nine months previously, Sarah's mum without any warning disappeared out of Sarah's life, and Sarah was forced to live with her dad and step-siblings for a short period. It later materialised that Sarah's mum had been in prison briefly and both parents had wanted to spare Sarah the details.

In order for individual therapeutic work with Sarah and myself to become possible, I approach our beginning very carefully. Sarah and her mum are used to depending on each other. Although Sarah is my client, I feel that it is crucial to develop a secure relationship with mum before attempting any work with Sarah.

By gaining mum's trust, I can help hold and contain both of them in the transition towards Sarah beginning individual sessions. I choose initially to meet individually with mum, then we have two joint sessions with mum and Sarah together at her school. Mum helps by supporting Sarah's introduction into the therapy room and to some of the potential activities on offer.

In our first joint session, Sarah's mum draws a flower and we laugh together. Seeing mum's enthusiasm and experiencing her ease of relationship, helps Sarah to find the courage to tentatively pick up a pencil and slowly start to shade in one of the petals. In the second session, Sarah takes a further step and experiments with some clay. Led by her mum they both craft a clay version of themselves. Towards the end of the session, mum joins the two forms by linking their arms and Sarah leans into her mum and rubs her cheek against mum's sleeve.

For the first few individual sessions, mum brings Sarah to the session but this isn't sustainable due to her work commitments, so Sarah has to make the enormous step of bringing herself to our sessions.

A Sausage Dog Called Daisy

(Lens cited here refers to "Five Lenses of Theoretical Anchoring" (Souter-Anderson, 2010) explored later in the chapter.)

Sarah arrives suddenly through the therapy door. I can already feel her tension in the room. She stands by the closed door looking for direction from me, breathing rapidly. Her shoulders are hunched giving her the appearance of being smaller than she actually is. A long fringe covers one of her eyes and she fiddles with a piece of blue-tac in one of her hands. I notice how clammy her hands are and how sticky the blue-tac has become and I feel an immediate warmth towards her, aware of how difficult it must have been for her to arrive.

Sarah is almost immediately drawn to the clay. I start by asking her if she would like to choose a bit of clay from an assortment of pieces I have laid out on a slab. She chooses quickly. I suggest that she spends some time just getting to know the clay, to develop a sense of the touch, shape, texture, temperature, smell and weight (Lens 1). Then when Sarah seems ready, I encourage her to create something. Sarah looks up at me through her fringe. "What?" She pauses "It can be whatever I like?" she asks. I smile and nod.

Sarah starts by smoothing out the clay. The clay is quite firm so she adds some water to soften it a little. As I watch her smoothing out the clay, I notice her breathing begin to slow and I feel some of her tension begin to dissolve. It feels as though Sarah is smoothing out some of her own tension through the clay almost as though it has become an extension of herself (Lens 2 and Lens 3). I check out with her whether she would like me to make something alongside her. She nods. So while I am focusing on her and her model, I allow something to begin to form in my hands.

Sarah starts to roll the clay saying: "I'm making a dog. It's a Sausage Dog called Daisy." She rolls the clay into a long roll and starts to make legs. She struggles to fix the legs to the body, so that the dog can stand up independently. She makes

Figure 1.1 A Sausage Dog Called Daisy.

repeated attempts to secure the legs to the dog's body (Lens 4). I put this into words: "It seems difficult for that dog to stand up. Those legs are just not wanting to do what you want them to do."

Without looking at me, Sarah asks if I have watched a particular film. I haven't, so I ask her about it. Sarah explains: "It's about a dog who runs away from home because her Mum is too protective." We think a little more about this and Sarah says: "The dog is being cuddled too much." I respond by saying: "I guess it would be difficult for that dog, difficult to have much freedom to just be herself, to do her own things ..." (Lens 4).

When the legs have been successfully fixed on and the dog is able to stand, I give it what I have been making: a food bowl and a water bowl (see Figure 1.1). Sarah stands the dog next to the water bowl to drink from it. I explain that we are coming to the end of our session. I conclude: "It feels really important that this dog can stand on her own feet." Sarah pats the dog on her back. "Yes it is." She replies (Lens 5).

Reflection

Sarah's sausage dog, Daisy, seems to have held much potent meaning for her. Initially, the dog was unsteady and unable to stand on its own, and "being cuddled too much" as it seems Sarah might have felt at times. In this example, it seems that the embodied image, Daisy the sausage dog, moves from being a scapegoat of many of Sarah's complex feelings with regard to her mother into being a talisman for Daisy (and perhaps Sarah) and being able to imagine what it might be like to stand independently and be in her own space.

Sarah's need for independence has emerged through her clay image of Daisy the dog and this offers us a real opportunity to work with new awareness. Now visible to both of us, we can begin to explore in metaphor how it might feel for Daisy to be cuddled too much. I move it along further by suggesting a way that Daisy may feel restricted by too much cuddling. The session ends with Sarah clarifying that it is important for Daisy to be able to stand independently. I think we both know that Sarah is referring to herself, but we stay in the safety of the metaphor and I feel that Sarah is leaving with a sense of feeling understood.

The Rat and the Toilet Seat

(*Several weeks after her first session*)

Sarah is concentrating hard today. She presses her lips firmly together as she rolls out a piece of clay with her hands. She frowns as she starts to work the clay. "This feels heavy today," she says in a slightly accusatory manner. I remind her of the bowl of water available in case the clay needs more moisture, but I am also alerted to the possibility that Sarah is showing me some hard-to-reach material. Sarah looks at the water bowl but chooses not to add any water to the clay. She starts to slap the clay into shape, transferring it from palm to palm. The clay slaps loudly as it makes contact with her palms. Sarah directs me to make something while she works. I sense that she wants my attention to be slightly diluted from her activity. I feel a jarring sensation in my stomach and experience the sense that I'm being emotionally pushed away a little.

Sarah screws her face up as she pushes one end of her clay with her thumb and index finger. She leaves two indents where her fingers have been and moulds the end into a point. She rolls two small balls together and places them into the indents. I recognise these as eyes. Four legs are moulded and fixed to the body. A lot of time is taken on moulding the feet which are quite large and act to support the body to stand firmly onto the work board. I comment on how well the feet support the animal. Sarah doesn't respond. I may be interjecting too soon here or perhaps Sarah is too deep in her process to hear or respond to me in that moment. Next she makes a small bowl, which she fills with water and Sarah places this down below the animal's head. Then a tail is fixed to the animal. For the remainder of the session, Sarah concentrates on rolling tiny balls which she places around the animal.

"It's a rat." Sarah announces. "What have *you* made?" She asks in a slightly dismissive way. I look down into my cupped hands. "Some sort of bowl." I reply. I place the bowl next to the rat on the board and notice that it is in fact the shape of a toilet bowl. I feel curious about this creation. Why have I made a toilet? Sarah calls our joint work: "The Rat and the Toilet Seat" (see Figure 1.2).

On reflection after our session, I sense that Sarah is starting to explore emerging feelings of anger. I wonder if these are feelings within the transference of anger she felt about being rejected by her mum when she disappeared without explanation. Interestingly in our very next meeting, we share a very explosive session involving large amounts of runny clay and Sarah speaks about some angry feelings she has with her teacher, who she perceives has rejected her.

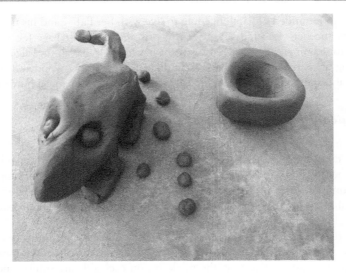

Figure 1.2 The Rat and the Toilet Seat.

In this session by working in metaphor with clay, Sarah is able to connect with some angry feelings for the first time. She struggles with the process initially commenting that the clay "feels hard today" and I am alerted to the fact that we may be moving into an area of the work that is hard to reach. Sarah perseveres and develops a rat and a bowl of water. The rat's excrement is scattered about. When working with children creating excrement in art therapy sessions, Felicity Aldridge came to the conclusion that "the work was about getting the feelings from inside, out" (Aldridge, 1998). My felt sense in the session with Sarah is that she is "getting out" some angry feelings.

Clay therapy allows the opportunity to attune deeply with the child's experience. Stern (1985) describes the beautiful dance between mother and infant, as the mother mirror's the infant's response and reflects this back to the infant. Similarly, an intimate dance can unfold between the therapist, child and the clay. "When the therapist is working intuitively with a deeper level of empathy and understanding, that is when the therapist is attuned to the client's needs, a knowing 'contact' is made" (Souter-Anderson, 2010). It is in this knowing 'contact' that I believe the clay toilet seat is formed, by me, as an unconscious response to Sarah's need for a container for her anger. Souter-Anderson explores the attuned relationship in detail in The Five Lenses of Theoretical Anchoring for use of Clay in Therapy (Souter-Anderson, 2010). This is cited in full at the end of this chapter.

I am curious about the choice of a rat and any potential meaning attached to this. A rat is thought to be a very intelligent creature. Interestingly in the Chinese culture, rats are considered to bring wealth through their intelligence. However, rats are also described as vermin and are often considered unwelcome visitors. They live off other people's food scraps and are often found in dark shadowy places. I am reminded of Sarah needing to live with her father and his new family, when her mother was suddenly placed in prison. This must have felt incredibly difficult for Sarah and I wondered if part of her had felt like an unwelcome guest, becoming an extra in this already established family. I also wondered if the rat perhaps also symbolises Sarah's desire to ease her mother's financial burden.

The Vandalising of the Tower of Connection

(*Before a holiday period towards the end of Sarah's therapy*)

Sarah takes a lump of clay and transfers it from one hand to the other. She doesn't seem sure what to make today. We talk about our break and the plans for Sarah's summer. Sarah is going away for a week to stay with her dad. She is feeling excited about spending time with him but also feeling anxious about leaving her mum.

Sarah takes a knife from the selection of tools. She cuts her lump of clay into two. She sits the two pieces so that they are facing each other. We look at the image together and notice how the markings on each side are similar and reflect back to each other. Sarah is about to move on when she suddenly decides to add a lolly stick across the top of both pieces. We notice together that the stick connects the two pieces of clay. Sarah calls her creation "The Tower of Connection." We have worked together for some time now, and it is our last session before a long summer break. I offer Sarah some self-drying clay to take home to use during the break if she chooses. She accepts the clay and wraps it in a separate plastic bag. I am hoping that the clay will act as a kind of transitional object for Sarah during our break, helping to maintain a link between us and her work (Figure 1.3).

Figure 1.3 The Tower of Connection.

Figure 1.4 The Vandalised Tower of Connection.

Just as Sarah is preparing to leave, she suddenly turns back. She runs over to the clay structure takes the lolly stick connecting the two halves and plunges it into one half. "What's happened here?" I ask. "It's been vandalised." Sarah replies, as she picks up her bag of holiday clay and runs out the door (Figure 1.4).

I sit and reflect over what has just happened. Our ending for the summer break has been so sudden, so abrupt and I am feeling stunned. I look at the clay image now "vandalised" and I am aware that my breathing has tightened and feels uncomfortable. In that moment, I am feeling in pain. I am reminded of how Sarah's relationship was severed with her mother so abruptly when she went into prison and how shocking and painful this must have felt for Sarah. Also the power in which the stick was forced into the clay has connected me to Sarah's anger and painful feelings around this. I am also reminded of our imminent break from therapy and despite preparing us as best I could, Sarah was perhaps letting me know how angry she felt about it. Sarah was possibly also letting me know that in her experience connections can become damaged in separation.

Reflection on Sarah's Therapy

Playing with Clay

Sarah directed her own work through the clay, although it was laid out in an accessible and manageable way to encourage its use within her sessions. Children play out many themes within Non-Directive Play, according to Ryan and Edge (2011). When the therapy is child-centred and the play is open to the child's choice, it is interesting to see what the client naturally chooses.

In Sarah's therapy I could recognise several themes being worked through as she made her stories of: The Sausage Dog called Daisy, The Rat and the Toilet Seat and The Vandalising of the Tower of Connection. Her work also included the more specific themes of independence/dependence, abandonment, and separation anxiety. Ryan and Edge's article is directed towards Non-Directive Play, but in reality, the choice of materials available provides a degree of direction on the part of the therapist. So, for instance, I discover that Sarah seems drawn to the clay after her joint sessions with her Mother at the beginning of the therapy and so I have slabs of clay displayed ready for her each session when she arrives for her therapy.

In a paper titled "Beyond Directive or Non-Directive: Moving the Conversation Forward," there is reference to a study by Britton et al. in 2005, where they found that directive and non-directive theoretical approaches in therapy with children produced comparable levels of overall effectiveness – ranging from moderate to high levels of therapeutic change. As a result of this, *integrative* play therapy is rapidly becoming the model intervention in the use of play in therapy.

The authors of this paper suggest that the either-or (black and white) debate is outdated. Which of these is used, is influenced by the therapist's personality and training alongside their world view, which ranges across: reactive: driven from without (behaviourism), driven from within (psychoanalysis) or seeing individuals as self-actualising (humanism) (ibid). Obviously, the unique needs of the client or their presenting issue will also influence whether the play is more or less directed by the therapist. Moreover, the authors state that it doesn't seem to be possible to be completely one or the other. Carl Rogers refers to client-centred therapy. It would appear that even when using a directive approach within a particular session, the therapist works from Rogers' core conditions (1961) of: unconditional positive regard, empathy and genuineness/congruence.

The authors conclude that the famous question by Paul of "What Treatment, by Whom, is Most Effective for This Individual with that Specific Problem, and Under What set of Circumstances?" (Paul, 1967), would seem to have moved the debate on to a "client-focused theoretical approach" tailor-made to the individual client. We would add that this could be a more or less client-centred or therapist-directed approach that could change from moment to moment within each session. For Sarah, I moved in and out of directing and not directing within each session, allowing it to be client-led in that she chose what to do next but equally co-creating how the work unfolded.

When to Stay in the Metaphor or Come Out of the Metaphor

Freeman states that: "A symbol can be thought of as the smallest unit of metaphor, it can be a word, an object or a mental image" (Freeman, 1990).

In the Five Lens of Therapeutic Anchoring, Lens Four points to a potential space that can produce both symbolic and metaphorical meaning through the active engagement with the imagination. Souter-Anderson describes Storying; working with the story created in the clay, Personifying; interviewing and having dialogue with the clay and Labelling; giving the clay form a title, as techniques that invite the therapist and child to work creatively within the metaphor.

We will now seek to understand Sarah's work further by taking a more detailed look at working through metaphor. A metaphor "…always communicates on at least two levels" simultaneously (Freeman, 1990). It "… combines what is already known in a new way to produce a new thing not yet fully understood" (Siegelman, 1990). Hence an image, an object in the therapy, or a story, is often able to be multi-dimensional and multi-layered and (this means it) can thus communicate on many levels all at once, some being conscious and others remaining unconscious. Hence to ask a child to explain their creation (clay piece, painting, sand tray) in words might be asking them to reduce it to one dimension only or indeed the client may not have any spoken words to explain what they have expressed in their therapeutic art work. In addition, Gordon reminds us that these multi-dimensional meanings can be surrounded with powerful feelings with a numinous quality. This he suggests is the essence of their importance for the potential for change in therapy. This idea is similar to Schaverien's concept of the "embodied image" where the image is imbued with powerful meaning that can include negative aspects and be a scapegoat for positive emotions or be a talisman for the client (Schaverien, 1999). I feel that Sarah's Sausage Dog held both these aspects in that it was a scapegoat for her difficult feelings and also a talisman for the possibility of change.

One of the key questions that therapists ask is when to stay in the metaphor and when to make the meaning of the metaphor more explicit to the child or to encourage them to do so themselves. A comment made by Lori Gottlieb in her fascinating books "Maybe you Should Talk to Someone" springs to mind here. She says it may seem that the patient often feels that they lead the way (or control the session) in their own way but in fact we therapists "pull the strings in our own ways – in what we say or don't say, what we respond to or hold on to for later, what we give attention to and what we don't" (Gottlieb, 2019). So when a child is working through metaphor, the therapist responds to this from moment to moment in what feels like the most appropriate way at that particular time in "what we say, or don't say, what we respond to or hold on to for later…" In order to gain some further perspective on this, it is helpful to apply something we have termed The Metaphor Continuum. (See Table 8.1, pg. 119.)

The Metaphor Continuum

With A Sausage Dog Called Daisy, Sarah indicates what the issues are for Daisy as she acknowledges the therapist mentioning that Daisy "needs to stand on her own feet" and this leads Sarah to refer to a film she has watched where the dog is "cuddled too much" and she allows the therapist's comment: "I guess it would be difficult for the dog, difficult to have much freedom to just be herself." This would seem to imply that therapist and client are moving between Level 2 in the table and Level 3.

In the "Rat and the Toilet Seat," we both seem to stay at Level 1. When I am reflecting on the story afterwards, I wonder if it's a way of Sarah preparing for an expression of her anger towards her mum for seeming to disappear out of her life when she went to prison and which is expressed through anger towards her teacher who she imagines is rejecting her.

In the "vandalising of the Tower of Connection," the multi-dimensional role of the metaphor within the clay work becomes apparent. Sarah makes explicit the connection between the two towers. I wonder if this is Level 1 of the Continuum Metaphor, as we both know it's about connection (between client and therapist) but don't refer to other connections that are important to Sarah. When Sarah names it "The Tower of Connection," she is perhaps moving to Level 7 for a fleeting moment – but in terms of the therapist and client rather than connecting it to her family story. Fascinatingly right at the end of the session, Sarah turns back and "vandalises the connection," naming it when the therapist asks "What's happened here?" Here she acts out how the metaphor may be connected to her own story and names the act (Level 3). Could this be Sarah moving from Level 2 to touching upon Level 7 to herself for a fracture of a second without naming it and dramatically leaving the room (Level 3). Equally maybe it could be better understood that she was at Level 2 in that she acted out her feelings of anger towards a broken connection (or the upcoming break in therapy with me) from the deep emotion of what happened when her mother disappeared without explanation.

We are not suggesting this is a precise or definitive way of speaking about the way symbol, metaphor and play may work in therapy. Instead, we are aiming to demonstrate the multi-dimensional, multi-layered and complicated ways that it can reach the client, and enable their psyche to be healed.

Conclusion

This chapter has described Sarah's use of clay in therapy with particular reference to the theories of clay, play, symbol and metaphor. Two frameworks, one for clay and one to understand the relevance of metaphor in Sarah's therapy, are utilised to try to understand the work more thoroughly. Having said this, I am very aware that some of the mercurial and alchemical processes in therapy are beyond logical explanation. Sometimes we just have to put theory aside and stand by in wonder at the way a client considered initially hard to reach can be reached by being given a bridge through the right arts medium at the right moment within the right therapeutic relationship.

Souter-Anderson – Five Lenses of Theoretical Anchoring for Clay Use in Therapy (with Examples of How This Applies to Sarah's Therapy)

Reprinted by permission from Dr Lynne Souter-Anderson

Note: This is not meant as an entirely linear process but one that can also oscillate between the Lenses.

Lens 1 – Making Contact

This is the stage of touching the clay physically and thereby making contact with the actual substance. If we are playing with clay, we are working with earth and this naturally links closely to Jungian theory. According to Stevens, psychologically the *prima materialis* are identical to the primal self.

I suggest that Sarah spends some time just getting to know the clay, to develop a sense of its touch, shape, texture, temperature, smell and weight.

Lens 2 – Play Space of Potential

Here we have the space of potential where through touching and playing with the clay, body and mind work together as one. Movement, massage and hypnosis with neuro-chemical processes may take the creator to altered states of consciousness.

I notice her breathing begin to slow and I feel some of her tension begin to dissolve. It feels as though Sarah is smoothing out some of her own tension through the clay. It feels as if the clay has become an extension of herself.

Lens 3 – Clay Play in the Presence of Another

As the creator plays with the clay in the presence of a therapeutic practitioner, the emotional contact often contributes towards an essence of exploration. What transpires through the play in the presence of another transmutes and "vaporises" up through the conical flask image into Lens 4.

As I watch her smoothing out the clay, I notice her breathing begin to slow...

I check out with her whether she would like me to make something alongside her. She nods. So while I am focusing on Sarah and her work, I allow something to begin to form in my hands.

Lens 4 – Bridging Space of Potential Lens

A second space of importance is that between Lens 4 and Lens 5 where an alchemical process enables symbolic and metaphorical contact by actively engaging the imagination.

Sarah struggles to fix the legs to the body, so that the dog can stand up independently. Sarah makes repeated attempts to secure the legs to the dog's body. I put this into words. "It seems difficult for that dog to stand up."

Lens 5 – Emerging Theme

The creating period now has an end result whether it is an image or process. Exploration of the created image or process often identifies existential themes.

I conclude: "It feels really important that this dog can stand on her own feet." Sarah pats the dog on her back. "Yes it is." She replies.

References

Aldridge, F. (1998). Chocolate and shit; aesthetics and cultural poverty in art therapy with children. *Inscape*, 3:1, 2–9.

Freeman, J. (1990). *Symbol, Story & Ceremony: Using Metaphor in Individual & Family Therapy*. London: W.W. Norton.

Gottlieb, L. (2019). *Maybe You Should Talk to Someone*. Australia/London: Scribe.

Jung, C.G. (1964). *Man and His Symbols*. London: Aldus Books.

Kalff, D. (1980). *A Psychotherapeutic Approach to the Psyche*. Boston, MA: Sigo Press.

Paul, G.L. (1967). Strategy of outcome of research in psychotherapy. *Journal of Consulting Psychology*, 31, 109–118.

Rogers, C.R. (1961). *On Becoming a Person: A Therapist's View of Psychotherapy*. London: Constable.

Ryan, V. & Edge, A. (2011). The role of play themes in non-directive play therapy. *Clinical Child Psychology & Psychiatry*, 1, 1–16.

Schaverien, J. (1999). *The Revealing Image*. London: Jessica Kingsley.

Siegelman, E.Y. (1990). *Metaphor & Meaning in Psychotherapy*. NY: Guildford Press.

Souter-Anderson, L. (2010). *Touching Clay, Touching What? The Use of Clay in Therapy*. Dorset, England: Archive Publishing, 157–159.

Stagg, E. (2020). Jungian sandplay for adults. *Therapy Today*, 31, 38–41.

Stern, D.N. (1985). *The Interpersonal World of the Infant*. US: Basic Books.

Turner, B. (2005). *The Handbook of Sandplay Therapy*. Cloverdale, CA: Temenos Press, 33, 45–49.

Webber, A. (2017). *Break through Moments in Arts-Based Psychotherapy*. London: Karnac.

Chapter 2

My Heart Hurts

Elizabeth Bond

Introduction

"I might not be here next week" my client had said, when her therapy sessions were well underway and in full flow. This unexpected ending brought to a close many months of therapeutic experience that had a profound effect on me as a clinician. Here is the story of this client's therapy and my reflections on it. When she scored her name into a clay model of her face (which she made for me as a gift when the therapy ended), it felt symbolic of her carving into me the experience of our time together.

When she was referred to me initially, there had been a lot of stress expressed by those managing her in school. She was described to me as being "unreachable", and containing her behaviour to keep her and the other children safe had become the main strategy of the school staff. Here you will see laid bare the struggles we had in connecting and reaching one another, and how I was eventually able to reach her by working with the Arts which formed a bridge over and under which her work could flow.

After giving some background about the referral, each therapy session is written in the present tense to show the immediacy of the encounter. After each session, I reflect on the therapeutic work and provide some of the theory underpinning it.

Referral and Preparation

Lily. A child of seven. How could such a young child already have such a reputation?

Everyone I talked to about Lily's referral in preparation for the commencement of her therapy emphasised how difficult she was. They described to me the volatility of her moods and behaviour and advised me of the need for a risk assessment and to have some help on standby during the therapy sessions.

She was so disruptive and violent in class that she was restricted to only very short mornings (mostly outside the classroom) with a teaching assistant (TA) in attendance. It was almost as though she was coming to therapy with something that you find on an electrical appliance – "Warning: Do not remove this label" followed by a list of possible hazards.

DOI: 10.4324/9781003163015-2

Lily had by then been at the school for five months. I was told that it was hard to predict how Lily would react in any given situation as nothing seemed consistent in her behaviour. The times were few and far between when they felt able to get alongside her and "get through to her". This was daunting and set up a tension in me – would I cope? Would this work? Would she even stay in the room? Was I experienced enough for such a child? As I prepared myself, Lily struck me as such a pretty name. What I had heard about her behaviour seemed incongruous with this, but I pondered: lilies are strong, tall, beautiful architectural flowers emerging from bulbs. I was interested in the layers of the bulb from which *this* Lily sprang and the soil in which she was planted.

I was informed that Lily had three older brothers and that her Dad was no longer allowed contact with his family. She had witnessed ongoing domestic violence when she was younger and her mother was caring, but herself traumatised and at present ineffective in managing her children and giving them boundaries. She was, though, open to receiving the support she needed and was concerned to get Lily some help too.

When I first met Lily, she was sitting with her TA at a table in a corridor near to her classroom. She was colouring when I appeared holding a tiger puppet and the TA introduced me enthusiastically. "This is Elizabeth, do you remember I talked about her, she has a room with lots of things in it to make and do, and you can go every week until break time to have some time with her". Lily carried on colouring, head down and focussed, as though she was thinking.

"Shall we try it next week?" I said, hopefully and then added "Tim would like to meet you, he likes colouring too." I sat the puppet on the table and Lily glanced up and took him in with a quick sweep of her brown eyes. "Okay", she said without a glimmer of a change in expression. The TA looked reassuringly at me over her head. "Tim and I will be waiting for you at this time next week", I said, "and we are looking forward to showing you all the things in the room".

Your First Mark

As I sit waiting for Lily to arrive with her TA, I take a deep breath and make a mental checklist that all is ready. To me, it does not seem likely that Lily will be unmanageable in her first session, but the extension numbers to ring for help from those on standby are tucked under a paint pot near the phone in the room. I have thought long and hard about how many of the resources to put out – enough for variety, but not too many to overwhelm. Tim, the tiger puppet, is sitting on my hand as we wait, wondering, how it will go. We remind each other that we are meeting a very young child who has experienced difficult things in her short life.

Lily arrives with her TA who, it has been agreed, will come in with her for the first five to ten minutes. Lily has a serious expression on her face in contrast to the TA's bright, smiley expression of encouragement. On the table are several pipe cleaners twisted and knotted together. "Can you help me untangle these", I say, "they are all in a jumble?" Lily picks up the tangled pipe cleaners and makes light work of the muddle. Now they are all separate. She does not speak and does not

look at me. As I start to explain that when she comes here we can sort out mud-
dles, jumbles and tangles, Lily goes over to the paint bottles and brings them over
to the table. The TA says goodbye to Lily and exits quickly, reminding her that
I will bring her back to her table near her classroom and she will see her later.

"Ah, painting!" I exclaim. I realise that less is more with Lily, and I need to not
overwhelm her with the expression of enthusiasm I feel that she is choosing to stay
and get stuck in. I ask what size of paper she would like, and she points to a medi-
um-sized piece. She picks up two brushes and I get her the palette container to put
the paints in and some water too. Lily pours the black paint into the container and
fills it just stopping at the brim. She dips a thick brush into the paint and paints a
downward line and then a horizontal line across it.

"You have painted a shape", I say. "It is a cross", she says. "A cross?". "Yes, it is
the cross of Jesus". Our verbal dialogue has begun. There is no eye contact, as she
stares at her image. I am curious. "The cross of Jesus?", I say, "Where did you hear
about that?" "At the holiday club, she replies".

My mind is working overtime, wondering about this. As a Christian, this image
is laden with meaning for me; however, Lily is now starting to pour different colours into another container, in a very controlled way. She mixes these to make a
murky brown and slowly covers the cross with the brown paint. Lily's focus is
intense, and I am dragging my surprise away, to be present with her. She then fills
each palette container with a different combination of colours, mixing murky
greens and greys. With each mixed colour, she paints over the previous layer as I
narrate what is happening. As the colours blend in the palette and on the paper, I
see Lily locked in an intense expression of concentration. Is my attempt to make
contact with her through my soliloquy an intrusion or a help to her, I wonder?

The paper is now heavy with the layers of thick paint as she puts her brush
down – and I summarise the story of her painting. "You painted a black cross and
then you mixed all the colours and painted over it lots of times, and now we can't
see it anymore". "Have you finished?" She nods, looking straight ahead. She gets
up quickly and goes to the play dough, ripping off the top of the plastic container
and easing the play dough out with her very painty hands.

I move quickly to make a space at the table away from the paints for her. "Shall
we wash your hands first?" I ask her. She shakes her head, "No" – too late anyway
and it really doesn't matter. I tell her that we have ten minutes left, so we can wash
them before she goes back.

Reflection

I remember, looking back on this first session with Lily as I returned to the therapy
room to clear up after the session. The tangible sense of relief and elation I felt that
Lily had stayed in the room and nothing unmanageable had happened. It made
me realise that many of the adults around Lily in school would be experiencing
an unsettledness when they were with her, as I had in this first session as I was
wondering if at any moment she would react in an aggressive way to something
she was experiencing.

I also recall a later occasion when I had been asked to take Lily to a different room after her session instead of her table (as her TA is away). This had made Lily angry and so she ran back to her table instead. As she hurried along the corridor, she swept everything onto the floor from all the surfaces outside the classrooms, with me in hot-footed pursuit frantically trying to calm her!

There is no doubt that Lily's engagement in this first session with the art materials (particularly the paints and the modelling clay), which then continued on in many sessions, was pivotal in enabling communication between us to take place. It was clear that Lily found it difficult to trust adults and her defences against any kind of perceived threat were strong and acted upon very quickly. It seemed that Lily had developed what has been termed "blocked trust in response to frightening and painful relational experiences with adults" (Baylin & Hughes, 2016).

Her engagement with the arts materials, however, seemed to provide a bridge between us whereby she could communicate and therapeutic change could slowly emerge. Waller describes how Art as a means of communication in therapy can be a non-verbal and symbolic language, a "container" for powerful emotions, an expression of feelings that are difficult to form into words and also an opportunity for physical and playful creative exploration (Waller, 2006). In these early days, I was facilitating Lily to express herself through the paints and her pouring, mixing and increasingly messy use of the paints as sessions went on seemed to be a metaphor for the fluidity of our developing communication and exploration of her thoughts and feelings.

Unfathomable Violence Played Out in the Sand

Today, Lily walks determinedly to the sand. To my smile and welcome, there is no response. Lily is frowning, her mouth is a straight line and she looks paler than usual. She pulls the plastic box containing figures towards her with her small hands and sits down. I sit down next to her feeling as though I am a violin that has just been muted.

Lily throws the figures into the sand tray with force. While the Storm Trooper is face down in the sand the Incredible Hulk jumps on him grinding him further into the sand and bashes him several times. I start narrating as Lily drags the Hulk away to the other side of the sand tray, while the Storm Trooper is lifted to face him on the opposite side. With a verbal "Pow" Lily brings them together in mid-air, crashing onto each other with huge force. They fall to the ground and this time the Storm Trooper bashes the face of the Hulk who is lying on his back prostrate in the sand. "Wow, that must have hurt the Hulk", I say. I am ignored while Lily is now grabbing the box of vehicles and is scrabbling to find what she wants. She chooses a double-decker red bus and a police van. She struggles to hold the bus and the Hulk in one hand but manages to attack the Storm Trooper with both several times, hitting him repeatedly. "Gosh is he dead", I say? Without replying, Lily flings the Hulk on his back in the sand, raises the Storm Trooper out of the sand with one hand and grabs the police car with the other. She then brings them both down with a whack on the Hulk's face, bashing him several times.

I am struggling. I am trying hard to stay with this onslaught of violence between these two characters, but it seems relentless – this has gone on for weeks at the start of many sessions, and the ramming of the vehicles onto the figures today has escalated the violence to a higher level. I am trying hard to muster and match the energy of Lily's battle in my narration, while inwardly experiencing shock and resistance within myself to do this. When I express empathy for the characters for their physical wounding, I am feeling blocked and unheard. I feel shut down and my words are ricocheting off Lily, just as her characters are bouncing off each other. I am no longer a person but am reduced to an object in the room. Who am I to Lily? Am I just part of the furniture, or am I a wall watching, witnessing, absorbing all her shock, pain and struggles as they are flung around the room? Is Lily manoeuvring me into feeling how she has felt?

Reflection

After Lily has left the room, my mind is churning over our sessions so far. At no point has Lily asked for help or shown any recognition of us playing mutually. Games are on her terms alone and played without rules despite my protestations about fairness. When she gets fed up with Connect 4, she just releases the catch to end the game by letting the counters clatter over the table in noisy mayhem. Her toleration of frustration is so limited. In the fishing game, she peeks over the top of the cardboard fish tank and hooks up the big fish first, and then says she has won and the game is done, taking all the fish on her turn and leaving me with none. I feel powerless and hard done by in the face of her actions and am gaining understanding how adults around Lily are finding it difficult to break through her defences and have a two-way conversation. I do wonder though if Lily is enabling me to feel how powerless and hard done by she feels in her life.

Violent Sandplay

Lily's engagement in sandplay would often come at the beginning of our sessions and seemed like an activity that made way for more sensory work with paint, clay and water. The escalating violence between her characters resulting in the scene described above, of the characters bashing each other relentlessly with vehicles, has left me with hard questions as a therapist. Has Lily's experience of domestic violence in the home and the ongoing culture of violent behaviour amongst the siblings (with her mother unable to establish and maintain safe boundaries for her children), led her to playing out this trauma (past and present), in the sand? When upset and distressed in school, Lily's aggression towards peers and property was behaviour to be contained. It felt in the room as though Lily had to get this violent play out of her system each session, and for me to narrate and verbally acknowledge the hurt, the pain, the scariness and the hopelessness of these encounters. Lily's desensitisation to the empathy I expressed for the characters in her battles, concerned me greatly.

We know that trauma leaves a neurological imprint when traumatic events that "generally involve threats to life, or bodily integrity, or a close encounter with violence and death" (Herman, 1992) can overwhelm the psyche. As I reflect on the violent sandplay in Lily's sessions, I wonder was I just reinforcing the trauma of her experiences over and over again, colluding with this primitive language of violence and harming her further by triggering her into a constant hyper-vigilant state? Or was there a more healthy pattern of processing traumatic violent experiences going on?

Klorer states that trauma is expressed in right brain deficits in the processing of social, emotional and bodily information (Klorer, 2005), so perhaps through the sandplay, I *was* enabling Lily to process, with the provision of a container (termed in Sandplay "a safe and protected space" (Kalff, 2003)) the traumatic material and Lily's unprocessed feelings. Through the play was I tracking the hurt and pain of the characters and in so doing giving congruent feedback and validation of her own experiences and feelings?

The fact that the original energy of Lily's battles dissipated over time leads me to ponder that the discomfort of witnessing and staying with the excruciating violence that Lily was showing me, although hard in the counter-transference, was processing traumatic material in a safe way. I am reassured by Cattanach's appraisal that:

> while telling a story can revive a strong experience, it does not usually create the same intensity of feeling as the actual experience. The creation of a story where the events and characters are similar but 'not me', also creates an effect of distance from the terror and trauma of the actual events.
>
> (Cattanach, 1993)

Connecting

Lily has found the clay. After two sessions where she has hammered, pummelled and punched the grey lump, punishing it for its resistance to her, she has pulled a small bit off and has shaped a circle, poked holes for a pattern and has presented it to me and said "A cake for you". After all these weeks of feeling like another object in the room, I am like the cat that got the cream. My expressed delight "Oh Lily thank you so much, it is a lovely cake, I am so lucky!" spills into the room like a shaft of sunlight, hopefully bathing Lily in its warmth. The clay play and painting continue and necessitate a big clean-up at the sink afterwards as Lily's use of the paints is getting more free and less controlled.

There are spillages, paint overflows the palette seeping onto the table, and her hands and arms with pulled up sleeves, are a riot of various coloured splodges. Lily enjoys the clean-up time at the sink. Standing on a chair with the taps flowing, she tips the palettes into the water and watches the thick paint get diluted and swirl down the plughole. She uses the paintbrushes to get the palettes clean. She is engaged and delighted with this and a little grin is playing on her flushed face. Once the washing up is done, I put the plug in and fill the sink with warm water.

She immerses her hands and arms in the water, swishing them to and fro, getting her sleeves quite sodden. I swish my painty hands around with hers in the water and reach for the towel as she pulls out the plug. She grabs the towel from me and dries herself. She waits for me to dry my hands and then shouts "High Five" and swings her arm towards mine. My hand reaches hers and we connect for a moment. She laughs and glances away quickly.

Lily now reaches for a lime green bottle of bubble mixture and starts unscrewing the top. She holds the bubble blower up to her mouth and tries several times to blow a bubble. She hands it to me. I dip the blower in and blow a tiny bubble which hangs in the air. She catches it with her clapping hands. I am now blowing more slowly and a stream of bubbles trails high into the air. Lily jumps up to catch them and claps her hands over them. She is now watching me as I blow and I deliberately wait for her catching and chasing to finish before I start again. Her gaze is fixated on me and we hold eye contact over and over again before the bubbles flow and her catching erupts into a twisting, jumping, clapping dance. We share the joy with squeals of delight and exclamations: "Look at that one!", "Where has it gone?", "Catch it!".

My heart is singing. Today Lily is tolerating my presence as a person! In one session, she has initiated physical contact and held my gaze over and over again. We have shared excitement, joy and laughter.

Reflection: Neurobiology of Early Attachment/ Trust Established

The journey Lily took me on involved a revisiting of some of the earliest attachment behaviour between a baby and its mother. Lily's minimal eye contact, dysregulation and inability to self-soothe, pointed most likely to the unavailability of her attachment figure very early on in her life. This is not at all surprising as her mother had been experiencing the trauma of sustained domestic violence from an abusive partner, which was carried out over many years. Perry asserts that: "The first relationship determines the biological and emotional 'template' for all future relationships" (Perry, 2013). It is more than likely therefore that Lily would not have been able to develop an internalised model for self-regulation, or a template for security. Perry continues:

> Without predictable, responsive, nurturing and sensory enriched caregiving the infant's potential for normal bonding and attachments will be unrealised. The brain systems responsible for healthy emotional relationships will not develop in an optimal way without the right kinds of experiences at the *right times* in life.
>
> (Perry, 2013)

From our first meeting, it was evident that Lily was not giving me eye contact and this continued through many sessions. Her gaze often focused on what she was doing, such as painting, or playing in the sand with figures. She would give me brief glances sometimes when I was speaking but would quickly look away. Her head was often down rather than inclined in my direction when I spoke to her. Intuitively, I knew both to respect the distance she wanted to keep from me, and wait, but also to help encourage her to engage with me in a more direct way as her tolerance of me allowed.

Lily's facial expressions were quite often not responsive to mine because her gaze was averted, although she was especially expressive when she was playing in the sand tray with her figures. At these times, she would make verbal noises to simulate violent encounters and I would mirror or echo these in my narration of her play to validate her responses. She would display affective responses by her face becoming flushed, and by grimacing, frowning or smiling and laughing during the play.

In his article "The Meeting Eyes of Love: How Empathy is born in us", Mark Matousek signifies the importance of eye contact with the mother in these words:

> You learn the world from your mother's face. The mother's eyes especially are a child's refuge, the mirror from where children confirm their existence. From the doting reflection of its mother's eyes, a baby draws its earliest, wordless lessons about connection, care and love and about how being ignored – which every child is sooner or later – makes the good feeling disappear.
>
> (Matousek, 2011)

Through my offering of the "core conditions" of the Person-Centred Approach of sincerity, unconditional acceptance and empathetic understanding (Rogers, 1957), I had sought to provide Lily with a nurturing presence, staying with her while she explored the play and art resources, validating her verbal and non-verbal responses. Her lack of eye contact concerned me as a practitioner, but the way in which it was eventually established surprised me. It was achieved through Lily's initiation and my intuitive responses to her through the play with the bubbles. From that point on I sought opportunities like the "Fishing Game" to proactively work on this with her.

Daniel Siegel in his work explains how the discovery of "mirror neurons" in the brain which respond to eye contact and facial expressions, teach the infant (if the caregiving is responsive and nurturing) through imitation of behaviour to "imagine empathetically what is going on inside another person" (Siegel, 2012). The "connecting" with Lily with the bubbles felt as though a breakthrough had occurred in this most fundamental area of early development. Daniel Siegel clarifies the meaning of this process in the infant in the following statement:

> How we come to know 'who we are' is shaped by the communication we have had with others … being around caregivers early in life who are attuned to our internal worlds in a reliable way will provide us with the 'mirror experiences' that enable us to have a coherent and flexible sense of our selves in the world.
>
> (Siegel, 2012)

The non-verbal communication between Lily and myself was enabled through Lily's engagement with both artistic and play experiences. The creative arts used therapeutically provide experiences for the client which are multisensory (Malchiodi, 2014). Through painting, clay, sand, water and bubbles, she was exploring visual, tactile, kinaesthetic and even aural sensations. There was a sensory dynamic present associated with the art materials and their flexibility which seemed to enable Lily to developmentally regress to a pre-verbal stage where she could re-negotiate early childhood needs from the therapeutic relationship.

The soothing flow of paint, water, sand and bubble mixture and the pliability of clay seemed to support Lily to feel calmer and less stressed helping her to feel regulated and safe. This in turn was giving her positive sensory experiences to process both attachment issues and also traumatic experiences. Malchiodi (2014) advocates "Trauma-informed expressive arts therapy" as a model for addressing the attachment difficulties that arise from traumatic experiences which she describes as embracing the responses of both mind and body through traumatic events and "recognising that symptoms are adaptive coping strategies rather than pathology" (Malchiodi, 2012 cited in Malchiodi, 2014).

Nursed by a Tale

I am waiting for Lily to arrive with her TA. She is late. Five minutes after the time of the session, the TA pops her head round the door looking concerned.

"Could you come?" she says, "Lily is having a bad morning, I can't get her to come to therapy".

When I arrive, Lily is sitting hunched up at the table near her classroom, with hands clasping the sides of her face, looking straight ahead. The TA says quietly and breezily, "Elizabeth is here Lily". Lily remains looking ahead at the wall, "I don't want to come, go away!" I wait and then say quietly, "That's okay Lily, we can leave it for today, but if you change your mind, I'll be waiting in the room. I'll leave Connect 4 with you in case you want to have a game with your TA." Lily takes her hands from her face and glances at the game. She then puts them back again, stares at the wall and shouts loudly: "Go Away! Go Away!".

I make a retreat, while I hear the TA talking quietly and soothingly to Lily trying to distract her. This has not happened before. Lily has had her ups and downs, (mostly related to being internally excluded after violent episodes when she has hurt others or damaged things), but she has always come willingly to her sessions. My mind races, what has been happening to Lily? Is she safe? We seemed to be making progress, will this be a permanent rupture? What could I have done differently approaching her today? I replay the picture of Lily clasping her face, those hands forming a barrier, shutting us out, hanging onto herself as though she is under threat.

Twenty minutes after the session's start time, Lily appears at the door clutching the Connect 4 game, followed quickly by her TA. She sits down without looking at me, pushes Connect 4 away, and picks up The Fishing game. Lily's face is blotchy and her eyes red-rimmed from crying. She sets up the game and hands me the green rod, while she tips the fish into the cardboard pond and dangles her red rod into it. She hauls out a little fish and detaches it from the magnet.

My turn…I bounce my magnet around and also catch one of the fish. "Oh good, I've got one too!'", I exclaim. Lily looks up at me, acknowledging my success. I smile. More recently, Lily has begun to play more fairly and when she has been cheating by looking over the top of the cardboard pond, I have said "Look at me" and she has held eye contact with me to stop herself from cheating. I am wondering if she can tolerate this today? I decide to risk it.

Lily dances her rod around in the pond and tries to peak over. "Look at me" I say quietly, holding my breath. Lily turns her head and holds my gaze, looking serious. There is a click as a fish clings to her rod, it is a big one this time. We continue and on Lily's turn I say each time, "Look at me, look at me" and her eyes lock onto mine and disconnect again when we hear the click and the fish is drawn up and also disconnected. Lily has won and grins from her little pinched face. Together we pack the rods, fish and pond back into the box.

I tell Lily that we have ten minutes left and then I will take her back to her TA. Lily picks up a book. It is a book that we have read before about a small shark who has adventures with a friend and finds himself lost, gets scared and finds his way home again, back to his Mum. Lily lies down on the bean bag and I squash onto it with her. I say to Lily, "You've had a difficult morning, how are you feeling now?".

Lily turns and looks at me "My heart hurts" she says. She puts her hand on the top part of her tummy, and before I can empathise, quickly commands: "Read it" while giving me the book. I go with Lily's command. I could have questioned her further, explored the depth of her words with her, asked her about the top part of her tummy where she placed her hand, but I sense this would be too much for her today, she is too fragile. Perhaps an opportunity missed, but I go with my intuition. I read to Lily, in a quiet soothing voice. Lily puts her thumb in her mouth and strokes her nose with her index finger. My heart is full. I am aware of the preciousness of these moments. This little person is drinking in some nourishment and sustenance from my presence, my voice, my calm. And I sense she is soothed and held like a baby at the breast. She knows what she needs this morning.

I feel exhausted by the emotional roller-coaster of today's encounter – from staying with Lily in her distress, waiting, watching and wondering from moment to moment how to respond in a way that can hold her and help her to feel safe and understood, in spite of so much unknowing.

Reflection: Stories in Therapy

It was interesting that in the last ten minutes of this session Lily chose a book for me to read to her called "Gilbert in Deep" (Clarke & Fuger, 2007). This is a story of a small shark who set out on an adventure and became frightened by going beyond the coral reef into deep waters. Eventually, he found his way back to his mother. This seemed to be a metaphor for Lily's dysregulation at the start of the day and subsequent need for nurture in the session. In the countertransference during the session, I felt like a mother working hard to calm a distressed infant. A lot of the communication was non-verbal, with me trying to sense Lily's fragmentation and vulnerability and provide a safe gentle presence through eye contact, tone of voice and facial expressions. This was punctuated by a small amount of verbal interaction between us. This did seem to enable Lily to directly express to me that "her heart hurt" when I checked in later with how she was feeling towards the end of our session.

Thinking about the drama evident in Lily's session from start to the finish, and the dramatic narrative of the story she chose for me to read to her, two things seemed particularly pertinent to Lily; firstly, the story described scary feelings of the little shark (who thought he wasn't afraid of anything) creating tension which was resolved at the end of the story. Secondly, my "story voice" and vocal expressions most likely conveyed empathy. This possibly enabled Lily to experience a "safe emergency" (Baylin & Hughes, 2016), in the story, which may have paralleled her own real-life experience.

Stories can be powerful tools in therapy to provide attunement with the client. Baylin and Hughes (2016) describe how synchronicity in brain activity between a storyteller and listener (can dissipate cortisol and release oxytocin) and has been seen in neuroimaging studies (reported by Zak, 2012). They conclude: "This is why the use of storytelling for engaging mistrustful children can be so helpful, such a powerful process for helping deactivate the child's self-defense system long enough for a compelling narrative to be completed" (Baylin & Hughes, 2016).

A Time of Uncertainty

As I get the room ready today, I feel relieved that Lily's move to a new school (a therapeutic environment more suited to her needs to which she has been referred), is taking longer to happen than anticipated. The school has told me that Lily has been there on a visit but the date when she will move there is uncertain. It could be in a few weeks or longer. What we do know is that we are ending our time together and I need to manage this uncertain time as well as I can with a child who has already experienced a lot of change in her short life. I find this daunting and disappointing.

Lily's head appears round the door. "Hello" she says with a grin as she sits down and pulls the sand tray towards her. She reaches for her characters; the Storm Trooper and the Incredible Hulk now have teams which include animals and female figures. As she arranges them at opposing ends of the sand tray ready for battle, she looks up at me and says:

"I went to visit my new school, yesterday".

"Oh, what was it like?" I ask.

"It was awesome" she exclaims loudly. "It has a huge garden, and in one corner there is a wood and there are benches where you can sit round a big fire and you can eat sausages!" Lily's brown eyes are alight, her face is slightly flushed, her lips pressed tight in a little smile. Her hands are scooping up the sand, letting it flow off her fingers, over and over.

"And how do you feel about moving schools?" I ask.

"A bit sad", she says, looking down. "I'm going because I'm bad". Lily's hands move in faster little movements.

"Lily", I say gently, "Look at me". Her hands stop in the sand as her eyes look into mine.

"Lily, you are not bad, you are going to the new school because it is a better fit for you. There will be grown-ups there who can help you with the things you find difficult and help you calm down when you're feeling upset."

"Okay", says Lily, and lifts the Storm Trooper out of the sand and knocks the Incredible Hulk off his feet into the sand. The Storm Trooper's team join in by fighting the Incredible Hulk's team, but within minutes the play loses energy and peters out and Lily leaves the character's face down in the sand. She picks up the list we have made of the things she wants to do before we say goodbye and puts it in front of me and reaches for a blue felt pen.

"What would you like to do today?" I ask her.

"Let's make our models", she says. She puts a big blue tick next to "Make models" on the list.

She then puts the felt pen down and reaches for the clay and struggles to pull off two large lumps. I hold the clay while she pulls.

"One for you, and one for me", she says. "I'm going to make a swan for you".

"What are you going to make me"?

Reflection: Transition to Verbal Engagement

I hope the above dialogue gives a glimpse of the very different communication compared with earlier sessions that was happening between us towards the end of Lily's sessions. Lily's communication had developed from being largely non-verbal (with very few sentences uttered, but sounds and words in the play and gestures, nodding or shaking her head in response to questions I asked or comments I made) to her initiating conversation, replying verbally in sentences, asking me questions like an alert seven-year-old child. She also gave me eye contact, acknowledged me in the room, asking for help when she needed it, and was able to make and follow a list of all that she wanted to do in the last few sessions.

In this verbal dialogue between Lily and myself, it is possible to see the way that Lily was now able to express directly in conversation that she felt both sad about moving schools and that she had concluded that the reason she was going to the new school was because she was "bad". Her ability to use her thinking skills and cognitive function by the end of the therapy had changed significantly.

It was interesting to see that early on Lily created a routine to our sessions where often she would play in the sand with her figures in an aggressive way, then she would move on to painting, with lots of mixing and experimenting with colours, finishing with playing games. This perhaps gave her an opportunity to discharge and play out her trauma and strong feelings with me witnessing and validating them for her. This seemed to enable a creative exploration of the paints and lead on to the more cognitive activity of playing games near the end of the session. Her routine also hopefully provided her with the containment, control and sense of security she needed in our developing relationship because was able to direct the pace she could tolerate and manage within each 50-minute session.

Through growing trust, because she was able to feel safe, Lily was then able to experiment with trying new ways of playing with me in the last couple of months of therapy, venturing into dressing up and role play, using puppets with dialogue and making up songs. In all these scenarios she was playing creatively with me as a play-mate and she was bringing her imagination to bear in these play scenarios.

Epilogue

I still have the clay models and card Lily made for me.

The swan is red and has an interesting lump on its head (a bit like some dinosaurs). It also has a pattern scored on its back. It looks like a mythical "swan-dragon" creature. As I look at the swan, it reminds me that when I was with Lily I felt like the typical description of a swan – sailing along, maintaining a calm exterior, while furiously paddling, observing, thinking, wondering and responding to whatever Lily was being and doing.

The redness is curious; I was often helping to contain Lily's anger and rage expressed in her play, so the swan's coat of red paint is perhaps a reminder of this? The pattern on the swan's back is symbolic to me of the way the work with Lily was scored into me, teaching me so much about the rawness of being present and exposed to whatever the child is bringing, and experiencing and witnessing the patterns which the child creates in therapy to bring about their own healing.

The other clay model Lily made for me was of her face. It is a thick tile, heavy to hold, painted yellow with clown like red cheeks. It looks rough and primitive. What strikes me today are the eyes. They are see-through holes and they seek my attention. All that work on gaining eye contact and the eyes in *this* face let you see right through them. Lily's smile and name are carved into the face. She did not want me to forget her.

On the cards Lily and I made for each other, she wanted both our hand prints on each one. My yellow hand is overlaid with her two red handprints. Whenever children paint their hands in therapy and make prints, I tell them about the uniqueness of their fingerprints: that no one else in the world has exactly the same pattern of ridges on their fingers as they have.

I wrote a poem after the therapy had finished to help me to process the work with Lily as well as how the ending came so much sooner than anticipated. An extract from it is presented here.

Lily

An old lady in a seven-year-old's body
Carrying the burden of badness.

★★★

Into the sand you went:
The bashing and thrashing
Pounding and hurting
Over and over again...
Until it became lethargic.

★★★

Then we were:
Together.
Meeting
Connecting like a newborn
In the bubble blowing
Watching and catching the popping rainbows.
Catching our fish and holding
Each other's gaze
In the fish game

★★★

And then with art and box
You left
On your way to the next part of
Your Journey
May you thrive Lily.

References

Baylin, J.F. & Hughes, D.A. (2016) *The Neurobiology of Attachment-Focused Therapy*. New York: W.W. Norton.

Cattanach, A.C. (1993) *A. Children's Stories in Play Therapy*. London and Philadelphia: Jessica Kingsley.

Clarke, J. & Fuger, C. (illustrator) (2007) *Gilbert in Deep*. London New York Sydney: Simon & Schuster Children's.

Herman, J.L. (1992) *Trauma and Recovery*. New York: Basic Books.

Kalff, D. (2003) *A Psychotherapeutic Approach to the Psyche*. Cloverdale, CA: Tremenos Press (Originally published in English in 1980).

Klorer, P.G. (2005) Expressive Therapy with Severely Maltreated Children. Neuroscience Contributions. *Art Therapy*, 22(4), 214–220.

Malchiodi, C.A. (2012) Trauma-Informed Art Therapy with Sexually Abused Children. In P. Goodyear-Brown (Ed.), *Handbook of Child Sexual Abuse: Prevention, Assessment, Treatment* (pp. 341–354). Hoboken, NJ: Wiley.

Malchiodi, C.A. (2014) Creative Arts Therapy Approaches to Attachment Issues. In C.A. Malchiodi & D.A. Crenshaw (Eds.), *Creative Arts and Play Therapy for Attachment Problems* (pp. 10–12). New York: The Guildford Press.

Matousek, M. (2011) *The Meeting Eyes of Love: How Empathy is Born in Us.* Psychology Today posted April 8, 2011. Sussex Publishers, LLC.

Perry, B.D. (2013) Bonding and Attachment in Maltreated Children. *The Child Trauma Academy,* www.childtrauma.org (Adapted in part from: "Maltreated Children: Experience, Brain Development and the Next Generation". New York: W.W. Norton & Company, in preparation).

Rogers, C.R. (1957) The Necessary and Sufficient Conditions of Therapeutic Personality Change. *Journal of Consulting Psychology,* 21, 95–103.

Siegel, D.J. (2012) *The Developing Mind* (Second Edition). New York/London: The Guildford Press.

Waller, D. (2006) Art Therapy for Children: How it Leads to Change. *Clinical Psychology and Psychiatry,* 11, 271.

Zak, P.J. (2012) *The Moral Molecule: How Trust Works.* New York: Penguin.

Chapter 3

The Toad Croakers in the Land of Noise

Koren Wilmer

Act I

Introduction

Oliver arrives at my house with his parents. His mother encourages him to ring the cast iron bell at the side entrance gate. I open the gate and greet him with a cheery smile. He is wearing a serious expression which makes him appear older than his six years. He looks past me and spots the Music Box (a purpose-built log cabin for my therapy practice) at the far end of the garden. He runs excitedly towards it. There is no pause for social niceties – no "hello" for me or "goodbye" for his parents.

I hurry after him, observing his awkward gait – head down, arms flapping from his elbows and wrists. Oliver arrives ahead of me, opens the door, steps purposefully into the small lobby area and then opens the door to the playroom. I follow him inside.

"Hello Oliver, I'm Koren and this…"

There is no acknowledgement of me from Oliver, not so much as a glance. He stops briefly. There is a tension in his body (and mine) – it feels like a mixture of excitement, anxiety and apprehension.

Oliver is drawn to some strange-looking objects encased in bubble wrap (I have only recently moved in to a new therapy space and not finished unpacking).

"Would you like to help me unpack these?" I ask. Oliver does not respond verbally but watches intently as I pull at the wrappings. He seems hesitant about joining in, preferring to wait for the contents to be revealed. Very quickly we have a collection of small percussion instruments and a pile of bubble wrap. The bubble wrap holds more interest.

I take some and scrunch it up, enjoying the sensory delights as it squeaks and pops. I start to mould it into a ball, securing it with tape and toss it spontaneously into the open loft area. Oliver joins me and does the same until we are soon engaged in making and lobbing balls into the space together. I feel our initial social anxieties beginning to ease.

Another anxiety niggles – one that is entirely my own. I'm supposed to be a music therapist, hardwired by my training to get joint musical interaction going!

DOI: 10.4324/9781003163015-3

So I risk our fledgling relationship, take a beater and now accompany each of Oliver's throws with a drum beat. I am lucky – Oliver is quick to appreciate the connection between my activity and his action. Realising he has a degree of control over me, he relaxes further and smiles. He picks up a beater and drums loudly on the bass drum, allowing me to join in. This is a good feeling – I begin to relax too and suggest that Oliver might like to take off his coat. He is happy to do this and puts it carefully on the table.

Oliver continues to explore the available instruments, stopping occasionally in one spot and vigorously flapping his hands. With one finger he sounds all the notes of the piano in order, from top to bottom, and learns the word for the resulting chromatic scale.

He unpacks the xylophone and arranges the note bars in order, singing the pitch of the next note before placing it. He blows a few wind instruments and dances with some bells strapped to his feet and wrists. He sorts pictures of the instruments into three categories: wind, percussion and string. He seems pleased with all that's on offer.

Oliver is methodical in his investigations – sounding notes in order and trying different types of beaters to find out how they change the tone. He is keen to tell me what he knows about the instruments and how the sounds are made. There is a focused intensity in him. I watch and listen, impressed by his knowledge, and intrigued by his adult expression and serious tone of voice. I am his assistant now, handing him beaters and moving instruments to enable his ease of access as he paces the room in excitement.

As our session nears its end, I draw Oliver's attention to the time on the clock. His response is immediate. He picks up his coat and abruptly leaves the Music Box. He runs back up to the house to meet his parents. When I catch up I want to assure Oliver that if he has enjoyed his time he can come back next week. But he is already making his way up the side passage to the gate. His parents want him to say "goodbye" and "thank you", but Oliver is running towards the car, already anticipating the next part of his day's itinerary.

About Oliver

It is October 2003. Oliver is six years old. He is my 39th tour guide into the world of autism – a world so alien and yet so close to home. It is our world but, for the most part, not as you or I could imagine experiencing it. This is what makes it hard for us to reach one another.

Oliver is the only child of two creative and intelligent parents, both with teaching backgrounds. Growing up in a stimulating and nurturing environment he has been able to feed his voracious appetite for knowledge about the physical world. He learned to read early and books, both fact and fiction, are an important part of his life. He has developed many areas of special interest (Dinosaurs, Ancient History, Natural History, Astronomy, Geography, Archaeology) in which he has become highly informed. He loves making up stories and games which revolve around his specific interests.

His mother estimates that before he went to school on a full-time basis, they spent at least three hours a day playing games and telling stories. Stories were also used to motivate Oliver, through otherwise seemingly-pointless activities such as toiletting, dressing and eating.

As a small child, Oliver enjoyed adult company. As an only child, he was used to being the sole focus of attention, but he could not tolerate his mother's attention being taken by another adult.

More difficult to understand was Oliver's intolerance of other children. They frightened him. He would scream and cry when they came close. It became impossible to leave him with a child-minder who cared for two other children as Oliver could not tolerate being in the same room as them. At playgroup, he was unable to sit with other children or share their activities and became distressed if they disrupted one of his games. He hit out a lot, especially at his mother, and threw spectacular tantrums. At nursery, he refused to enter the classroom and often had to be carried in by his teacher.

Oliver was four and a half years old when he was diagnosed with Asperger's Syndrome – a condition which has since been removed as a separate diagnosis from DSM-V (2013) and incorporated into Autistic Spectrum Disorder. This is, in my opinion, a welcome development. As Mike Stanton states, "Not everyone with autism has Asperger syndrome. But everyone with Asperger syndrome is autistic" (Stanton, 2000).

Autistic Spectrum Disorder is diagnosed from a cluster of behavioural features which are shared to some extent with all children with autism:

- Resistance to change
- Attachment to routine
- Social naivety
- Rigidity of thought
- Over-literal interpretation of language
- Potential to become obsessive and elevate routines into rituals that must be followed to the last detail.

(Stanton, 2000)

Oliver's mother described his condition as "a kind of social blindness. He cannot interact with his peers, or do group work alongside them. He can't follow a teacher's instructions when given to the group. If things go wrong for him, he cannot contain his distress."

Oliver did not appear as physically well co-ordinated or as adventurous as his peers. His gross and fine motor skills were underdeveloped for his age which frustrated him intensely.[1] He expected that one should be able to produce perfect results first time in all activities and had a low tolerance for making mistakes. This in turn made him reluctant to practise skills such as writing, drawing and colouring.

Oliver could see no point in mastering self-help skills and learned to cooperate only very slowly. He would sing to occupy himself while he was dressing which would distract him from the task in hand.

Oliver was hypersensitive to particular sounds, for example: babies crying, children shrieking, vacuum cleaners, lawn mowers and hand driers. He would cover his ears and run. Playgrounds were a nightmare for him.

Autistic author, Gunilla Gerland, in her book, *A Real Person: Life on the Outside* (1997), describes the devastating impact of hypersensitivity to noise:

> Certain sounds frightened me, dogs barking, mopeds, tractors and cars, engines of various kinds. They would explode inside me and make me lose all sense of the way my body related to my surroundings. It was like being flung out into space... Sometimes I screamed and covered my ears.

At the time of Oliver's referral, I had been working for nine years with children with special needs as a music therapist in my own private practice. Many of my autistic clients were very young children with little or no language.

One of the main tools of a music therapist is the ability to reach people (especially those with verbal and or emotional communication difficulties) through joint improvised music making – a non-verbal method of two-way communication requiring no formal musical skills on the part of the client but requiring sensitive and skilled musicianship on behalf of the therapist. Through their music making, a relationship of trust is nurtured, enabling the client to express something of themselves, while feeling heard and supported by the therapist.

In this way, the client is helped to access deeply held emotions and feelings making them audible and, therefore, accessible. Enabling a person to express themselves in this way in a supportive and safe environment is generally regarded as the key role of a music therapist. However, in truth, I often struggled to reach my autistic clients through joint improvisation.

Before training as a music therapist I had worked in a long-stay hospital for adults with learning disabilities. Many were autistic but as I then had no real understanding of the condition, I simply fell into the trap of accepting their bizarre behaviours as "autistic" and learnt to "manage" them. There was a sort of pride amongst us as staff in being able to cope and not be phased by the behaviours exhibited.

In the nineties, before the advent of the internet, I scoured libraries and bookshops for information about autism. The few books I found were academic tomes – informative but cold. Then one day my sister told me of a book she had recently read by Donna Williams called "Nobody Nowhere." This astonishing autobiography of an autistic person's early life as a child opened the doors for me to an amazing, shocking and fascinating world. "The more I became aware of the world around me, the more I became afraid. Other people were my enemies, and reaching out to me was their weapon..." (Williams, 1992, p. 13).

Suddenly I could begin to see the children I was working with in a new light. From then on, I devoured every book that I could get my hands on, especially those written by autistic authors, that could help me understand and connect with my autistic clients.

In 2000, I had the privilege of travelling with one of my clients and her family to America for a week's intensive training in "Son Rise" – a programme using volunteers to work at home with the autistic child in a specially designated play-room. The main tool was to make yourself interesting to the child by joining them in their behaviours, picking up on their own specific interests and learning to experience life from an autistic child's point of view. This experience gave me confidence to be more playful and experimental with my clients; however, my professional training and qualification to practise was still confined within the remit of being a music therapist.

My practice at the time of working with Oliver was housed in a brand new purpose-built log cabin at the end of a long garden. I called it The Music Box. It backed onto allotments offering a peaceful retreat in a busy town environment. Inside was a small entrance lobby with a door to the main room. It was light and airy with windows to the side and front and double doors looking out to the garden. A vaulted ceiling and an open loft area gave it a sense of space and airi-ness. The walls had been soundproofed and plastered. On a high shelf, within sight but out of reach, there were a number of baskets containing small percussion and wind instruments and a collection of miscellaneous playthings. Around the room were the larger floor-standing percussive instruments; a piano, some xylo-phones, a bass metallophone, a cymbal on a stand, various drums and a large free-standing glockenspiel in the shape of a zebra – the note bars forming the zebra's stripes.

Act 11

Trying to Reach Oliver – Or More Accurately – How Oliver Finds a Way to Reach Me

Oliver was referred for music therapy by his mother as she recognised his inher-ent love of music (which included a sophisticated appreciation of classical music including string quartets). She knew he would respond well in a one-to-one rela-tionship with an adult and wanted to find an activity outside of home and school that he would be able to enjoy.

The sessions that were to follow developed in quite a different way than either his parents or I had anticipated. After a few sessions in which Oliver joyfully and systematically explored the different instruments, he stopped using them as poten-tial music makers. He had enjoyed discovering how instruments made their sounds and organising them into their categories; wind, percussion, etc. He appreciated too their visual characteristics, but their function as objects with which to make music was on the whole avoided.

If I detected a rhythmic pattern or a melodic fragment in his explorations and used this to join with him, Oliver would shout "Stop! Don't drown out my music." The professional therapist in me copes with the rebuff. I have felt it so many times

I am ready for it, perhaps even resigned to it – but it still smarts. Like many of my autistic clients, the idea of the two of us making music together was clearly not on his agenda.

My inner music therapist grew anxious – Oliver was a smart kid – when he has explored all the instruments what then? Will he get bored? How will I join him? Will he just leave when he feels he's seen everything? I feel the expectation of his parents who have invested their trust and money in me. I wait – containing my niggling fears…

Oliver on the other hand, reflects none of my anxieties – he's not concerned with the theoretical niceties of developing a "social" relationship with me. He is enjoying the space to do his own thing, unimpeded by someone else's wishes and expectations, and keen to continue in the same vein each week.

At the end of his fourth session, Oliver spots a couple of sound-makers that fire his imagination. Two carved wooden toads of different sizes sit on top of the piano. They are beautifully tactile with a serrated ridge running across the centre of their backs. Oliver picks them up and I show him how he can make them "croak" by drawing a small stick across the serrations on their backs. Oliver quickly named them "Big Toad-croaker" and "Little Toad-croaker."

Act III

The Land of Noise – Reaching Oliver, Oliver Reaches Me

Oliver runs excitedly towards the Music Box. His mother says he is very excited, he has been planning for this session all week. I follow him down the garden with eager anticipation.

Oliver takes off his coat – a lovely sign that he feels safe in the playroom. He fetches the Toad-croakers from the piano and while pacing around the room, launches straight into his narrative:

> There are two Toad-croakers – Big Toad-croaker, and his son, Little Toad-croaker.
>
> (see Figure 3.1)

Oliver continues to pace around the room, head down, flapping his hands vigorously as he prepares his next move. His face is serious, he is clearly thinking hard. I sit on the periphery of the room – all ears and eyes. Oliver picks up the heavy zebra-shaped glockenspiel and shifts it to the centre of the room (see Figure 3.2).

"Episode One," he declares triumphantly, "The Fate of the Villainous Zebra…

The Toad-croakers are out on a mission to find the best noise made by a violin bow."

Oliver takes the violin bow from its case. He tries it on several instruments with varying success.

> They were attacked by a villainous Zebra. The Zebra brayed and showed his teeth.

Figure 3.1 The Toad-Croakers.

Figure 3.2 The Zebra.

I grabbed a notebook as I suspected I would be expected to remember every detail of the story for next week.

"The Toad-croakers fought back." Oliver picks up a large drum beater and places it in front of the Zebra.

They put a big bass drum beater in front of the Zebra which tripped him up.

Oliver roughly collapses the Zebra onto the floor. I fear for my instrument but know this is not the time to interject.

Oliver returns to the Toad-croakers and clunks them across the metal bars of the bass Metallophone[2] stopping at the end.

> They came to a cliff-edge and looked down. They saw Zebra kicking madly with his legs but not getting up. Big Toad-croaker warned: "Don't make noises or you'll wake him up. I've thought of a plan: we put the violin bow down so that it attaches to the Zebra, then we slide down the bow. Then we walk across the Zebra without stepping on any grooves and making a noise. Then we climb up the sides of the xylophone and we are there."

Oliver fetches the violin bow and places it as a slide from the metallophone to the Zebra. He gingerly manoeuvres the Toad-croakers according to the plan and stands Zebra up again.

> Zebra got up and bared his teeth. Big Toad-croaker said "run, run or he'll bite you."

Oliver knocks Little Toad-croaker off the xylophone.

> Big Toad-croaker rescues him by swinging on the angel chimes.[3]

Oliver takes the Toad-croakers, crashes them against the bars of the angel chimes, clonks them across the Rota-Drums[4] and up onto the piano where the violin rests.
Oliver draws the violin bow across the strings of the violin which alerts the Zebra, requiring the Toad-croakers to think up new ways to get rid of him. He drags the Zebra closer and begins to batter it using woodblocks, collapses it again and covers it with some coloured cloths.

> The Toad-croakers attempted lots of ideas to get rid of the Zebra; bashing him with wood blocks, covering him with sheets, whipping him, tripping him up, until finally, a combination of factors beat him.

I listen intrigued, delighted and slightly amused by the formality of the language Oliver uses to express himself. I also make a mental note to myself – make cardboard cut out of Zebra for future sessions!!
Oliver quickly picks up some beaters, sounds the temple blocks and bashes the cymbal with great gusto.

> The Toad-croakers made triumphant music on the cymbal and woodblocks. The Zebra slopped off. Until next week's adventure…

Oliver comes over to me interested in what I have been able to write down.
We have reached the end of our session. I thank Oliver for his amazing story and promise to type up our script in time for next week's session. Oliver collects his coat and hurries back to greet his mother and tell her about today's adventure with the Toad-croakers.

I am blown away!

The following week, Oliver runs excitedly to the Music Box. I show him the typed manuscript of last week's story. Oliver seems to have expected no less and glances approvingly. I read him my introduction to his story, which I have written based on his verbal descriptions.

> The Land of Noise is a place where nothing is quiet. There are musical instruments all over the place. You cannot move without making a sound. It is very stormy and there are lots of tape recorders. Some strange characters live in the Land of Noise.
>
> There is Zebra – Zebra is greedy and grumpy. He loathes the thought of creatures having fun and making music together. He tries to make the Land of Noise less noisy by driving the other inhabitants away. The Zebra lives in a dark creepy lair with his larder of food and his money. The Toad-croakers are cunning and not easily fooled. They think up many plans to get rid of the grumpy Zebra.

Oliver listens, pacing about the room and excitedly flapping his hands. He seems to be satisfied with my synopsis and loses no time in announcing:

Episode Two – The Toad-Croakers and the Exploration.

I am ready for my job as scribe, prop mover and solver of various technical issues to enable the smooth running of the adventures. Oliver acts out the story as he narrates:

> The Toad-croakers were making their way across the piano unaware of a lurking danger.
>
> The Zebra came out of his lair as he could smell Toad-croakers – a damp, squidgy, slimy smell.
>
> The Zebra snapped at the Toad-croakers but they were ready with their weapons. They blew on the farty whistle.[5] The Zebra couldn't bear the sound of the farty whistle. It made his ears ring and his teeth chatter and he ran back to his lair.
>
> The Toad-croakers continued their journey across the land of the dangerous Zebra. Jumping from high platforms they bumped into a triangle and drum, making noises that woke the Zebra.
>
> The Zebra came saying "I smell Toad-croakers."
>
> Quickly Big Toad-croaker grabbed the violin and began to play (Oliver swiftly draws the violin bow across the open strings). The Zebra fell to the ground for this was the most painful noise (Oliver collapses the Zebra onto the floor).
>
> The Toad-croakers took advantage of the Zebra lying on the ground. They covered him with a duvet and attacked him with woodblocks until he ran away.

A bell was sounded to tell all the creatures in the Land of Noise that it was safe again.

The next week's adventure followed on as if there had been no break:

Episode III – In which the hungry Toad-croakers discover the secret of the golden eggs and move to a new home in the "xylohome."

Poor old Zebra is further tortured and bullied by the Toad-croakers and retreats back into his lair, leaving the Toad-croakers free to explore.

The Adventures in the Land of Noise continued seamlessly for a further 13 weeks and included lots of storms, a burglary, hypnosis, and some magic golden eggs – while all the time the Toad-croakers pit their wits to keep the grumpy Zebra at bay. The episodes were full of violence and usually ended in scenes of chaos where all the instrumental props involved were piled in a heap on the floor. Fortunately for my stock of instruments, Oliver did not need to literally act out the violence; he seemed happy for me to arrange the props appropriately as if we were setting up individual photo shots.

Eventually I grew tired of the repetitive nature of the storyline – i.e. the never-ending feud between the Toad-croakers and the Zebra. I have always been uncomfortable with confrontation and recognised this as my own feeling and not necessarily counter-transference from Oliver. But still I craved some resolution.

I had managed to replace Zebra with a cardboard replica as the instrument was in danger of getting damaged from being collapsed too often. Oliver was initially a bit thrown by this unexpected change (something out of his control) but after a few moments of thought, he regained his control of the story and called the next episode "Derek the Duplicate."

Derek the Zebra has changed. He has gone into an invisible black Zebra with no stripes. He has made a duplicate of himself because he didn't want to be bashed up any more.

Eventually Derek (the duplicate Zebra) is driven out of the Land of Noise. But...

He had a son Denis, who was much better than him. More intelligent and could do complicated sums like: 10×100. He has a different glint in his eyes. He is more cunning than his father or uncle before that. He is not easily fooled and could easily work out what the Toad-croakers were planning.

I am ashamed to say at this point I groaned inwardly. I decided that at the beginning of the next session I would carefully confront Oliver with my feelings. Oliver arrived for his next session in great spirits and ready to carry on with the next episode. I plucked up my courage and as gently as I could suggested that the storyline

Figure 3.3 The Land of Noise Explodes.

was, maybe, getting rather predictable. Oliver listened and after a short pause in which he paced thoughtfully about the room he surprised me by announcing with great conviction:

The Land of Noise came to an end with a mighty explosion.

(see Figure 3.3)

We spent the session upturning instruments, banging drums and cymbals creating a fabulous scene of chaos as everything ended up once more in a cathartic and highly charged heap on the floor. In the brief silence that ensued I wondered where our next sessions would go.

Reflections

Looking back on Oliver's narrative, there is so much to unpack. The Land of Noise shows his experience of how sounds and music can have both emotional and physical impact. He exploited this by using various instrumental sounds as weapons and traps. For instance, the Toad-croakers discovered that Zebra liked the sound of the triangle. They decided to exploit this to lure Zebra into their traps. "Then the singing bowl began to sound, hypnotising Zebra so that he did foolish things like walk in front of a rolling bass drum which knocked him flat."

This extract shows an interesting development in Oliver's understanding of the way different minds can respond in different ways to the same stimuli – The

Toad-croakers are unaffected by particular sounds that literally drive the Zebra mad. This is part of the development of the Theory of Mind (Baron-Cohen and Leslie, 1985) which children with autism often struggle with.

Sadly the metaphor of Oliver's initial adventure passed me by – I had not yet trained in the use of story in therapeutic work. My training was in non-verbal expression through sounds and music. I knew the story was an important vehicle for Oliver and that was enough for me. He had found a way to use the instruments to express himself in a unique and imaginative way and joy of joys he clearly wanted to share this adventure with me.

Thank goodness it is not necessary to dig deeper into a child's thinking or reflect back to the child your own thoughts in order for therapy to be effective. But re-reading Oliver's stories some 17 years later, I am fascinated by the metaphors he uses and a little sad that I didn't fully recognise them at the time.

As a child with autism, Oliver's world was bombarded with unwanted sounds – sounds he was unable to control which caused him great anxiety. "The Land of Noise is a place where nothing is quiet."

Zebra is an interesting character – Oliver describes him as greedy and grumpy, he loathes the thought of creatures having fun and "making music together." That might have been an interesting idea to reflect back to him. If Oliver identified with some aspects of Zebra I wonder about the "dark creepy lair" and also whether Oliver was bullied perhaps by other children at school for wanting to keep them at bay. The Toad-croakers are the heroes of his story but they are also quite cruel.

The Number One Orchestra of the World

The following week, Oliver notices I have labelled instruments with numbers and marked up numbers on the xylophone and metallophone bars. I introduce Oliver to the idea of composing music by number. After some experiments with this technique, Oliver finds a safer way to proceed and transfers the idea back to his characters – thus gaining back his control and showing me that blowing up the Land of Noise had simply cleared the way for a whole lot of new adventures. A new character "Green Frog" emerges as Oliver finds a green flannel frog puppet and adds him to the story. Green Frog becomes the Toad-croakers' teacher and helps them to form a band of instruments made up from instruments labelled with the number 1. Oliver announces: "the Toad-croakers and Green Frog play in the 'Number One Orchestra of the World'."

★★★★★★

The Adventures Continue with New Characters

Oliver's stories become more and more elaborate as the weeks and months progress with each series of adventures covering his "special interest" at the time. Through his stories, he shares with me his passion and interests in the natural world both past and present and uses these to explore and play with ideas and experiences. He gathers further characters rather like a snowball rolling downhill gathers more snow. He animates almost every instrument available to populate his worlds with new characters for the Toad-croakers to come across and interact with in their travels.

Oliver then develops a new style of narration – a radio drama serial called: "The Toad-croakers and the Marvellous Machines." Oliver dictates the script, I type it up and we record the episode. Because we have a script to follow, Oliver is able to enjoy the experience of working together as he knows exactly the order in which we are going to speak and what we are going to say. He expresses his surprise at how I am able to make his characters sound the way he had imagined they would! This work shows a development in Oliver's use of his imagination as he no longer manipulates objects to tell his story. He is working with mental representations and using the instruments to make sound effects. In the development of the radio drama, Oliver also demonstrates that he can embrace Team Work.

I Undertake Further Training

As we embark on the radio play, I undertake my first assignment on a course for professionals working with people on the Autistic Spectrum. It is titled:

> It has been traditionally thought that people with Aspergers have an impaired imagination. Examine this concept in the light of a case study.

Oliver's stories showed an incredibly rich and inventive imagination. I had always been confused by this marker in autistic diagnosis. In what way did Oliver have "impaired imagination"? This assignment reminded me how the type of imagination used in fantasy was different from the type of imagination needed to plan and carry out everyday tasks and in the development of empathy. Oliver did struggle with the latter uses of imagination.

A lovely example of Oliver's rather "black and white" empathic response is illustrated in a game of Ten pin bowling he set up between Big Toad-croaker and Little Toad-croaker. Oliver bowls for both of them. Little Toad-croaker loses the game. I ask him: "What do you think Little Toad-croaker might be feeling because he has lost? What might he have said?" Oliver replies "I need to do more practice." I laugh because the answer surprises me. Oliver asks "why did you laugh?" I explain "I thought Little toad-croaker might have been a bit upset." Oliver replies "Only if someone had cheated."

What Makes a Child with Autism Spectrum Disorder Hard to Reach?

Oliver was an incredibly bright, sensitive child with an enormous capacity and desire for engagement with the world. His autism brought with it the challenges of a brain wired differently from his neurotypical peers. For Oliver, the behaviour of his peers was a complete mystery. He had little understanding of why they behaved as they did and why they didn't want to hear about the things he felt passionate about. He was unable to join them in play as he didn't understand the unspoken rules of social interaction. He had difficulty reading faces to give clues as to what they might be thinking and planning and found the unpredictability of children alarming and anxiety provoking. In summary, some of the specific issues that made Oliver hard to reach are given here (many of which I like to think we addressed together in The Music Box).

- His sensitivity to sound.
- Feelings of being ostracised for being different.
- His desire to play with others.
- His low threshold for error.
- His bombardment by external environmental stimuli.
- His difficulty in understanding other people's reactions.
- His overwhelm when things don't go to plan.

For Oliver, I believe his child-led sessions provided him with an oasis, free from the stresses of his day-to-day struggles. He found his own unique way to explore his experience of life and so enjoy the opportunity of sharing what excited him with someone outside of his family environment.

I believe thinking about Oliver can help the reader towards understanding some of the difficulties the person with autism faces in trying to reach out to us. This is beautifully illustrated by Dr. Camilla Pang (2020) in her introduction to her book *Explaining Humans – What Science Can Teach Us about Life, Love and Relationships*:

> It was five years into my life on Earth that I started to think I'd landed in the wrong place. I must have missed the stop. I felt like a stranger within my own species: someone who understood the words but couldn't speak the language; who shared an appearance with fellow humans but none of the essential characteristics.

She goes on to state that she feels she needs: "a guidebook, something that explains why people behave in the way they do?"

I feel the irony and the injustice in this – I have spent many years reading material attempting to explain why people with autism behave in the ways that they do. I have never thought of writing a manual for my clients explaining the ways in which *I* behave!

In looking back over my notes on Oliver's adventures in the Music Box and my development in helping him and other children on the autistic spectrum, I re-discovered a personal inscription from the author inside my copy of *Learning to Live with High Functioning Autism* (Stanton, 2000):

> Remember, it is better to teach autistic people how to manage our behaviour than how to manage their own.

(Stanton, 2000)

Notes

1 The most common movement disturbance is Apraxia, this is, having problems with the conceptualisation and planning of movement, so that the action is less proficient and coordinated than one would expect. Studies have indicated that children with Asperger's syndrome have problems with the mental preparation and planning of movement but have relatively intact motor pathways (Minshew, Goldstein and Siegel, 1997; Rinehart et al., 2001; Roger's et al., 1996; Smith and Bryson, 1998; Weimer et al., 2001; Claire Sainsbury-Martian in the Playground, 2009, p. 9).
2 A large free-standing instrument with metal bars sounded with beaters.
3 A free-standing set of metal chimes sounded by brushing or hitting with a metal beater.
4 A free-standing set of three drums which can rotate to produce different pitches.
5 An Acme duck call that can sound like a fart when you blow it!

References

Baron-Cohen, S., & Leslie, F. (1985) Does the Autistic Child Have a Theory of Mind? *Cognition 21*(1), 37–46.

Gerland, G. (1997) *A Real Person: Life on the Outside*. London: Souvenir Press Ltd.

Minshew, N. J., Goldstein, G., & Siegel, D. J. (1997) Neuropsychologic Functioning in Autism: Profile of a Complex Information Processing Disorder. *Journal of Autism and Development Disorders 38*, 1485–1498.

Pang, C. (2020) *Explaining Humans – What Science Can Teach Us about Life, Love and Relationships*. London: Penguin Books Ltd.

Rinehart, N., Bradshaw, J., Brereton, A., & Tonge, B. (2001) Movement Preparation in High Functioning Autism and Asperger Disorder. *Journal of Autism and Developmental Disorders 31*, 79–88.

Rogers, S., Benneto, L., McEvoy, R., & Pennington, B. (1996) Imitation and Pantomime in High Function Adolescents with Autism Spectrum Disorder. *Child Development 67*, 2060–2073.

Sainsbury, C. (2009) *Martian in the Playground*. London: Sage Publications.

Smith, I., & Bryson, S. (1998) Gesture Imitation in Autism; 1. Nonsymbolic Postures and Sequences. *Cognitive Neuropsychology 15*, 747–770.

Stanton, M. (2000) *Learning to Live with High Functioning Autism*. London: Jessica Kingsley.

Weimer, A., Schatz, A., Ballantyne, A., & Trauer, D. (2001) "Motor" Impairment in Asperger Syndrome: Evidence for a Deficit in Proprioception. *Developmental and Behavioural Paediatrics 22*, 92–101.

Williams, D. (1992) *Nobody Nowhere*. London: Doubleday.

Chapter 4

Florence Nightingale Is Just Outside the Door

Jane Unsworth

This chapter tells a story about an extraordinary encounter with a child that happened some years ago now, when I was a trainee therapist on my clinical placement. When I met the little girl, I shall call Poppy, she was presenting as selectively mute and frozen. She seemed so far out of reach that I thought it might be impossible to work with her, yet the experience of reaching out to her and what that could actually mean transformed my sense of what being a therapist could be.

If you will indulge me, I would like to ask you to imagine you are watching a slide-show of images taken on a journey I went on in the past, grainy and with the enthusiasm and imperfections of a rather amateur photographer. I made these 'snapshots' for my Master's thesis using a heuristic approach to re-explore and examine my experiences (Moustakas, 1990), and have taken them out to look at them afresh. The following commentary is the re-telling of the story of the therapy journey we made together, reflected on from my more experienced perspective.

Before I begin our slideshow, I'd like to tell you some more about Poppy. At the time I met her, she was five years old and had retreated so far away from the world outside her immediate family that she could barely exist. She did not speak in school and, over time, had shown a gradual falling away of other aspects of the presentation of a living, autonomous child. By the time she was referred for therapy, her teacher described a 'pretty and perfect' little figure who stood, statue-like, in the classroom apparently unable to speak or move, even to meet the most basic of bodily functions such as asking to use the toilet. She was both frozen and mute and seemed completely out of reach.

My first thoughts were of a profoundly distressed and anxious child. The term 'Selective Mutism' used by staff in relation to Poppy has been re-classified in the most recent DSM V as an anxiety disorder. My now more experienced self also thinks about an aspect of a "Disorganised/Disorientated attachment style"... "behavioural stilling, when all movements cease, suggesting confusion or depression, and dazed expressions suggestive of conflicting systems producing a frozen state" (Geddes, 2006). The result of attachment trauma being that incoherence pervades the development of self, described by Fisher (2017) as "patterns of compartmentalisation" which the child adopts as "trauma-related procedural learning: it is safer to adapt using a system of selves rather than becoming a fully integrated 'self'" (Fisher, 2017).

DOI: 10.4324/9781003163015-4

Little did I know of the extraordinary and complex journey we were about to embark on together. Over a period of 26 months, we travelled through some difficult and dangerous terrain. We shared struggles and delights along the way and eventually arrived at a place where she, and also I, had become more integrated and actualised, in a sense more 'real'. As I hope you will see, this is a tale of the therapeutic process of reaching out to a client who may seem unreachable also being one of reaching in for the therapist, and that these are indivisible.

Now, to begin.

First Meeting

I look across the classroom and am struck by her ethereal fragility, as though a little fairy had stepped out of a story. Her stance is stiff and static, unmoving apart from her bright, alert eyes that fix intently on my face. I look directly into them and everything else in the classroom fades and dulls, still there but distant now, outside of and not part of the intensity of our shared gaze.

This is not what I had been expecting. I give a little smile and gently speak to her. She does not move but continues to hold me in deep eye contact, as though she were somehow searching beyond my words and demeanour into my essence. This feels powerful and, in that moment, reasonable and comfortable. I hold her gaze and simply am. After a time I gently speak again.

Do you think you would you like to come with me to my room to see my toys and art things next week?

Her eyes imperceptibly widen and somehow convey the sense of a tiny nod. I smile warmly.

"OK. I'll look forward to seeing you then" I say. I hear a small intake of breath and her eyes glisten.

"See you next week" I say, almost in a whisper, and smile directly into her eyes. Those eyes sparkle and remain fixed on me as I walk towards the door. As I stand in the doorway, I look back to her and we make eye contact again. Again, the bustle of the classroom falls away and what exists is our connection, powerful to us but invisible to others. As she holds my gaze, I smile and give a small wave. Her eyes give another bright sparkle for a moment, and then she looks away.

I am released, and walk out of the room.

This first encounter shows a shift in my way of relating with Poppy that was to prove absolutely central to the therapy – from doing to being. In a moment I describe leaving my own thoughts and expectations behind and devoting my whole bodily attention to Poppy and her experience in the here and now. Indeed, I can feel it again as I think about it. The focus on shared eye contact and strongly felt sense of our connection being very powerful evokes Stern's ideas about the mother–infant dyad and the 'shared affect state' (Stern, 1985) that is the foundation of a secure attachment. Even though I didn't know it at the time, I was now ready to meet her, exactly as she was. Her response to this was to be extraordinary…

First Session

I feel excited at the prospect of our first session. I have read about selective mutism and *been given ideas from my supervision group* and I am confident and prepared to manage a silent 50 minutes.

When I arrive at the classroom, she is perched on a chair behind all the other children, who are sitting on the carpet in front of the teacher. I am met by the same powerful eye contact and shining eyes I had encountered the previous week and feel myself drawn towards her. I have been told that she is unlikely to move without physical assistance and, as I come close to her and we continue to look into each other's eyes, I feel my hand reach forward and see her hand rise to meet it. It is almost as though we are engaged in a dance together as we move from the chair and across the classroom, walking at her pace and connected by our joined hands and joined gaze, negotiating without words how we journey through the school corridor in partnership until we reach the door of the therapy room. Here there is a pause and a strong sense of being on the threshold of something. I say

"Shall we open it together?" and she reaches forward to push on the wooden surface with me.

We step through the entrance side by side, no longer looking at one another as we pass into the therapy space. The door closes behind us and I look towards her again. We stand facing one another as we hear the catch click into place. She lifts her chin and I lean towards her.

"I've got a secret" she says.

I feel a moment's astonishment, but almost immediately a powerful sense of rightness and recognition that she had planned to do this.

"Oh," I say, matching the volume and tone of her voice. "Would you like to tell me about it? You can if you want, or not if you don't want to."

She sits down at the table of art materials and I sit beside her, now both looking at the materials rather than each other.

"I'm a princess, but nobody knows except Mummy" she says.

Amazing! The moment when Poppy spoke to me was like a lightning bolt, simultaneously experienced as a shock and absolutely inevitable. My higher 'left brain' response was intellectual and had been concerned with thinking about selective mutism and how I would work with her, so I was not consciously expecting speech. However, my more embodied 'right brain' response had been engaging with her creatively in a felt and co-created relational way. The re-establishment of close eye contact and full, embodied connectedness it evidenced led to our shared 'dance' towards the therapy room. Schore describes "reciprocal interactions within the mother–infant regulatory system" (Schore, 2003) communicating to the child that she can feel understood and understand herself whilst feeling safe within the regulation of the caregiver. In the context of this understanding of the meaning, we were beginning to make together, the possibility that the 'Princess' part of Poppy might be able to feel safe enough to speak to me is no longer a surprise.

She had begun to allow me to reach out to her, and her Princess-self could perhaps see the possibility of my fingertips in the distance, but my hand was still a very long way from hers.

'Baby's Birthday' 1st Stage

The baby doll is dressed entirely in pink: its hard plastic limbs and head attached to a soft-stuffed torso; blue glass-like eyes staring, petal lips slightly parted, cheeks forever rosy. Poppy begins her now-familiar routine.

"It's Baby's birthday! We need to get her party ready."

She proceeds to direct me to hold Baby (the doll) and keep her occupied, giving me a small ball from the box to do this with, "While we get the party ready." As usual, she does not touch Baby and requires that Baby should not look at her.

As I hold Baby and play with her I began to feel drowsy.

Poppy gets to her usual activity, using the plastic tea set to create mixtures of sand, water, paint, glue, play-doh and glitter. She examines the ones saved from the week before and re-mixes them. As she does this she gives a running commentary, her voice light and with a sing-song quality. She presents as busy, happy and content.

As she engages in this 'happy' task I, as in previous sessions, become increasingly sleepy. I find my eyes frequently drawn to the clock on the wall and my attention drifting away from the room. I feel physically uncomfortable and find myself shifting position as we sit on the floor. An unpleasant fizzing/itching feeling in my legs grows. I feel a little queasy. As I hold Baby in my lap, I struggle with the strong desire to end the session and leave the room.

Whilst being painfully aware of my own difficult feelings, I work on maintaining my focus alongside the child, staying with her in her activity and matching her affect. She appears to enjoy my engagement with her and my summarising responses to her utterances, smiling, laughing and making eye contact. I have found in previous sessions that any question about her experience of the activity would be met with a response almost beyond ignoring, rather as though I simply had not communicated at all. I find myself wanting her positive engagement with me and really enjoying moments of shared attention and feeling.

She directs my participation in the play, mixing 'cakes' and pouring liquids with absorption, referring to Baby but not engaging with her in any way. I continue to work to notice and be alongside her contented play, whilst managing the increasingly unpleasant physical and emotional experiences I am aware of in myself.

This activity continues until the end of the session, when we follow the now-familiar routine of choosing those 'cakes' and 'drinks' to be saved for next time.

I was becoming aware of some profound fragmentation in my experience in the therapy room with Poppy. This iteration of 'Baby' appeared to represent another aspect of idealised, appealing femininity and childishness alongside the presentations of Poppy herself as the unreal fairy Poppy who had stepped out of a story in Snapshot 1 and the Princess Poppy with the magical power of speech who first came into the room. Our play together felt repetitive and limited, with a sense of being both there and not-there simultaneously. Poppy felt more distant than ever.

However, something about these characteristics now belonging to an object (the doll named Baby) that could be passed between us seemed to begin to evoke a deeply contrasting set of experiences within me that did not seem concordant with my authentic self. Grant and Crawley (2002) describe a projective identification as a blurring of the boundaries between self and other, where the client engenders in the therapist aspects of herself that feel too unsafe to experience, so the therapist experiences them instead.

Perhaps Poppy's retreat into an idealised, limited and safe aspect of herself where she could engage in contented play and keep her difficult and painful feelings apart was beginning to change? Perhaps in opening myself up to the possibility of such deep connectedness with her, I was reaching out to these withheld aspects of her experience, and beginning to touch some of them?

'Baby's Birthday' 2nd Stage

Baby is waiting as we begin our session. The familiar routine begins, as it now has for many sessions before. "It's Baby's birthday! We need to get her party ready."

Poppy directs me to hold Baby and keep her occupied, giving me Baby's current toy, as chosen by Poppy, a small, solid fairy figure. This is still, as in previous sessions, to distract Baby "while we get the party ready." As usual, Poppy does not touch Baby and requires that Baby should not look at her.

The baby doll is still dressed entirely in pink and maintains her idealised baby girl properties. However, her slightly parted petal lips are now crusted with the dried residue of 'food' mixtures we have made from sand, glue and paint during previous sessions. Her candy-pink clothes are stained around the neck with the dribbles of this 'food', which has poured out of her mouth and down her chest over numerous episodes of forced feeding during previous weeks. The blue glassy eyes continue to stare and the rosy cheeks, slightly dimpled as though smiling, continue to shine. I feel the now-familiar disgust rising in my chest.

Poppy continues to engage with creating and re-mixing mixtures for the party food, chatting brightly in a sing-song voice about what she is doing and how much fun the party is going to be. She reminds me, as always, that Baby shouldn't see us as the party will be a surprise for her. As she does this, I hold Baby and her hard fairy 'toy' and feel increasingly sickened. I struggle to keep my attention in the room. As in the many sessions that have come before this one, my own strong feelings of discomfort, inattention, drowsiness, nausea and disgust are directly at odds with Poppy's presentation as engaged, focussed, happy and content. She does not appear to notice any change to Baby's appearance.

I feel the time in the game approaching where it will be my task to 'feed' baby with some of the prepared food. Poppy presents it to me and, as usual, tells me that Baby does not want to eat it. She watches with apparent fascination as I use the small pink plastic spoon that she has given me to put repeated spoonfuls of the grey, sloppy mixture to Baby's lips and to continue to do this as the 'food' pours out again and again, covering Baby's face and chest. As in the previous sessions, I feel panic rising and my throat becomes strained and painful. My own breath quickens and my heart pounds as I resist a powerful desire to run from the room. I focus on slowing my own breath to regulate and maintain my position beside Poppy, both physically and emotionally.

At this point in previous sessions, I have tried to think with Poppy about what this experience might be like for Baby and for the maker of the food. I have spoken in my own voice and I have spoken as Baby. On all those occasions, she has responded, as she often does, with a lack of recognition so total that it is tempting to think that she has not heard me at all. The result of this has been that I simply continue to act and re-enact this process with her week after week, following her instructions and being alongside her as we act it out together.

This time, as we follow the familiar pattern of this feeding process, I feel a sudden change in my own emotional state. Far from sick and drowsy, I feel intensely alert and present in the room. I look at Poppy who appears to be unchanged, continuing to watch with an apparent detached interest. I lift the spoon of 'food' to Baby's lips yet again and, for the first time, I turn Baby's head away and say "No!".

Suddenly, Poppy's facial expression and physical demeanour totally change. She breathes in sharply and audibly. Her stiff, mannered presentation is transformed as her shoulders rise, she leans a little forward and her hands lift towards me, open-palmed. She looks at me and Baby wide-eyed and open-mouthed, with a smile beginning to form. She appears to be both amazed and delighted.

"No, I don't want to!" I say again as I move Baby's head away from the spoon, more vigorously this time, all the while looking at Poppy's face as she looks at baby and then back at me. She repeatedly makes close, engaged eye contact with me and laughs with apparent delight.

"What's it like when Baby says No?" I ask her.

"It's amazing!" she replies.I feel absolutely present, alive and more connected to Poppy than ever before in this moment. We continue to enact Baby's refusal to be fed for the rest of the session, sharing warm eye contact, talk and laughter as we do so.

Oh yuck. Even re-reading this account years later evokes very uncomfortable emotions and bodily sensations for me. The panic and desire to avoid contemplating the 'feeding' aspect of this play is still an active memory.

However, my real experiencing and processing of these feelings of panic, nausea and being trapped were key to the therapeutic shift in this session. Grant and Crawley (2002) cite Ogden (1982) in stating the therapeutic value of this is that "the recipient is different from the projector" (Grant and Crawley, 2002, p. 28) and can therefore respond to the feelings differently and more maturely. The therapist can digest and present the feelings back to the client in a way that can be tolerated, offering new ways of handling deeply disturbing feelings that could not previously be owned.

The deeply felt connection and consequent embodied, empathetic experiencing between us allowed this moment to happen phenomenologically, when I was suddenly really able to reach out and touch another previously out-of-reach aspect of Poppy's emotional life, and she was able to feel the touch and tolerate it as safe.

Fragmentation and escape from trauma through dissociation processes can lead to the development of dissociative aspects of self described by Fisher (2017) as "Structurally dissociated parts", where an individual appears to inhabit different and very distinct aspects of themselves at different times and in different contexts, often with limited awareness that this is taking place. Poppy had already been presenting different versions of herself – at home and at school, outside the therapy room and inside. This snapshot shows very clearly how she is dissociated from the repeated traumatic experience being enacted on 'Baby' in our play until the moment we are connected through my felt sense that, after weeks of processing happening in me, baby could resist this time. In a rush of adrenaline, we are both suddenly engaged with Baby's experiencing at a heightened level 'wide-eyed'.

However, these are realisations I had not fully made at the time. I felt out of my depth as I was becoming more drawn in to this relationship, and questioning what it meant to my practice as a student therapist. I was experiencing things that were difficult and frightening and could, at times, feel like a lost girl myself. I needed a hand to reach out to me, which was offered at a key moment by my clinical supervisor…

Super Supervision Session

I am feeling absolutely stuck. What am I going to say *about my work* to my colleagues and supervisor *in today's fortnightly supervision group*? What is happening? What am I doing? What is the point?

I sit on the cushion in my usual spot and listen to my colleagues talking about their cases. Poppy is in my mind, but out of reach somehow. I can't seem to formulate any words to talk about her or even collect any coherent thoughts about her. It comes to my turn and I feel a sense of anxiety and impending failure. I don't have anything to show. I have a lump in my throat and my mouth is dry. I can't feel my body and am only aware of my head and its strange, simultaneous emptiness and weight.

My calm and kind supervisor looks at me warmly and gently reminds me to 'trust the process' and just choose some objects to arrange. I look at her face and am able to imagine that, yes, this might be possible. I begin to feel my breath in my chest and it is slowing. As I stand up and look at the very many objects arranged on the shelves, my arm rises and I reach towards a figure with absolute certainty. The little grey pewter fairy sits solidly in my hand and I can feel my senses returning to my body in a rush. Impotence is replaced with agency and inertia with action. I quickly select a vine of abundant green leaf growth and a small wooden, articulated figure of a girl with rosy cheeks and brightly coloured clothing. I sit down and arrange them in front of me on the floor placing the grey pewter fairy to the left and the colourful wooden girl to the right with the growing leaves as a pathway from fairy to girl (see Figure 4.1).

As I finish, I become aware of my supervisor and colleagues and look up to see them all looking between my created image and my face with interest.

"I think I've realised" I say.

> This (gesturing to the fairy) is Poppy when I first met her, like a little changeling – beautiful to look at but grey, cold, stiff and lacking life – an absence where she should be. The leaf growth is what is happening in the therapy somehow and the little wooden figure (picking it up and holding it gently in my hand) is what she is becoming – a colourful, warm, moving, imperfect and alive girl. Poppy is turning back into a real girl!

I feel full of energy and warmth. I am excited to continue the therapy journey at our next session.

Figure 4.1 Supervision Image.

When I see this again, I am reminded of the image of a Russian doll, with me containing Poppy and my supervisor containing me. Remembering my supervisor holding eye contact and communicating her empathy with my plight, remaining calm and feeding my self-doubt back to me in a way that I could digest makes me feel the process of her enabling embodiment and integration in me. My exclamation that "Poppy is turning back into a real girl" could just as easily have been applied to me in that moment, the processes parallel.

My confirmed confidence following this supervision allowed the process of the therapy to evolve and my capacity to contain the difficult emotions that were evoked in the process created opportunity for further fragmented aspects of Poppy's experience and self to manifest and come within reach. The first and most extraordinary of these was "Florence Nightingale"…

Florence Nightingale on the Phone

As usual, it is Baby's birthday. Baby is no longer a Baby and it is now usually her fourth birthday. Preparations are underway. We are getting everything ready for the party as we usually do. We are chatting about how Poppy's week has been and exchanging warm laughter and eye contact. Poppy is updating me about the whereabouts and exploits of her imaginary friend 'Florence Nightingale' who is an adventurer and explorer. Florence is on her way to the party, as she usually is, but is coming from a very long way away and has to overcome many obstacles. I am feeling engaged and interested. I follow Poppy's talk and play with delighted interest and track what is happening with her. She seeks eye contact and receives my empathy – communicating facial expressions positively.

Over the previous weeks since Poppy introduced Florence Nightingale, we have gradually wondered about her together, with Poppy providing the answers: how old she is – a few years older than Poppy; what she looks like – just like Poppy; how Poppy knows what she is doing – they share the same thoughts. It has been established that nobody else can see her or knows about her but that I can know about her. This gradual involvement of, understanding and talking about Florence Nightingale has become an established part of the play and I feel quite fascinated to find out more about her.

I ask Poppy where Florence might be now and whether she might come to the party in time. I feel my fascination rise and look at Poppy, who is looking directly at me, wide-eyed and alert. My own level of awareness rises sharply as I look into Poppy's eyes. "Why don't you ask her?" she says. My senses have become very sharp and I am suddenly aware of a toy mobile phone in the box of objects and pick it up. Holding it to my ear I say "Hello, is that Florence Nightingale?"

"Yes, it is" says Poppy.

"Oh, I'm so glad to talk to you Florence" I say. "What are you doing? I know you have lots of adventures on your travels in the world. Where are you now?"

"I'm just outside the door" says Poppy. My scalp tingles and the hair stands up on my arms. I look at her, mouth open and questioning.

"Listen," she says. "Can you hear her?"

I look over to the therapy room door. "Shall we let her in?" I say.

"Yes" says Poppy, "Open the door."

Seeing this snapshot takes my breath away all over again. The journey and promise of arrival of "Florence Nightingale" made the process we were engaged in together so real and explicit. Fisher (2017) suggests that processes of integrating fragmented aspects of self are complex, and involve meeting them as clearly differentiated in order to study and then befriend them before linking in a way that "fosters a transformed sense of the client's experience, facilitating healing and re-connection" (Fisher, 2017). It is as though me reaching out and making a connection with Florence through the toy phone is a tentative step towards the possibility that she may join us – it can be tasted and digested through the safety of my experience before being fed to Poppy when she is ready for it.

Excitingly, over the following weeks, Poppy did indeed begin to express aspects of character that had previously been attributed to Florence. She started to take independent action in school and was seen beginning to talk to other children. This process of integration began to up in pace from now on.

All the Friends

Poppy and I are discussing all the imaginary friends that are in the room with us for every session now, floating above our heads as we play. I am trying to track what is happening in the play as she chatters busily and am starting to feel very confused and unsure as to the distinct identities of the friends.

"Hang on a minute," I say. "Can we just look at the list of names because I am getting very mixed up about who is who?"

Poppy laughs and agrees to me getting the list we made several weeks ago out of her folder. As we look at it together, her eyebrows knit and her face reveals some confusion. "But that's wrong!" she says. "Those aren't their names." She looks down the list and then takes a pen to correct it, giving each friend the same surname and age as herself. She then gives some of them the first name Poppy.

I feel clarity and relief. We are able to continue our play.

The process of reaching out to previously unfelt aspects of herself had really begun and the following weeks saw great change. Other imaginary friends joined us in the intersubjective space of our therapy, more quickly and easily now than Florence had done. Friends such as Becky and Isla who could do things Poppy couldn't do and soon morphed into Poppy. Then came Charlie who played in a band and was confident and funny which were attributes Poppy found it hard to embrace. Then Grumpy Greta arrived and she was able to be oppositional and defiant in ways Poppy had never been able to show before.

The kind of dissociative fragmentation of self in response to trauma described in relation to Poppy's play with 'Baby' can, at its most extreme, lead to a diagnosis of Dissociative Identity Disorder, described in DSM – 5 as having distinct personality states that "involve(s) marked discontinuity in sense of self and sense of agency, accompanied by related alterations in affect, behaviour, consciousness, memory…" (DSM – 5, 2013). Interestingly in relation to Poppy's play with me Muller (2006) highlights studies finding a much higher incidence of childhood imaginary companions in adults who went on to be diagnosed with Dissociative Identity Disorders than in normative samples. Poppy's imaginary companions, brave and adventurous Florence Nightingale (Snapshot 6) so different to Poppy and yet sharing her looks and thoughts; and 'all the friends' floating above her (Snapshot 7), different and yet somehow having the same name as Poppy, could be understood as aspects of self that she has developed in response to early attachment trauma.

It remained important that I met and understood all the friends and their individual characteristics in some way, but this became harder for us both to track as the process got faster, leading to a list being created. I think my feeling of 'clarity and relief' here is at the recognition that, through my experiencing and managing the initial connection, Poppy was able to engage with them safely in the process of achieving coherence described by Fisher (2017).

The pace of this process continued to increase. Poppy showed more and more agency both in the therapy room and in the wider world. She even began to experiment with whispered speech to adults in school. The next snapshot shows how the final stages of integration were beginning…

Brave Bear

Poppy and I are playing with art materials that she has been able to get from the resources cupboard herself, as she usually does now. She is chatting to me about what she has been doing this week and games she has been playing at home with a favourite toy, Billy Bear.

"Billy climbed up the stairs all by himself, even though it was really steep!" she *says*, looking at me with wide eyes.

"Wow!" I *say*, conveying empathy at the enormity of this achievement "That sounds as though it might have been tough and scary! Good for Billy!"

"Yes," she says. "I am teaching him to be brave, just like you teach me to be brave."

I feel sudden surprise and a warm rush of feeling in my chest. I look at Poppy in amazement and wonder as she gives a little smile and continues to play, apparently unaware of the enormous impact on me of what she has just said. To her, it seemed simply a matter of fact.

I loved this moment we shared and am still so moved and amazed by the way it evokes the Kleinian idea of the healthily internalised relationship, incorporating representations of the self, the other and the emotion that connects them (Klein, 1952). This is the converse to the fragmented Poppy with split-off aspects of self we had seen at the beginning of our journey.

It was around this time that Poppy participated in a whole class assembly, standing on stage and singing with her peers in front of an audience. She really was becoming herself.

Ending – Integration

It is our last session. I am looking at Poppy with feelings of intense pride and admiration. She is looking through the images and objects we have made together during the long journey of her therapy. She picks out the list of names and ages of her imaginary friends. "What's this?" she asks. I feel quite astonished, but try to moderate this in my answer.

"Those were the names of some friends who used to come with you, do you remember?" She furrows her brows and scrunches her nose. "I couldn't see or hear them but you could?" I prompt further. She looks at me thoughtfully and says "Oh yes, I think so. I've forgotten about them, they've gone now."

She *discarded* the list on the floor and carried on looking at her other images, packing them up to take away with her.

The result of the process of forming coherence out of fragmentation is demonstrated most clearly here, our penultimate session together. I retained a memory of the distinct selves that joined us in our shared therapy space but Poppy revealed that "I've forgotten about them, they've gone now." I felt I had "taken them into myself and digested them for her" to enable her to take into herself what she needed from them.

Ending – Together Forever

Poppy and I are sitting opposite one another at the little table covered with art materials. We had previously planned to make cards for each other to take away from this last session. I am feeling calm, very connected to her and a little sad. "Would you like to make cards, or do something else?" I say. "Make cards!" she replies, emphatically. She looks at the materials laid out between us and up at me. "Let's do hand prints!" she says. She begins to squeeze paint from the large tubes onto paper plates, appearing to be fully engaged in the pouring and mixing. I am reminded of the play from our early sessions when she had become so engrossed in mixing sand, glue and paint to make 'food' for Baby's birthday, except that now the mixture is smooth and colourful. "What shall I do?" I say. "Mix some paint," is her reply. I join her in squeezing bright colour onto paper plates, enjoying the sensory experience of the smooth, soft paint as it spreads across the surface. We each hold our brushes and look at each other across the table covered with our mixed pigments. I begin to paint my hand, and Poppy does likewise. She looks at me and says "I want to paint your hand!" I feel a warmth in my chest as I reach out my hand, palm upwards, towards her. She gently takes my large hand in her little one and begins to stroke the paintbrush across it. I feel nurtured and valued – at once separate and distinct from her and yet intensely connected to her. She offers her little hand to me in an echo of my palm upwards gesture, and I gently take it and stroke the paintbrush across every finger and her palm. We have not spoken during this exchange, but I feel a deep sense of calm and contentment. I look at my painted hand and up at her face. I wait. Suddenly, she draws breath audibly and becomes much more lively and animated. "I know, I know!" she says, "You put yours and I'll put mine." "Both on the same one?" I confirm, although I feel a deep sense of the rightness of this and am sure this is what she means.

"Yes!" she exclaims excitedly. I place my right hand down on the card, pressing firmly and feeling every part of the skin as I do so. I peel my hand off the paper and we both look at the imprint. She then places her left hand on top of the image of my right, herself pressing the whole surface of her skin onto the print of my hand. She lifts her hand away and looks at the image. I look at it too. I feel a sense of achievement and contentment. There is a completeness and perfection about it that is deeply satisfying. "Now let's do yours!" she exclaims, and we repeat the process on the other piece of card, this time using my painted left hand and her painted right.

We look at them both, side by side. She picks up a felt pen and writes both of our names across the bottom of each image. "Look," she says, "Now we can both be holding hands for ever."

This snapshot of our final session reveals the process of intense connection, co-creation and internalisation that has taken place, allowing Poppy to manage a healthy separation. It describes our deeply attuned state and my internal experience of being: "at once separate and distinct from her and yet intensely connected to her." This time Poppy experienced the moment of alertness and took action phenomenologically, devising an activity that resulted in the creation of a transitional object for each of us that symbolically represents our connectedness in the co-creation of joined handprint images. We have shared feelings and understandings that will remain inside each of us and will be carried forward, beyond a space shared physically. This will indeed be with us forever.

★ ★ ★

Thank you for sharing in this slide show with me. As I hope I have shown, the therapeutic journey with this child who had seemed so far away as to be unreachable, and the process of revisiting it through auto-ethnography, was one of reaching into myself and my own experience. In order to reach out to Poppy, I learned to reach into myself, and in this gained a profound sense of what can be possible in a therapeutic encounter when one is able to open oneself to a level of being with another that is so embodied and intersubjective. As the once seemingly so unreachable Poppy said as I reached out my hand to her for the last time across the space we had created together: "Look, … now we can both be holding hands for ever…"

References

American Psychiatric Association (2013). *Diagnostic and Statistical Manual of Mental Disorders* (5th Ed.). Washington DC: American Psychiatric Publishing.

Fisher, J. (2017). *Healing the Fragmented Selves of Trauma Survivors – Overcoming Internal Self-Alienation*. New York: Routledge.

Geddes, H. (2006). *Attachment in the Classroom*. London: Worth Publishing Ltd.

Grant, J. and Crawley, J. (2002). *Transference and Projection*. Maidenhead: Open University Press.

Klein, M. (1952). Notes on some schizoid mechanisms. In J. Riviere (Ed.) *Developments in Psychoanalysis* (pp. 292–320). London: Hogarth Press.

Moustakas, C. (1990). *Heuristic Research: Design, Methodology and Applications*. Newbury Park, CA: Sage.

Muller, R. T. (2006). Childhood trauma, imaginary companions and the development of pathological dissociation. *Aggression and Violent Behaviour* Vol. 11, Issue 5, pp. 531–545.

Ogden, T. H. (1982). *Projective Identification and Psychotherapeutic Technique*. New York: Jason Aranson.

Schore, A. N. (2003). *Affect Regulation and the Repair of the Self*. New York: Horton.

Stern, D. (1985). *The Interpersonal World of the Infant*. London: Karnack Books.

Chapter 5

The Ripple Effect
Supervising Jane

Aileen Webber

Introduction

This chapter is the retold story of the remarkable therapeutic work undertaken by Jane Unsworth with her five-year-old client Poppy, presented in the previous chapter. It describes supervision carried out in a small group of four therapists with myself as supervisor. Amongst other things, I aim to show that when a therapist brings the therapeutic work of a client who is *hard-to-reach* to supervision, there is sometimes a knock-on effect of the therapist also becoming *hard-to-reach*.

Snapshot 1: Supervision Session before Jane Meets Poppy

A hush seemed to descend on the supervision group the first time Jane spoke about her new client Poppy. We listened attentively with concern and fascination to this child's unique difficulties. Jane had found out from her teacher that Poppy was unable to utter a single word at school or to show any sense of agency (although she had no difficulty in speaking or moving about at home). As the therapy room was within the school, Poppy was clearly not going to speak in therapy and she therefore already sounded *hard-to-reach*. Poppy, Jane told us, stood stiff and immobile in class, for example finding it too difficult to even put up her hand to ask for something. During this first introduction to Poppy, who at this stage Jane had not yet personally met, the supervision group seemed to be almost over eager to share their combined understanding and experiences of useful approaches when faced with Selective Mutism. Ideas included throwing bean bags, playing board games, blowing bubbles and generally having fun. Between us, we also recommended two books: "Selective Mutism in Our Own Words" (Sutton and Forrester, 2016) and "Can I tell you about Selective Mutism": a guide for friends, family and professionals (Johnson and Wintgens 2012). I was feeling confident that we had set Jane up with some useful practical suggestions as to how she could reach Poppy – despite the fact that she had never spoken at school. Even at this early stage, I was conscious of feeling responsible for supporting Jane so that she could reach this new client. We were full of anticipation as to what would happen when (or indeed if) Poppy accompanied Jane to the therapy room.

DOI: 10.4324/9781003163015-5

Snapshot 2: Supervision Session after Jane's First Meeting with Poppy

The anticipation in the room was palpable when Jane arrived for our next supervision group. I believe I spoke for all of us when I said to Jane that I was unable to contain myself any longer and would she please recount what had happened with Poppy in the intervening two weeks. My mind (and I sensed the minds of the other therapists) was full of questions. Would Poppy have agreed to go with Jane to the Therapy Room? How would Jane have managed to work with her Selective Mutism? Would Jane have utilised any of our suggestions for what she could do in a silent session? Would she have been able to reach Poppy? The scene was set with our combined curiosity. But nothing could have prepared us for what Jane was going to say next. She described how she walked with Poppy to the therapy room and how the door clicked closed and Poppy whispered in her ear: "I've got a secret … I'm a princess but no-body knows except Mummy!" There was a collective gasp from the group. Poppy had spoken in school for the first time ever!

I can remember with complete clarity how in that moment I pictured all that reading about how to work with Selective Mutism flying out of my head. Later I made a collage in my arts journal to depict the feeling of this moment (see Figure 5.1).

Figure 5.1 Ideas Flying Out of My Head.

What was this? It was most certainly not what we had anticipated. Yalom makes the important point, that guides my practice as a professional, that we need to think about our clients, read about their difficulties, imagine how we will work with them, and then leave all that thinking and theory outside the therapy door and tailor the therapy to the client in a unique way that is informed by the present moment (Yalom, 2001). In this instance, we needed to push all our preconceptions about Poppy and her therapy outside the *supervision* room door and stay with Jane as she was describing what had *actually* happened. We also had to deal with our mutual amazement and shock.

Reflections on Being a Supervisor

At this point, it is perhaps helpful to pause in the telling of this particular supervision story and step outside the supervision room in order to think about what supervision in this context actually involves. One of the many exceptional and wonderful things about this profession is that there is a *requirement* to take part in supervision. At a very basic level, supervision implies that a clearer (*super*) view (*vision*) of what is happening in the client's therapy is sought by the therapist speaking with another more experienced therapist. This very particular meaning of the word supervision within psychotherapy is summed up clearly by Carroll: "The supervisee is given a space, within a trusted relationship to reflect on their client work and explore ideas and creativity in the presence of an experienced other who enables that reflection" (Carroll and Tholstrup, 2004).

So, what should this "experienced other" provide? This can be thought of as a twofold aim to always have in mind: (a) the welfare of the clients whilst also encouraging (b) the development of the therapist. This is best achieved within a relationship between therapist and supervisor that is based on mutual trust, regard, and respect. The supervisor's function has been stated to provide: educative, supportive and administrative aspects (Kadushin, 1985). A lofty aspiration but one to which all supervisors must strive. Supervision also has a monitoring role to ensure that all clients are properly supported and the therapist is able to reflect on the therapy so that they can help their clients in the best way possible. It also provides a place where the therapist can talk through any safeguarding issues, assess any risks and discuss any ethical dilemmas.

Where a client is hard-to-reach, understanding the layer upon layer of interwoven relationships can be very complex as is shown in this chapter. It is my belief that the inclusion of art-based approaches within the supervision can help to untangle some of this complexity. The art made by both the therapist and supervisor in response to the client work can produce unconscious aspects of the therapy previously not grasped. The supervisor and the art also provide containment – particularly where the client is *hard-to- reach* and the unfolding of the therapy is difficult to manage or uncomfortable for the client, therapist or supervisor.

After completing my Gestalt and Integrative Arts Psychotherapy trainings and gaining many hours of experience working with clients, I was lucky enough to undertake a further qualification as a supervisor where the use of arts-based media was a key part of the supervision. This involved therapists giving central importance to describing their client's art, play, and metaphor in the supervision. Additional arts-based approaches would be brought into the supervision session itself in order to understand the therapeutic work further.

As described in the introduction to this book, where art or play are included in the therapeutic relationship it moves from a dyadic to a triadic relationship (Dalley et al., 1993). It is my belief that the introduction of art and play is central to the efficacy of the therapeutic work, especially in reaching *hard-to-reach* young people. Using art within the supervision provides a whole new dimension to the understanding of the therapy. This leaves the door open for the unexpected: synchronicity, silence, humour, fun, creativity, unconscious elements, and the opportunity to look at the therapy from multiple directions.

What is happening in the therapy can often be fascinatingly paralleled in the supervision. In Jane's case, this was within a supervision *group*. It was my job to try to unpick the echoes of the therapy that arose in the supervision group, in order to try to provide Jane with a new understanding of how to reach Poppy. Conversely we therapists and supervisors frequently marvel at how sometimes merely exploring something in the supervision may by unconscious osmosis (or almost magically) seem to shift something in the therapy. Practical suggestions may frequently help the therapist, but equally as in Jane's case, these may not seem to help much at all. But now to return to the supervision room.

Baby Being "Force-Fed"

Over many weeks, Jane described the "force feeding" of Baby and how sleepy and nauseous she would feel in the sessions. This was not something Jane had ever felt with a client before and we wondered if it was countertransference and what it might be telling us about Poppy. It was deeply disturbing to hear how Poppy's play was being experienced by Jane and I felt helpless to assist. Other therapists in the supervision group were affected by feeling deeply uncomfortable in various ways when hearing how Poppy would insist that Jane must continually, week on week, "force-feed" Baby. Instead of feeling sleepy, I would find myself going into overdrive: ruminating around the conundrum of what and how Poppy's play related to her story and *why* she was selectively mute. When I checked in with my body, I had a really uncomfortable feeling of being over-full or "stuffed" with too many unwanted and undigested thoughts and feelings swirling around in my head and feeling powerless to help.

At this point, I utilised my own art to try to understand what was happening. I was aware of the concepts of parallel process and countertransference in supervision, but in this case, I was not feeling Jane's feelings of nausea and tiredness so what might be going on? I sketched the pictures shown here and these images went some way towards helping me to come to the realisation that this over-full feeling of muddled and stressful thoughts was like carrying around a tornado of tangled responsibilities (see Figure 5.2) or feeling swallowed up by overwhelming

Figure 5.2 Tornado of Tangled Responsibilities.

feelings (see Figure 5.3). This meant I felt unable to think logically about how to support Jane.

On further reflection between supervision sessions, I began to realise that Jane had no other choice than to sit with these disturbingly uncomfortable feelings and I had no other choice than to hear about them and to sit with my *own* difficult feelings. The way I reacted at the time was to try to come up with different suggestions as to what Jane could do to persuade Poppy to allow her to cease "over-feeding" Baby. When reflecting on this later I began to realise that I was perhaps "over-feeding" the Supervision Group with ideas, suggestions, practical ways that Jane could change the situation, in a similar or parallel way to Jane feeling compelled by Poppy to "over-feed" Baby. We were all "stuffed" and uncomfortably full.

This felt like an example of a phenomenon that can arise in supervision called "parallel process". Mattinson describes this as:

> The processes at work currently in the relationship between client and worker are often reflected in the relationship between worker and supervisor.
>
> (Mattinson, 1975)

Perhaps with hindsight, we needed to stay with what Jane was telling us, whilst having an awareness of any feelings that emerged in us as she opened a window into the therapy room and expressing these to the supervision group.

Figure 5.3 Swallowed Up.

In psychotherapy and supervision trainings, much emphasis is put on the concept of countertransference. This is a complex issue including the conscious and unconscious aspects of client and therapist and their relationship. Within supervision, this includes both conscious and unconscious elements of the supervisor and the therapist and their client and their interwoven relationships. One way I have found helpful in attempting to unpick the many layers of countertransference, is to separate out *proactive* and *reactive* countertransference. Although it is in no way as simplistic as this might infer, it is possible in this analysis to think of *reactive* countertransference as being the feelings experienced in the therapist (or supervisor) in *reaction* to the client, whereas *proactive* countertransference refers to the therapist's (or the supervisor's) *own* feelings. For example, perhaps my feelings of wanting to provide practical suggestions and move Jane away from "force-feeding" Baby included *proactive* countertransference that was about my *own* history and experience of "over-feeding" myself to counteract difficult situations and feelings.

Luckily I was not left on my own with this unresolved dilemma. A supervisor in turn has a requirement to discuss the therapists under their supervision (and their client work) with a supervisor of their own. As it brought up so many conundrums, I frequently presented Jane's work with Poppy to *my* supervisor and together we reflected on how this urge towards "over-feeding" Jane and the supervision group, was most probably a kind of parallel process. Looking back I can see that I would often try to deflect or diffuse Jane's and my own uncomfortable feelings in the supervision sessions. I would make suggestions as to what Jane could do to resist having to keep "over-feeding" Baby (perhaps to prevent myself from feeling swallowed up).

My supervisor and I thought together about how this could be me having a need to "over- feed" Jane and the supervision group with ideas and suggestions in a kind of overcompensation for my feelings of being impotent to change things for Jane and Poppy. In hindsight, I can see that it would probably have been much better to voice my feelings of countertransference to the group, and then we could have collectively attempted to untangle the interwoven layers of intertwined relationships. This might have led to a useful discussion around the feelings of the supervision group, tracking through from client-to- therapist perhaps giving us some helpful additional information about what was happening in the therapy.

In subsequent supervision sessions, when Jane was describing her work with Poppy, I too started to feel disgust and distaste at the cumulative crusted layers of "food mixture" on Baby's lips from all the weeks of "force-feeding." After taking this new feeling to my own supervisor, I made a multi-layered image (see Figure 5.5) using Emotion Stones (www.yellow-door.net). Figure 5.4 is a close-up of Baby encrusted with "food mixture" taken from my diagrammatic image. After creating this image, *my* supervisor and I thought of the metaphor of a stone being dropped in a still pond and the semi-circles of ripples spreading out from the centre depicting the impact of Poppy's therapy.

Figure 5.5 shows the first circle of Poppy as the frozen fairy and the "force-fed" Baby equivalent of a stone being dropped into a pond. This is experienced in the first ripple effect by Jane as tiredness and nausea. In the next ripple effect, it is experienced by me, Jane's supervisor, as an uncomfortably full sensation of over-thinking with doubt pressing down on me. It is experienced by *my* supervisor (at the next ripple) as a bloated, over-full feeling in her stomach. This would seem to be an example of countertransference tracking through (as a ripple effect) from client-to-therapist-to-supervisor and finally to the supervisor's-supervisor.

Figure 5.4 Baby Being "Force-Fed".

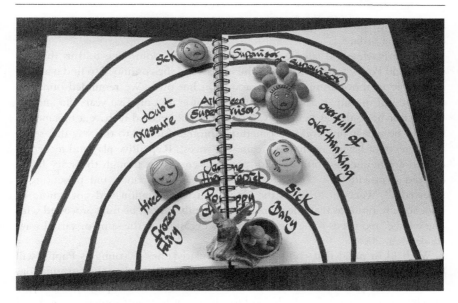

Figure 5.5 The Ripple Effect in Supervision.

This image helped provide me with some understanding of this complicated interwoven network of relationships. This in turn supported me to feel more fully present when sitting with Jane within our supervision group – which meant I could consciously avoid giving too many "helpful" suggestions. But many questions still remained for Jane as to what was happening in the therapy.

Was Poppy perhaps splitting off some of her unwanted feelings into Baby? Then Jane, as her therapist, and I as her supervisor, and Lottie as *my* supervisor, were experiencing these split off feelings, and finding ways to begin to digest Poppy's disgusting and rejected feelings, so that Jane could give bits back to Poppy in smaller, digested pieces? Donald Winnicott speaks about how a therapist can "hold" their client's difficult feelings and feed them back in small and manageable chunks so that the client can process them (Winnicott, 1985b).

Where the therapy is triadic (that is it involves client-art/play-therapist), Schaverien (1999) speaks of the *image* (or the play) "holding" unconscious unwanted feelings in a similar way. Was Baby "holding" Poppy's unmanageable feelings? Was Jane being "force-fed" them and "holding" them for Poppy and after an extended period of play in the therapy starting to digest them and give them back to Poppy in manageable bits?

Using journal drawing, poetry writing, collage making, and diagrams with miniature objects, supported me as I supervised Jane's work with Poppy. I agree with Barbara Fish when she says: "The heart of art-based supervision is response art that is made by both supervisees and supervisors before, during, and after sessions" (Fish, 2012). Response Art is the term used for a therapist or supervisor using their own art in response to the client's therapeutic work. The art I made helped me to gain a deeper form of empathy and allow unconscious factors to come to the surface.

Despite playing and talking freely in the therapy room, Jane told us that the teacher said Poppy was still not speaking in class and she continued to find it almost impossible to move around the classroom on her own. We reminded ourselves frequently in the supervision that Poppy was after all only five years old and we voiced our hope that as her play was repetitive she seemed to have a therapeutic need to be repeatedly working something through (similar to the way that some clients recount having recurring dream sequences). Repetitive play and recurring dreams are frequently suffused with powerful energy, as though the story being enacted is providing a "coded message of great importance and presenting it repeatedly" (Webber, 2017) so the client will pay attention and not ignore it. Badenoch reminds us that "deep trauma frequently cannot be fully processed with one telling" and needs to be visited on many occasions in the same or varied ways (Badenoch, 2008).

We held in mind that child clients, particularly ones as young as Poppy, will frequently work in the therapy through metaphor, story, play, and imagination, and we as therapists don't always have to understand what is happening in the play or why specifically it might be helpful for the client to repeat something over and over again. We often reminded ourselves of Margot Sunderland's important statement that: "… everyday language is not the natural language of feeling for children. Their natural language of feeling is that of image and metaphor, as in stories and dreams" (Sunderland, 2000). I tried to impart this reassurance to Jane who could not fully understand what was happening in the embodied countertransference that was so uncomfortable for her. It is an important aspect of the supervisor's role, to show the therapist confidence that they are doing a good job despite any feelings of doubt or uncertainty the therapist (or indeed the supervisor) might be experiencing.

Patrick Casement (1985) states that through his reading of Winnicott, he came to think of supervision in terms of a "nursing triad". He says the new mother needs to be believed by a significant other to be a "Good Enough Mother" (Winnicott, 1985a) and then she gains confidence. She can then respond to the individuality of each of her baby's changing developmental needs. It seems that I needed to support Jane in a similar way to the nursing triad and to believe in her ability to be a "Good Enough Therapist" so that she could respond to Poppy's changing needs. Where the supervisor is able to imbue the therapist with confidence in their ability as a therapist, even where the client is hard-to-reach, the block or impasse experienced by the therapist may often, seemingly magically, be overcome.

As I came to increasingly understand what might be happening in the therapy I realised I had somehow to find a way to *tolerate* how I was feeling. Although I felt I was being less than helpful in supporting Jane, I was still able to honestly express my belief that she was a "Good Enough Therapist" (Casement, 1985). These feelings of doubt probably included some degree of parallel process, as Jane felt less than helpful towards Poppy, and I felt less than helpful towards Jane. My supervisor at times also expressed feelings of helplessness. Was this something of what Poppy was feeling? Did she feel helpless to avoid the onslaught of thoughts and feelings she had experienced during her short five years of existence? Was she unable to take them all in and so had to split them off and Jane had to take them in via Baby's "force-feeding?"

Baby Says "No!"

Going back to our group supervision story, during one memorable session Jane described how after all this time of having to act out "force-feeding" Baby, it was at last possible for Jane (as Baby) to say "No!" We felt total shock. I remember taking a sharp intake of breath and as I let it out I felt complete relief as my body relaxed and like Poppy and Jane in the therapy room, we in the supervision group all laughed. So many times we had imagined what might happen if Jane changed the play, but Jane was following her embodied felt sense and intuitively knew the play had to be enacted over and over again.

Oh the patience that Jane displayed and the persistence to remain with what was happening while feeling so nauseous and sleepy. But oh the wondrous release when at last the time felt right and Baby rebelled. Clearly Jane had managed the timing from her intuition just right, as when Baby did at last refuse to take in any more of the revolting mixture, Poppy was able to tolerate the change in the dynamics of the play. We applauded how Jane had followed Poppy and been led by *her* needs but none of us really fully understood what had happened to make it possible for Jane to enable Baby to at last refuse to be given this "food mixture" against her will.

My Experience of Jane's "Super Supervision" Session

In my supervision practice, I frequently encourage therapists to create an image from the many objects and materials present in my practice room. I noticed in one particular supervision occasion that Jane hadn't put anything in front of her. With all the client work that Jane had discussed in supervision she had showed herself to be an exceptionally intuitive and skilled therapist who had no difficulty in communicating verbally or with image making. So this was something entirely new. Jane was passively sitting on her floor cushion watching everyone else. I wondered what might be happening to her. Might it be countertransference from her client Poppy who found it so difficult to initiate actions in her world and was sometimes struck dumb although she clearly had much to say? Could it be that Poppy, like Jane today, just watched the others around her whilst seeming not to be participating? Was Jane today hard-to-reach in a similar way that Poppy had been hard-to-reach at school and in the therapy? When it got to Jane's turn she looked confused, bewildered and stuck, so I suggested that she could just "Trust the Process" (McNiff, 1998) and choose some objects. I was uncomfortably aware that my overstuffed shelves provided too much choice for someone feeling unable to make a decision. It was almost as if here too I was trying to "over-feed" Jane.

Figure 5.6 Jane's Image of Poppy's Therapy.

After a short pause, however, my gentle belief that she *could* select some objects seemed to unfreeze Jane enough to choose a pewter fairy, a wooden doll and a vine of green ivy leaves stretched out between them (see Figure 5.6, first shown in Chapter 4, as Figure 4.1).

This action seemed to enable Jane to speak about how Poppy would appear to be moving from a stiff, frozen fairy, to what Jane called "a real girl." I noticed that in fact here in the practice room, the symbol chosen for Poppy had moved from the pewter frozen fairy to a wooden doll – ironically not so real yet. However, I kept this thought to myself as I didn't think it would be particularly helpful for Jane at this stage. Sometimes being a supervisor seems to be as much about what is *not* said as what *is* said.

After this supervision session, I spoke to my own supervisor about it. My supervisor asked me for a mental image of how I was feeling in that present moment as I was sharing the session with her. I told her that I felt as though I had previously been frozen into inertia and scattered in my thoughts and feelings and I had been desperate to know what to do or say to support Jane in her work with Poppy. However, now at last I was beginning to thaw out and watch with curiosity as the work (and Poppy) were beginning to unfreeze and flow.

Unexpectedly what happened next in the therapy was yet another twist in Poppy's extraordinary tale.

Florence Nightingale Is on the Phone

Some time after the breakthrough moment (Webber, 2017), where Jane (as Baby) said "No!" to being force-fed, Jane described how Poppy would regale many adventures of a friend she called Florence Nightingale. This seemed to be a further split off part of Poppy who was brave, caring, and selfless enough to do many of the things that Poppy was not yet able to do. Florence Nightingale would frequently be on her way to Baby's birthday party but so far she had never got anywhere near. Nothing could have prepared us for the recounting of a therapy session where

Florence Nightingale was yet again on her way to Baby's birthday party (Baby was now about to be four). Florence Nightingale had never managed to get even close to the party but on this occasion Poppy suddenly announced that Jane could speak to her as she was "just outside the door." I remember feeling myself being pulled sharply into full attentiveness as though I was being flooded with adrenalin. With her usual intuitive inventiveness, Jane told us how she had reached for the toy telephone in the therapy room and talked to Florence Nightingale on the phone. We spoke about what an amazing example this was of an imaginary friend that had seemed to serve the purpose of acting out all the adventures and taking all the risks that Poppy was unable to engage in, and coming quite literally up to the door of the therapy room. Was Jane about to be able to *reach* the Florence Nightingale part of Poppy? Did this perhaps signify that this part of Poppy was coming closer and closer to becoming integrated into Poppy?

A Host of New Characters Enter the Therapy Room and the Supervision Room

Shortly after this, again totally unexpectedly, a crowd of new characters began to enter the therapy room one after another in quick succession. Jane told us that first came Isla and Becky. Poppy said they were her friends. Around this time Jane was told that Poppy had her first *real* friend that she played with in the school playground. We celebrated this in the supervision group with glee. As Jane told us about this wonderful example of how therapy can support change in a client's world "out there," I was reminded of what was said to Robert Akeret during a supervision session with Eric Fromm: "we never *cure* anyone, Dr. Akeret… we just stand by and cheer whilst they cure themselves" (Akeret, 1995). Now that Poppy and Jane were beginning to be unfrozen, it felt as though we in the supervision group were all metaphorically standing by and cheering with delight as Poppy went by on her therapeutic adventure. We had all tolerated an intolerable situation, but now Poppy could begin to come alive. Jane had found a way to *reach* the split off parts of Poppy (Baby, Florence Nightingale and these new characters) and I had found a way to *reach* Jane's frozen state.

Soon after this, Becky and Isla morphed into being called Poppy. We spoke in supervision about the totally fascinating way that Poppy's imaginary friends had perhaps moved from being split off aspects of Poppy who could do things at school that Poppy herself was unable to do, into becoming integrated into Poppy – giving her a fuller range of ways of being and behaving. Then a new character called Charlie arrived. He was an older boy who played in a band. He was confident and funny and after a while Poppy would act out being in the band with him, trying out for herself being self-assured and amusing. This continued for a short while and heralded the beginning of a lot of other friends rapidly joining into the play. There was a grumpy child, called Greta, who would never do what she was told. Grumpy Greta would feature in stories with Billy Bear (who had been spoken about in the therapy room for some while) and eventually transformed into him. I remember the deeply fascinating discussions we had around what each of the characters might mean for Poppy and how and why they would disappear as separate entities as if Jane had managed to *reach* them and Poppy had seemed to be able to take on some aspects of each of them as her own.

In delving into trying to understand more about the phenomenon of imaginary friends, I read up extensively into this fascinating and seemingly fairly common occurrence. Having an imaginary friend can "serve as a wonderful coping mechanism to help children through difficult times…" (Gavin, 2014). Sometimes, Gavin suggests, an imaginary friend will be blamed for exploits that a child is unwilling to own where the child is using the character as a scapegoat for unwanted behaviours. This sounded similar to Poppy's Grumpy Greta character.

As Poppy was so young at the time of her therapy, we thought of these characters as imaginary friends, but the similarity to the concept of sub-personalities was never far from our minds. The following theoretical ideas about sub-personalities seem particularly pertinent. According to Kevin Fall (2003), a sub-personality can be thought of as a "personality mode that activates (appears on a temporary basis) to allow a person to cope with certain types of psychosocial situations." This seems helpful in describing the arrival and merging of Poppy's characters. They seemed to appear to help Poppy cope with a particular situation by portraying characteristics that she could not yet master. Then they would disappear when Poppy could achieve the new behaviours. What seems particularly unique and surprising is the quick succession with which these new characters came along at this stage of Poppy's therapy and then went on their way.

We had by now been introduced to so many of Poppy's unusual imaginary friends. We had to keep reminding ourselves that this was a five-year-old child who possessed this extraordinarily fertile, active, and unusual imagination. Week after week we were invited into Poppy's many peopled world, following Jane's release from having to "force-feed" Baby. The video in my head playing and replaying Baby being "force-fed" had ceased.

Baby was four years old, and Jane was allowed to be fully present in the therapy room. I chose a postcard from my collection (see Figure 5.7) that seemed to resonate with how Poppy's characters made me feel when so many of them appeared one after the other (www.inkognito.de cards).

Finding this card seemed to settle some of my unease around Jane's therapeutic work with Poppy. Was it something about the child in the picture being asleep (like Jane feeling so sleepy) or was it about the characters climbing out of the pages of a book (resonating with Poppy's many imaginary friends arriving in the therapy room) and taking on a life of their own? Or was it that the first character was pressing a finger to his lips as if to silence the others (like Poppy when she wouldn't talk at school)? It is not possible, or necessary, to fully analyse why an image might be so important. Suffice it to say it resonated deeply with me and helped me to make emotional sense of both Poppy's therapeutic work and being Jane's supervisor through this therapy. Barbara Fish so aptly states using images in supervision facilitates the "communication of challenging and nuanced content" (Fish, 2017). Finding this image certainly helped me to express some of the depths touched by Poppy's magical imagination.

Figure 5.7 Characters Taking on a Life of Their Own.

Brave Bear Session

Jane spoke about how Greta Grumpy Girl used to play with Billy Bear and after a while seemed to become transformed or subsumed into Billy Bear. Jane explained that Billy Bear was different to all the other characters in that Billy Bear existed as a cuddly toy that Poppy played with at home. Jane described how he would be mentioned frequently in the sessions but he never came in person to the therapy room. Poppy had been given Billy Bear when she was born. It seems Billy Bear could perhaps be described as "a pretend friend with physical presence" (Gavin, 2014). As the therapy unfolded Jane described how Poppy's anecdotes of Brave Bear would seem to echo achievements and developments that could be seen in Poppy herself.

In one particularly memorable session, Jane spoke about how Poppy had told Jane that Billy Bear was helped to be brave in climbing up the stairs by Poppy's support, like Poppy had become brave through Jane's support. I said to Jane that it was as though Poppy had internalised Jane as a nurturing internal presence and taught her to be brave and Jane said that I, as her supervisor, had taught Jane to be brave. I remember being moved to tears.

In providing supervision for therapists, it is not easy to know if you are support-ing them in the best possible way to ensure that their many changing requirements are fulfilled. I felt at the beginning of Jane's therapy with Poppy that I was failing to adequately support her. Jane was struggling to *reach* Poppy and manage her own uncomfortable feelings and I was finding it so difficult to *reach* and support Jane in her struggle to *reach* Poppy. The British Association of Counsellors and Psychotherapists (B.A.C.P.) list the following personal moral qualities to which therapists and supervisors are strongly encouraged to aspire: "empathy, sincerity, integrity, resilience, humility, competence, fairness, wisdom and courage." How could I possibly be all these things at all times in relation to Jane? Particularly in her struggle to reach a *hard-to-reach* client like Poppy? Clearly I couldn't. But I did strive to do my best and remain open to my own continued professional develop-ment. For me the use of response art was a key way to support myself in this endeavour as well as the wisdom of my own invaluable supervisor – both sustained me in the supervision of Jane's remarkable therapy with Poppy.

Alonso (1985) puts the onus on supervisors poetically when she says that psy-chotherapy supervisors "serve as the keepers of the faith" and the "mentors of the young". Theirs she states is "a quiet profession that combines the discipline of science with the aesthetic creativity of art." She continues that supervisors: "teach, inspire, cajole and shape their students towards their own standard of professional excellence." Again an impossibly high ideal. Fascinatingly she makes the key point in her book titled The Quiet Profession that "it is a curious paradox that at their best they are the least visible" (Ibid). Hopefully, if I was not able to be less than visible in my support of Jane and Poppy, at least perhaps I was quietly serving as a "keeper of the faith" and a "mentor of the young" with the "creativity of art" being central to the endeavour.

Final Session

What happened in Jane and Poppy's final session was so unexpected and so mov-ing. Jane's job was done and so was mine (and that of my own supervisor too) and yet as Poppy herself stated in that last session, she and Jane would be "Holding Hands Forever." In a parallel process, I (and probably everyone else in the supervi-sion group) would hold the memory of this remarkable client's therapeutic jour-ney in our minds forever.

References

Akeret, R.U. (1995). *The Man Who Loved a Polar Bear*. London: Penguin.
Alonso, A. (1985). *The Quiet Profession: Supervisors of Psychotherapy*. London: Macmillan Publishing Company.
Badenoch, B. (2008). *Being a Brain-Wise Therapist*. New York: W. W. Norton.
Carroll, M. & Tholstrup, M. (2004). The Spirituality of Supervision. In *Integrative Approaches to Supervision* (pp. 76–91). London: Jessica Kingsley.
Casement, P. (1985). *On Learning from the Patient*. London: Tavistock/Routledge Publications.

Emotion Stones. (n.d.) www.yellow-door.net.

Fall, K.A. (2003). *Theoretical Models of Counselling and Psychotherapy*. London: Routledge.

Fish, B.J. (2012). Response Art: The Art of the Art Therapist. *Art Therapy: Journal of the American Art Therapy Association*, 29(3), 138–143.

Fish, B.J. (2017). *Art-Based Supervision: Cultivating Therapeutic Insight through Imagery*. New York/London: Routledge.

Gavin, F. (2014). *Your Child's Imaginary Friend: An Overview for Parents*. London: Wordwise.

Johnson, M. & Wintgens, A. (2012). *Can I Tell You about Selective Mutism: A Guide for Friends, Family and Professionals*. London and Philadelphia: Jessica Kingsley.

Kadushin, A. (1985). *Supervision in Social Work*. New York: Columbia University Press.

McNiff, S. (1998). *Trust the Process*. Boston, MA: Shambhala.

Mattinson, J. (1975). *The Reflection Process in Casework Supervision*. London: Tavistock Institute of Marital Studies.

Schaverien, J. (1999). *The Revealing Image*. London: Jessica Kingsley.

Sunderland, M. (2000). *Using Story Telling as a Therapeutic Tool with Children*. Oxon: Winslow Press Ltd.

Sutton, C. & Forrester, C. (2016). *Selective Mutism in Our Own Words: Experiences in Childhood and Adulthood*. London: Jessica Kingsley.

Webber, A. (2017). *Breakthrough Moments in Arts-Based Psychotherapy*. London: Karnac.

Winnicott, D.W. (1985a). *Collected Papers: Through Paediatrics to Psycho-Analysis*. London: Tavistock Publications.

Winnicott, D.W. (1985b). *Maturational Processes and the Facilitating Environment Studies in Theory and Emotional Development*. London: Karnac.

www.inkognito. (n.d.) de a German website for a range of unusual postcards (where I obtained the postcard with characters emerging out of the pages of a storybook; Figure 5.7).

Yalom, I.D. (2001). *The Gift of Therapy: Reflections on Being a Therapist*. London: Piatkus.

Chapter 6

The Boy Trapped in a Puffer Fish

Sarah Attle

Context

"Hard to reach" is a definition often used within education and community services to describe those families with whom such services find it hard to engage or work. The term often also includes those families who are seen as disadvantaged, and their children vulnerable, due to socio-economic factors. These children may also have suffered from a number of Adverse Childhood Experiences (ACEs), the consequences of which are wide-ranging (Fellitti et al., 1998). They may also therefore show signs of relational and developmental trauma.

Charlie was one such child. Ten years old, he was the oldest of four children and living with his Mum. I understood that he often felt responsible and anxious about her. Her ongoing mental health difficulties meant that she found it hard to provide consistent care and she was also unable to work in paid employment. Her own childhood also included several ACEs. Charlie often seemed angry and appeared cut-off from his peers, struggling to make positive friendships. He was referred to therapy within his school environment, where I worked, due to increasing concerns over his behaviour and its impact on his learning.

Snapshot 1: Finding Charlie

Charlie is a child who does not expect the world to like him. This is reflected immediately in his body language when we first meet: wary and watchful. I am surprised nonetheless to find him to be open and direct in his communication; albeit his narrative is to tell me that things aren't going well for him currently. He is disarmingly honest in saying that he has no real friends and that he really struggles at playtime. He says that others find him "annoying". And there is a palpable frustration that is almost visceral in the room. I also notice the challenge in Charlie's voice as he speaks of the "we" of his home life; a sense of weariness in feeling judged, of defensiveness in seeking to stand up for himself in a world that does not feel fair. Despite his openness, he seems to have already decided that he is not someone who has choices; he is telling me how it is because that is his concrete and unchangeable reality. It has the practised tones of a learned family script.

DOI: 10.4324/9781003163015-6

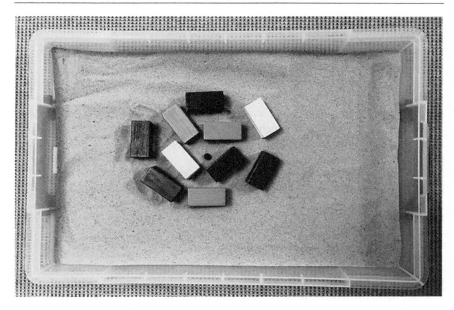

Figure 6.1 Little Black Dot.

I explain to Charlie that this is his time and space and that I am really looking forward to getting to know him. I sense that it is important to communicate from the outset that I expect to enjoy his company and that he is valued and valuable just as he is. I also want Charlie to know that I am really interested in understanding how things feel to him and that I come with only positive preconceptions. Inviting him to use any of the arts and play resources around the room, I ask Charlie to show me what it feels like to be him in those playground moments.

Charlie seems intrigued by the sand tray and moves this in front of him, smoothing the surface over with his hand. He then looks around and carefully selects a number of items. First to go into the tray is a tiny black pom-pom, which he places in the middle. He raises his eyes to check whether I am still watching and I lean forward as he carefully places first one and then more and more big, coloured bricks into the tray, surrounding the single black dot (see Figure 6.1).

"Oh, hello, little black dot", I say, "how does it feel to be you?"

Charlie looks at me and I have a sense of his curiosity, but I also notice his guardedness and hesitation in replying. I wait a moment longer, looking away and then back and smiling, hoping this will allow some space and enough safety for Charlie to risk a response. I am aware that for Charlie his day-to-day interactions come with many risks: a risk perhaps of not being seen, of being labelled, of disappointment, even rejection. The language of feelings is new, potentially exposing and challenging.

"I feel like everyone's on top of me", Charlie replies. I am intrigued by this boy who on the one hand seems so closed, so sure that his path is set and yet is willing to risk expressing this admission to me now and who can, even in this first session, use the resources to communicate a felt truth beyond words. An image comes to my mind of a boy within a boy; the exterior sharp and spiky, like a puffer fish, but the inside soft and vulnerable.

We both look at the little black dot together. I notice how small it seems, lost amidst all the coloured bricks around it, pressing in on it, confident and assertive in their colour, sharp edges and unity. By contrast, the black pom-pom seems almost not quite formed, monochrome and fuzzy. It is different and other and alone. I wonder whether this is just how it feels to Charlie when he is in the play-ground, or whether this a bigger communication about Charlie's sense of who he is: not quite belonging, restricted, stuck. I sense the weight of the bricks pressing in and the heaviness in the room and sigh out deeply. Charlie sighs out too. I feel aware of so many circumstances in Charlie's external world that I cannot change, but would I be able to help him to change his view of himself?

Reflections on the Work

During my first session with Charlie, I recognised that his self-confidence was low and that his self-image was quite negative, reflected through an equivalent Internal Working Model (IWM) (Bowlby, 1988). This did not surprise me, hav-ing regard to Bronfenbrenner's work on the impact of environment upon healthy development (1979). I surmised that his attachment model with his mum, his primary carer, was likely to have some ambivalent aspects (Ainsworth et al., 1978; Crittenden, 2006) and that some of his early developmental needs might not have been met consistently. As Winnicott observed: "…the mother's face is the mirror in which the child first begins to find himself" (1971/2005). Attempting to help Charlie to mobilise a more positive sense of self, then, by reflecting back to him an image of someone who is valuable, would need to form a key part of the work. In working with children who have suffered developmental and relational trauma, I find it helpful to hold in mind an image of multiple footprints almost physically embossed upon the brain, recognising the often-complex factors and impacts fre-quently co-occurring; affecting physical, mental, social and emotional maturation and as helpfully analysed by Treisman (2017). This image also emphasises the neu-robiological effect of such traumas and the therapeutic need for space to heal. I was aware that these footprints were likely to cause Charlie's body and brain to react in trauma responses that would make it harder still to reach him.

In seeking to provide Charlie with a firm foundation upon which to build (Maslow, 1943), I understood that I needed to pack into our sessions as many experiences that affirmed him as I could, given that he did not expect to be liked. Bowlby recognised that, although "logically indefensible", such patterns once internalised continued to operate throughout the child's lifespan as an expectation and therefore often became a felt and experienced reality (1973/1998). The first part of my work would be in creating together and holding an intersubjective therapeutic space in which Charlie could explore and grow safely (Stern, 1985; Schore & Schore, 2008), as well as connect with me. A good guide for this early groundwork is Siegel's reminder of our universal attachment needs: "We need to be *seen, safe* and *soothed*, in order to feel *secure*" (2013).

I am often reminded in the early stages of therapy of the childhood game of Hide & Seek, which is often physically enacted too, as the child expresses their unconscious need to be seen and validated; "to feel the gleam in the mother's eye", as Kohut puts it (1971). It also embodies the dilemma facing so many children who feel that their difficult circumstances are somehow their fault and that they are unloveable, not worthy of being found. I still remember the intense emotional response I felt when I first read Winnicott's distillation of this: "…it is joy to be hidden but disaster not to be found" (Winnicott, 1965/2007). Would I be able to encourage Charlie to make tentative steps out of the darkness, out of the learned patterns of behaviour that seemed to have become so set? Would I be able to reach him?

Finally, as well as seeking to address the first of Kohut's needs, to be "mirrored", I was very conscious of Charlie's deep-rooted need to feel a sense of belonging; to feel like one amongst others (Maslow, 1954/1987; Kohut, 1971, 1984). There were also broader societal factors to overcome here too; Charlie needed to feel that he was the author of his own story and that the ending was not already written. I held in mind Dalal's warning that: "Belonging means we have a place in the world, but it also means we are placed in the world. The fact that we find ourselves placed, reminds us that power relations are intrinsic to notions of belonging and community" (2015).

However, I began this work encouraged by Charlie's willingness to share how he was feeling despite his negative worldview, also inspired by my deep humanistic understanding of human motivation as growth-oriented (e.g. Rogers, 1961/2004) and a belief in the power of connection to effect change. What happened in our next session only served to deepen this understanding.

Snapshot 2: Trapped

Charlie arrives at our next session looking red and cross. There is an untamed energy in the room, bouncing off the walls, reflected in Charlie's clenching and unclenching of his fists and his jittery feet. I wonder aloud what has happened, although the muddy trousers and scuffed trainers give me a clue – another playtime football incident! "It's not fair – I always get in trouble!" Charlie exclaims. I say that I want him to tell me all about it, anxious for him to feel that his voice is heard, that this is his time and space once again. But first, to try to help him to dissipate some of that anger, to get rid of a few of those spikes and to enable the "pufferfish" boy to deflate a little … I invite Charlie to stand up. He looks at me curiously, having only just sat down and together we shake our legs out, then our arms, then our heads and he starts to laugh at me jumping around the room jiggling up and down and we laugh together and our eyes meet. His face is open now, less guarded and I feel a rush of warmth towards him: "There you are!" I think.

We talk about the events of lunchtime and he shows me using the whiteboard what had happened and who was where; eagerly drawn stick figures being positioned, moved, reflected upon. I gently encourage Charlie to talk about how it felt and also to wonder about how others might have been feeling too. The immediacy and the fluidity of the medium allows him to change what he has drawn, whilst the solid edges of the board are able to contain and control these overspilling emotions. I notice Charlie's ability to work out of metaphor, but beneath the anger I can sense a whole whirlwind of other feelings.

To deepen his response, I invite Charlie to have a look through the pile of Dixit cards (Libellud, 2017) upon the table and to see if there is one that expresses how he is feeling. He carefully goes through the cards, before stopping abruptly and says: "This is it!" (see Figure 6.2; Libellud, 2017).

Again, Charlie looks at me and there is an intense electricity-like connection between us, as we engage in the emotional experience communicated through his chosen image. A silence and pregnant sadness suffused with wonder hangs in the air between us, as we each consider what the card might be saying.

Figure 6.2 Trapped (Libellud, 2017).

Words come now, first one or two and then quickly a stream, as Charlie identifies more and more aspects of the card that he feels relate to him and how he sees himself, as well as how he feels others see him; his mind working to assimilate the meanings and truths this image encapsulates for him. I am in awe once again of the ability of art to bridge the gap between what is consciously known and what is felt and experienced. He explains that he is seen as the "bad guy" who should be punished, feeling stuck with this worldview of himself and his behaviour. He points out the man's sad eyes, giving expression to the sorrow within and the prison uniform. He looks again and comments on the "boring" landscape and I have a sense of a small admission that maybe Charlie too is bored of his own external landscape: maybe this provides an opportunity for us to work with and explore what he would like to change?

Another realisation now: Charlie notices that the bars have no sides, that the man could come around them if he chose to. "No-one listens, so I might as well stay there", he challenges: "I can't let go, there's no point". I am aware that Charlie is sometimes speaking of the prisoner in the third person, sometimes claiming his identity as his own. But then, more hesitantly he adds: "I might need a teacher to help me". I say that we will be able to work through these feelings together and I am struck powerfully by the poignant contrast between the young primary school-aged child sitting in front of me and the older, more haggard man represented on the card. I have a fresh insight into the impact upon Charlie of his many challenging life experiences and the way that these have shaped his developmental trajectory thus far. I recognise that as a therapist, I cannot change how some things are for him, but I can fill in some of the missing maturational foundation stones and equip him with resources that might enable that trajectory to become more normative.

I gently wonder aloud whether the image might have a title? Charlie does not hesitate: "Trapped". If Charlie was as yet unable to move from behind the bars, part of our journey together would be for me to join him where he was standing and for him to know that I was willing to be there with him and to look at the landscape as he saw it. My hope was that Charlie would at some point be able to take his own steps around the side of the bars… I could not carry him; my role was to give him the confidence and the tools to be able to do so himself.

Reflections on the Work

This snapshot represents a significant moment in the therapy, as Charlie made several connections: with the image, with his feelings, with his own understanding, with me; as shown in this representation created by me to understand what might be happening in such moments (see Figure 6.3). There was also a timelessness as the moment encapsulated aspects of Charlie's past and also where he saw himself currently in the present, yet with a forward-facing potential and dynamic. At the heart of change moments in therapy are key connective experiences, prismic in quality: reflecting, illuminating and refracting both the client's internal and

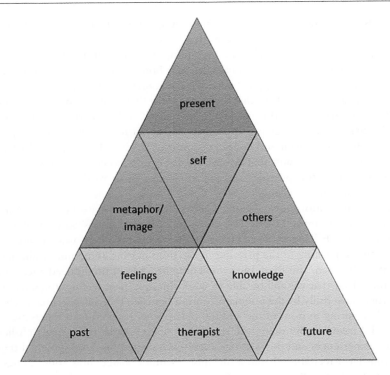

Figure 6.3 Sarah's Representation of a Change Moment and Its Key Connective Experiences.

external landscapes. They are experienced phenomenologically, not cognitively and as such have the power to heal and transform. As Siegel summarised:

> These moments of joining at the heart of healing bring our dyadic states of connection into a new level of integrative harmony... And with this fluid movement to connect within ourselves and with others, we come to live more fully alive.
>
> (Siegel, 2013)

Stern recognised that: "Sense of self is not a cognitive construct. It is an experiential integration" (1985). So too then is the work of change, with *experiencing* as the key to change as understood by Gendlin's affirmation of the "felt sense" in therapy work (1961). Charlie here was hard to reach not just because of the barriers that he felt others had placed around him, but also because of the barriers that he had placed around himself, as well as his bodily responses to the trauma that he had suffered. I recognised that some of these barriers were there to defend and protect and as such needed to be honoured, rather than viewed negatively. Porges' work is transformative in illuminating this understanding; as he summarises: "... when our body goes into certain states when it is traumatised, it is acting heroically.

The body is helping us, it is saving us, and our body is not failing us – it's attempting to help us survive" (Porges, 2017). In order to harness the healing power of prismic connection still further, Charlie and I would need to develop further our relationship of trust so that he felt able to let us look behind these defences together. Just as a puffer fish puffs up when threatened, so too did Charlie.

Among our young clients, play and arts media naturally harness the potential healing and illuminating power of metaphor (Piaget & Inhelder, 1966/2000; Haen, 2005). The use of metaphors and symbols within therapy is part of our daily work with children, originating in the right brain and serving to bridge gaps both therapeutically and neurobiologically (Pally, 2000; Modell, 2009). I have found that my research into the nature of metaphors has deepened my understanding of what happens when we use metaphor, firing new neural pathways and integrating left and right brain activity, towards greater wholeness (Gilchrist, 2009; Schore, 2019). As Modell recognised, metaphors represent "an emergent property of mind" (1997). Their polysemic quality also enables them to work with the flexibility of water; being able to get into the gaps and make connections in the child's psyche where needed; whether in the conscious or unconscious, or somewhere in between.

In noticing Charlie's dual use of both first and third person interchangeably, I recognised the way that the image enabled him to distance himself just enough to be able to tolerate the big feelings generated and so explore them further (as per Siegel's window of tolerance) (Siegel, 2015). Seligman summarises the safety and distance brought by metaphor as "a kind of 'me-not-me' language" (2007). Moreover, the tense being used did not matter; as Sunderland explains, it is because: "a major part of therapeutic change is the result of empathy. And you can empathise just as easily with the child's feelings as expressed through metaphor as you can if they were expressed through everyday language" (Sunderland, 2000). The image had unlocked a fresh experience, understanding and acknowledgement of feelings of which Charlie had been previously unaware, but the felt experience of which had shaped so significantly his behaviour; the "unthought known" (Bollas, 1987).

Even from the earliest times of Aristotle, metaphor was understood to contain a sense of change and movement, as well as inter-modality (Imre, 2010), and it is these characteristics that make their role so central therapeutically, working at what Wilkinson summarises as the "interface of what might be termed the cognitive-affective divide" (2017). As she further noted: "…emergent metaphor helps us to understand the emotional truth of our inner experience while still tolerating uncertainty" (Wilkinson, 2010). In this session with Charlie, it felt like he had been able to speak and share an important emotional truth about how it felt to be him through the Dixit card (see Figure 6.2) and that I had been able to witness and hold that for him. Our work towards freeing Charlie was underway.

Snapshot 3: Letting Go of the Mask

I look at Charlie at the beginning of our session. His face is once again flushed and his expression mutinous. I have just picked him up from the classroom, where he was sitting outside, talking to the class teacher. There were two other boys also waiting for the playtime debrief as to what had gone wrong. The scene was a familiar one, frequently revisited and representing the ongoing dilemma for Charlie: was it just easier to continue these deeply rooted patterns of behaviour? Did he really want things to change?

After a number of weeks of working together, I recognise that we have also experienced this ongoing ambivalence in the therapy room: sometimes Charlie feels fully present and keen to engage in our work together; at other times a different narrative emerges, where it feels like I am trying to communicate with a child who is half in the room and half not, who feels that although his behaviour gets him into trouble it is working well enough for him. I feel that our relationship is secure enough for me to be able to reflect on this aloud to Charlie, so that we can wonder about it together. I draw two circles: one with two stick figures fully inside, but the other with one stick figure inside and the other one breaking through the circle's frame, running away and with one foot either side of the frame. Charlie agrees that it sometimes feels like this for him too and he now feels fully in the room. He says that he likes to be the class joker and to make people laugh. He says this confidently, but then pauses and looks at me and then says: "But I don't think people always think I'm funny. But I just do it". The story of Goldilocks comes into my head; in the experiences, Charlie recounts to me he sometimes feels too big, like he is putting on a big, bright, false persona in the hope that he will be seen and liked. At other times, he seems too small; unconfident, with no clear idea of who he is; still embryonic, vulnerable. I long for Charlie to feel just right.

I invite Charlie to use the play figures to explore further how it feels to be him today, wondering to which one he feels most drawn. After some consideration, he selects two figures. The first is a Stormtrooper Star Wars figure that is: heavily armoured, anonymous, protected, almost monochrome (see Figure 6.4). Here, then, is the mask that I experience sometimes in the room. A pause and a silence and I am careful not to fill it: the space is one I hold open in which Charlie can rest, feel, wonder, reflect; I am a guardian as well as a co-creator of the process.

Do those feel right to you?", I eventually gently encourage, as he has settled on the two figures. The "as if" quality of the metaphorical figures allows Charlie once again to encounter unconsciously felt truths and I am invited still deeper into Charlie's world as he experiences it. He looks up and our eyes connect again. I notice audibly the armour and the fact that the figure really needs it. Charlie tells me that this is how he used to be and sometimes still feels; I recognise that without it he would feel too vulnerable and he would not be safe. He then tells me that the second, brighter Playmobil figure, dressed in bold colours and with sunshine yellow hair (see Figure 6.4) is how he feels most of the time now and I observe that this second bearded figure is still old before his time. When I am curious about this, Charlie lets me know that it was chosen for this reason. However, there is a sense of movement, of journeying towards a fresh sense of identity and Charlie feels less stuck, less hopeless.

Figure 6.4 Two Versions of Charlie.

Reflections on the Work

My "Goldilocks" phrase of "too big or too small, never just right" often came to mind as I spoke about Charlie in supervision and I believe it has applied to other children with whom I have worked too, where there has been relational trauma. Charlie's description of himself as the class clown made me think of Winnicott's "false self" (1965/2007), there to defend and hide the true self, self-perceived as unlovable; just like the puffer fish with its protective spikes. Where there is no secure attachment, the child instead becomes preoccupied with the love response that he finds lacking in the caregiver (Sunderland, 2003). There are also clear parallels with Rogers' analysis of the masks we wear and the therapeutic task of peeling back the layers to find the true self (1961/2004). As Stern observed: "The desire to know and to be known… can be a powerful motive and can be felt as a need-state" (Stern, 1985).

I viewed my work through these sessions as providing Charlie with the time, space and safety to allow this unpeeling to take place, understanding that his sense of self was still in very early formation. It could perhaps be viewed as a continuation of our game of Hide & Seek, except the term "game" implies something frivolous and transitory: I viewed it instead as life-giving and potentially transformative. The most helpful description of this process that I have found comes from Lanyado, who observed: "...it is like spotting a new bud on a plant that was none too healthy, and... giv[ing] it the best possible chance to grow. The emphasis is on natural recovery rather than emergency care in a hothouse atmosphere" (2004). This emphasises the developmental context and the maturational work being achieved and is itself a powerful metaphor. As Lakoff and Johnson summarise: "the essence of metaphor is in understanding one thing in terms of another" (1980/2003).

This snapshot also illustrates some of the theory behind the therapeutic process itself. McNiff reminds us to "trust the process" (1998), and as therapist we often work instinctively, as we seek to make and deepen the connections with our clients. As a self-confessed over-thinker, I have come to respect and trust the process of change itself, as understood through the many works of the Boston Change Process Study Group (2010). There is a clear link for me between intuition and embodied relating (Totton, 2015), harnessed as therapists as we respond to the affective connection in the intersubjective field. Marks-Tarlow defines clinical intuition as: "a right-brain, fully embodied mode of perceiving, relating and responding to the ongoing flows and changing dynamics of psychotherapy" (2012). She characterises the therapist as: "shuttling back and forth... between inner versus outer world, embodied versus conceptual self-awareness, feeling versus thought, and intuitive versus deliberating modes" (Ibid). There is an energy and sense of phronetic intentional endeavour in this description that I find apt, used in the service of the child, moment by moment (Holliday, 2015). As therapists, we seek to grow, hold and harness the potential of each moment to bring healing and therapeutic change.

Snapshot 4: What Happens When You Don't Belong

Charlie is now able to share more about his past as well as current experiences; sometimes directly through words, sometimes through play, sometimes through continuing to use the whiteboard to draw out different scenarios and then redrawing them. I am a witness and cheerleader to Charlie's growing sense of self, his emerging increased resilience and together we are contemplators of the possible. Today, Charlie is drawing and mapping out a football game at lunchtime, where he feels really aggrieved about how someone else has behaved and we wonder together about what might have been going on for this recalcitrant player. I comment on the fact that Charlie is physically and proportionately bigger and more central in these latest drawings compared to earlier ones and ask how it feels. He beams, then hesitates, saying: "It feels really good, but I kind of feel sorry for the people who aren't big". When I ask if he could show me how it feels not to be

Figure 6.5 "No Acceptance" (Recreated by Sarah from the original).

big, Charlie asks for a piece of paper. I notice the change from the more transitory whiteboard to the permanency of paper, and I am therefore aware of the more intense emotional response that this might evoke.

Charlie works furiously, the speed and certainty of his pen strokes communicating the depth and importance of the emotions being revealed, accompanied by a clear, determined narrative as he is all the time making connections: with his own experience, with the past, with how it felt (see Figure 6.5). He titles it "No Acceptance". Charlie uses his own assimilated psycho-education to make sense of the intense feelings of the rejection of not belonging:

> Your brain becomes cloudy and you can't think any more…sadness pours over your heart and it gets infected…then your heart gets blocked and there's no emotions…then your guts go all blue and you don't feel confident any-more…you feel really small and you stop talking to people and so your ears get blocked…and you get into really bad habits.

I feel almost overwhelmed with compassion for this young man who has struggled so much and yet is now able to express so rawly and powerfully how it has felt to be him. Yet I sense I need to scaffold these feelings a little too; to hold and to honour them. I tentatively offer a response: "All of those feelings and yet some-times no feelings…because there were too many feelings for your heart to hold". Charlie remembers now the "Trapped" card of his earlier session (see Figure 6.2) and connects the two and we grieve together for the losses and the "never-hads" that have punctuated his childhood so far.

"And how do you feel now?", I wonder. "All of this is unblocked and I'm more open to people and not depressed and my heart got bigger" Charlie responds, and I echo: "Your heart got bigger and you got bigger!".

Reflections on the Work

In affirming Charlie for the positive choices he had made, and was continuing to make, as well as emphasising his inner resources, particularly in relation to his emotional maturity, I was able to reinforce this new positive view of himself. I was also able to note the change in his IWM as discussed earlier, providing a powerful new internalised resource for Charlie to draw upon in the future.

By providing sufficient distance and containment for these big feelings through the relationship that we had developed and the use of arts resources (Bion, 1962; Kalu, 2002), Charlie's emotional experience was deepened and freshly experienced as if in the present, as per the Gestalt cycle of experience (Clarkson, 2014).

Haen notes that loss of language can occur in children following traumatic events: "Being able to further express the unspeakable is so often a long and difficult journey. It is for this reason that metaphor, play, symbol and enactment can become crucial therapeutic tools in working through the trauma" (Van der Kolk, 2005). Van der Kolk's work established that in trauma, the Broca's area (a language centre in the brain) shuts down, so that a client will not have processed the trauma in words and nor will they be able to express verbally their thoughts or feelings; therefore, non-verbal metaphor becomes key (Webber, 2017). Whilst Charlie came to be able to verbalise some of his felt experiences around friendships and not belonging, the bigger feeling of not belonging societally sometimes remained unspoken. Nonetheless, the presence of these feelings and their expression through his created image became part of the work of meaning-making and Charlie's growth of self; as Siegel noted: "Coherent narratives are created through inter-hemispheric integration" (Siegel, 2015).

Charlie's willingness to mentalise how others might be feeling was also encouraging in terms of his ability to form healthier friendships and to make wiser behavioural choices. Through this work, Charlie had come to be able to let me reach him, to reach himself and now to reach out to others too.

Snapshot 5: Growing Towards the Light

It is our last session together. We have spent time together reflecting on Charlie's journey, on his positive feelings anticipating school transitions and the metamorphic transformation in Charlie's sense of self-worth. He is proud and I am proud of him, and we celebrate this and delight in each other's company as we say goodbye. Many aspects of Charlie's circumstances remain unchanged, but he feels more at the centre of his own life, with a positive outlook on a world with more possibilities. He asks to look at the Dixit cards for one last time and selects one (see Figure 6.6; Libellud, 2017). Instead of an old man, he identifies himself as a small boy looking up at a tower; a tower that he has created with others. He tells me it is a tower of relationships and friendships, all working together. Tall and strong. I observe the

Figure 6.6 A Tower of Relationships (Libellud, 2017).

interwoven bricks and the hard work that has clearly gone into its creation and we marvel at it. Anticipating my now familiar approach, Charlie points out to me the light and the nest at the top, vocalising a link to hope and new things to come. I notice aloud the bird and Charlie says: "It reminds me of the people that helped along the way... and because it's very bright, it lights things up..."

Reflections on the Work

My work with Charlie was a reminder to me of the simple power of human connection as the bedrock of therapeutic work: the power of being reached and the power of reaching others. By accepting all aspects of Charlie that he was able to bring, I offered him an alternative experience from the relational and developmental trauma that had so shaped his life thus far; this felt sense is summed up by Hill powerfully: "Such viscerally experienced sympathy offers a reassuring and vitalising connectedness. One feels felt, known and accepted, nurtured" (Hill, 2015).

At the beginning of our work together, Charlie had felt almost unreachable; however, image and metaphor had bridged the gap where words could not; bringing healing, change and greater self-integration.

Through the work, I had also sought to equip Charlie for the choices ahead, recognising that humanistic theory accepts the child's self-agency and tendency towards self-actualisation (Maslow, 1943; Axline, 1974). Charlie had himself chosen to come out from behind the bars: he no longer felt trapped and by lowering some of the barriers he'd built around himself, he was able to see alternative paths forward, rather than the one that had felt so pre-destined.

Whilst it would be easy to portray this work as complete, it was in fact deeply understood by Charlie that the work was ongoing; as part of one of his own reflections, he himself drew a life cycle of a butterfly, recognising future hope in the sense of continued change and growth; repeating itself over and over. This sense of dynamic mobility was in marked contrast to the "trapped" image (see Figure 6.2) he had chosen early on. However, I felt that we had managed to complete our game of 'Hide & Seek' for now and we had also filled in some of the developmental building blocks that had been missing for Charlie, giving him the chance of a more normative developmental trajectory. My final tasks were to trust and let go.

Final Snapshot

For the moment, then, Charlie and I had completed this part of our journey together. I look at the small boy on the Dixit card and the small boy in front of me smiling and laughing and I see someone who is not too big, not too small… he is just right. From inside the big, spiky puffer fish, a ten-year-old child had been reached, found and freed to be himself (see Figure 6.7).

Figure 6.7 Child-Like Puffer Fish Freed from Spiky Puffer Fish.

References

Ainsworth, M.D.S., Blehar, M.C., Waters, E., & Wall, S. (1978). *Patterns of attachment: a psychological study of the strange situation*. Hillsdale, NJ: Erlbaum.

Axline, V. (1974). *Play therapy*. New York: Ballentine Books.

Bion, W. (1962). *Learning from experience*. London: William Heinemann.

Bollas, C. (1987). *The shadow of the object: psychoanalysis of the unthought known*. London: Free Association Books.

Boston Change Process Study Group (2010). *Change in psychotherapy: a unifying paradigm*. New York: W.W. Norton & Co.

Bowlby, J. (1988). *A secure base: clinical applications of attachment theory*. London and New York: Routledge.

Bowlby, J. (1998). *Attachment and loss: volume 2. Separation, anger and anxiety*. London: Pimlico. (Original work published 1973).

Bronfenbrenner, U. (1979). *The ecology of human development: experiments by nature and design*. Cambridge, MA: Harvard University Press.

Clarkson, P. (2014). *Gestalt counselling in action* (4th ed.). London: Sage.

Crittenden, P. (2006). A dynamic-maturational model of attachment. *Australian and New Zealand Journal of Family Therapy*, 27(2), 105–115. doi:10.1002/j.1467-8438.2006.tb00704.x.

Dalal, F. (2015). Specialists without spirit, sensualists without heart: psychotherapy as a moral endeavour. In J. Maratos (Ed.), *Foundations of group analysis for the twenty-first century* (pp. 249–273). London: Karnac.

Dixit Harmonies Expansion cards (n.d.) (see under Libellud).

Fellitti, V.J., Anda, R.F., Nordenberg, D., Williamson, D.F., Spitz, A.M., Edwards, V., Koss, M.P., & Marks, J.S. (1998). Relationship of childhood abuse and household dysfunction to many of the leading causes of death in adults. *American Journal of Preventative Medicine*, 14(4), 245–258. doi:10.1016/S0749-3797(98)00017-8.

Gendlin, E.T. (1961). Experiencing: a variable in the process of therapeutic change. *American Journal of Psychotherapy*, 15(2), 233–245.

Gilchrist, I. (2009). *The master and his emissary: the divided brain and the making of the western world*. New Haven, CT & London: Yale University Press.

Haen, C. (2005). Rebuilding security: group therapy with children affected by September 11. *International Journal of Group Psychotherapy*, 55(3), 391–414.

Hill, D. (2015). *Affect regulation theory: a clinical model*. New York: W.W. Norton & Company.

Holliday, C. (2015, December). *What informs our interventions?* BACP Children, Young People & Families, 4–8.

Imre, A. (2010). Metaphors in cognitive linguistics. *Eger Journal of English Studies, X*, 71–81.

Kalu, D. (2002). Containers and containment. *Psychodynamic Practice*, 8(3), 359–373. doi:10.1080/1353333021000019943.

Kohut, H. (1971). *The analysis of the self*. New York: International Universities Press, Inc.

Kohut, H. (1984). *How does analysis cure?* Chicago, IL: University of Chicago Press.

Lakoff, G., & Johnson, M. (2003). *Metaphors we live by* (2nd ed.). Chicago, IL: The University of Chicago Press. (Original work published 1980).

Lanyado, M. (2004). *The presence of the therapist: treating childhood trauma*. Hove: Routledge.

Libellud (2017). ASMDIX10EN Dixit Harmonies Expansion cards.

Marks-Tarlow, T. (2012). *Clinical intuition in psychotherapy: the neurobiology of embodied response*. New York: W. W. Norton.

McNiff, S. (1998). *Trust the process: an artist's guide to letting go*. Boulder, CO: Shambhala.

Maslow, A.H. (1943). A theory of human motivation. *Psychological Review*, 50(4), 370–396.

Maslow, A.H. (1987). Motivation and personality (3rd ed., revised by Frager, R., Fadiman, J., McReynolds, C., & Cox, R.). New York: Harper & Row. (Original work published 1954).

Modell, A.H. (1997). Reflections on metaphor and affects. *The Annual of Psychoanalysis*, 25, 219–233.

Modell, A.H. (2009). Metaphor – the bridge between feelings and knowledge. *Psychoanalytic Inquiry*, 29(1), 6–11.

Pally, R. (2000). *The mind-brain relationship*. London & New York: Karnac.

Piaget, J, & Inhelder, B. (2000). *The psychology of the child*. New York: Basic Books. (Original work published 1966).

Playmobil toys available from most toy stores (n.d.).

Porges, S.W. (2017). *The pocket guide to the polyvagal theory: the transformative power of feeling safe*. New York: WW Norton & Company.

Rogers, C.R. (2004). *On becoming a person: a therapist's view of psychotherapy*. London: Robinson. (Original work published 1961).

Schore, A.N. (2019). *Right brain psychotherapy*. New York: WW Norton & Company.

Schore, J.R. & Schore, A.N. (2008). Modern attachment theory: the central role of affect regulation in development and treatment. *Clinical Social Work Journal*, 36, 9–20. doi:10.1007/s10615-007-0111-7.

Seligman, S. (2007). Mentalization and metaphor, acknowledgment and grief: forms of transformation in the reflective space. *Psychoanalytic Dialogues*, 17(3), 321–344. doi:10.1080/10481880701413538.

Siegel, D.J. (2013). Therapeutic presence: mindful awareness and the person of the therapist. In D.J. Siegel, & M. Solomon (Eds.), *Healing moments in psychotherapy* (pp. 243–268). New York: W.W. Norton & Company.

Siegel, D.J. (2015). *The developing mind* (2nd ed.). New York: Guildford Press.

Stormtrooper Star Wars toys available at most toy stores (n.d.).

Stern, D.N. (1985). *The interpersonal world of the infant*. New York: Basic Books.

Sunderland, M. (2000). *Using storytelling as a therapeutic tool with children*. London: Speechmark.

Sunderland, M. (2003). *Helping children with low self-esteem*. London: Speechmark.

Totton, N. (2015). *Embodied relating*. London: Karnac.

Treisman, K. (2017). *Working with relational and developmental trauma in children and adolescents*. Abingdon: Routledge.

Van der Kolk, B. (2015). *The body keeps the score: mind, brain and body in the transformation of trauma*. London: Penguin Random House.

Webber, A. (2017). *Breakthrough moments in arts psychotherapy*. London: Karnac.

Wilkinson, M. (2010). *Changing minds in therapy: emotion, attachment, trauma and neurobiology*. New York: W.W. Norton and Company.

Wilkinson, M. (2017). Mind, brain and body. Healing trauma: the way forward. *Journal of Analytical Psychology*, 62(4), 526–543. doi:10.1111/1468-5922.12335.

Winnicott, D.W. (2005). *Playing and reality*. Abingdon: Routledge. (Original work published 1971).

Winnicott, D.W. (2007). *The maturational processes and the facilitating environment*. London: Karnac. (Original work published 1965).

Chapter 7

The Faceless Face
Reaching Shame without Words

Jude Adcock

Background

This chapter presents poignant moments in therapy with a transgender adolescent whose shame was reached within the context of the therapist's arts-based psycho-therapeutic counselling practice. The therapist's own shameful feelings are also reflected upon as part of the emerging process.

When Amardi was born, they outwardly presented with female sexual characteristics and therefore, unsurprisingly, were assigned to the female sex and gender binary. As Amardi developed into adolescence, their outward presentation and sexual characteristics no longer aligned with how they felt or perceived themselves. Amardi, who had also changed their name to be gender neutral, did not feel strongly male or female but rather occupied a mid-point on the gender continuum referred to commonly as 'non-binary'; meaning not identifying strongly with either the binary female or male position. Although Amardi's gender identity was not explicitly part of the reason for coming to therapy, I wanted to honour their request (disclosed at the initial parent meeting) that I use 'they/their/them' pronouns. I will therefore refer to Amardi either by name or they/their/themselves during this chapter.

Whilst it can be challenging to remember a client's requested pronouns, particularly for one whose appearance leans more typically to the binary genders, the most important thing, in my experience is to try and get it right but apologise and move on when invariably, on occasion we get it wrong. Gender identity and more explicitly transgender identity has garnered a lot of attention in recent years, ranking highly on the agenda of those adhering to the politics of critical social justice. As therapists, we may wonder about the origins of any client's expressed gender identity, be it inherent in their make-up or perhaps as an unconscious (or even in some cases conscious) reaction to developmental and/or environmental factors. No matter which, when working with a client expressing a particular gender identity, it is important to embrace this as an expression of their being – which may or may not become part of the therapeutic endeavour. It is important to never assume a transgender client is seeking therapy for their 'trans-ness' as the presenting issue may be unrelated.

DOI: 10.4324/9781003163015-7

Amardi had suffered significant trauma due to physical and psychological cruelty at the hands of a step-parent and unavailable mother who suffered with extremely poor mental health. Whilst all three children had experienced difficulties, as the eldest, Amardi had suffered the worst abuse. They were frequently compared to their 'brilliant' siblings whilst suffering constant criticism and shaming; admonished, it appeared, by virtue of simply being alive. Although effort had been made to alienate Amardi from their siblings, these attempts by the step-parent were largely unsuccessful. Amardi was living in safety at the time of the therapeutic work, but their previous experiences had caused a deep core shame to develop causing withdrawal into themselves and in turn inhibiting their ability to socially integrate. Increasingly concerned, Amardi's remaining biological parent and other step-parent, with whom they now lived, had contacted me.

Introducing the Work

The use of creative arts within the therapeutic relationship will be explored alongside how Amardi's shame was accessed and understood by the practitioner. The session vignettes will also demonstrate the progress made in reaching Amardi's shame in spite of little verbal dialogue during the sessions; whilst also attending to the sometimes stuck and inadequate feelings of the therapist concerned with not 'doing enough'. The importance of clinical supervision to work through these feelings will also be noted. Various art media were used throughout and many of the images were profoundly moving to the therapist. Thus, aged 15, Amardi and I began a therapeutic journey that would last three years.

Having taken a history at the parent meeting, prior to meeting Amardi, I had some idea of their background, presenting issues and likely hurdles in therapy; namely Amardi's ability or desire to join me in the therapeutic process. I was also aware that Amardi would likely be painfully shy, talk very little, be slow to trust and therefore might be hard to reach. Prior to meeting Amardi, I reflected on my own experiences of growing up as a lonely only child of acrimoniously divorced parents and the deeply rooted shame that, although much improved, I have never been entirely able to shake off. Implicit shame would become a notable feature of our work together, as if we recognised and understood it tacitly within each other.

Session 1 – Meeting Amardi

Amardi arrived with the kind and caring step-parent with whom Amardi and the other siblings now lived and with whom I had met at the initial parent meeting. Leaving their step-parent at the door, Amardi tentatively entered the room. Amardi's previous experiences were immediately and explicitly present in the room as a palpable embodiment of the shame they appeared to hold. A typical philosophical position on shame may view it as an emotion arising from self-assessment which causes the person high degrees of anxiety as they imagine how they are seen by others. Recognising this, I was immediately aware of my own shyness flirting with feelings of inadequacy and shame.

I welcomed Amardi into the room. They were unable to engage eye contact, spoke as little as possible and only then in a whispered tone. Amardi's non-verbal communication was, however, extremely powerful. Their demeanour was hunched with head down, eyes to the floor, almost contorted with an overwhelming air of uncertainty, perhaps even fear. I was struck deeply by a fragility that seemed to fill the room. I sensed Amardi was a similar height to me but slight in stature with the translucent skin of an embryo needing nurture and protection. Their hair was short, straight and slightly auburn with a fringe falling over one eye. I was struck by a withering sense of cold, a perceptible shivering but also metaphorically in relation to an example of a painful experience I had previously been made aware of: Amardi had been made by their other step-parent to search for lumps of coal in the snow one year as their Christmas 'present'. I sensed an embarrassed tension in the air, a palpable uncertainty between two people with shame at their core – yet both trying to relate to each other. This was not comfortable, not at all. I remember now the sense of awkwardness I felt, almost certain Amardi would be sharing this experience. However, with an awareness of what is mine I was able to regulate myself and remain calm. I warmly invited Amardi in, showed them where the bottled water was and offered a seat.

The green leather wing-backed chair appeared to consume Amardi and, in that moment, I wondered what on earth we would do next. In front of me sat a pale and frail-looking young person with an uncomfortableness about them I'd rarely experienced other than recognising it within myself. As I tried, somewhat in vain, to make conversation, any words Amardi was able to say were followed immediately by a redness to their face. And as their eyes met the floor, there appeared to be an air of desperation, as if willing it to open up and consume them. Yet, in spite of the apparent challenge ahead, I already felt a strong urge to be with Amardi, to find a way in which I might be able to reach them. I sensed already this was not going to be easy so I began with an awareness of consciously not colluding with Amardi's shame, and thereby 'muddying the waters' with my own experiences instead wanting to remain empathically attuned to Amardi's unique experience.

It was apparent from the outset that building a safe and trusting working alliance within the therapeutic relationship would be fundamental to any chance of reaching Amardi. Research shows that the therapeutic relationship is the key factor that produces positive outcomes regardless of theoretical modality (Wampold & Imel, 2015). As an arts-based counsellor and psychotherapist, I quickly suspected, from our brief exchange, that talking alone would not be enough. Through extensive training and personal experience as the client in therapy, I firmly believe that access to a broad range of art materials alongside the use of sand and clay can help the development of the therapeutic relationship when words are at best difficult and at worst impossible to find. To those unfamiliar with such work, it might be natural to wonder why using the creative-arts therapeutically can be so beneficial with shame-based clients and particularly with children and young people.

When working with young people, using arts media can reduce anxiety by enabling the client to communicate their feelings and experiences without having to find words (Malchiodi, 2012). When working with shame-based clients by using the creative arts, we are offering the client an alternative 'other' to the therapist and the created image can become the mirror with which their soul is given expression; through dialoguing with the image their self is given voice. By staying with the metaphor of the created image (no matter what material has been chosen to create it) the symbolic meaning is left undisturbed and this in itself can provide the possibility of change for the client. This was a useful reminder during the many times I felt the pangs of inadequacy as my own shame bubbled away in the cauldron of self-doubt. I often felt as if I wasn't doing anything useful, that I *should* know how to help Amardi find a way to move forward. Yet, with little dialogue between us, what Amardi wanted or needed from our work was far from explicit.

Supervision with my arts-based supervisor was particularly useful during these moments of my seemingly inevitable feelings of 'imposter syndrome'. My feelings of inadequacy were normalised and usefully we considered the importance of my 'bearing witness' to Armardi's psyche as it was being represented through the images they created each week. Souter-Anderson usefully illustrates this when describing working with clay. It's as if the client's psyche has produced through their hands what their eyes need to see in order to make sense of their world (Souter-Anderson, 2010). From this first meeting, not only did I sense that Amardi might be hard to reach but that I too would have a personal challenge in reaching deep into my own resolve as a competent and 'good enough' therapist as I was already aware of some similarities in our stories.

In this first session, aware of Amardi's shyness and propensity to create art, I soon asked if they would like to paint or draw. Amardi pointed to the paints. I busied about getting the necessary items ready as I encouraged Amardi to choose the paints they would like to use. Quietly, on brown paper, Amardi drew and then painted an image of a character in a long pale blue dress or perhaps a frock coat (see Figure 7.1). Dispensing tiny amounts of paint they applied it sparingly. I was struck by a sense of caution, as if something bad might happen if they were somehow uncontrolled. I was mesmerised as the image took shape. Striking long black hair contrasted the paleness of the garment whilst most poignant perhaps, the featureless face. I pondered the correlation between the empty face and the almost, at times, voiceless yet notable presence of Amardi in the room. After our brief introduction, the image creation took up (with some relief) the rest of the 45-minute session. No words were exchanged about the image – yet its powerfulness spoke a thousand. I felt as though already Amardi was showing me something important. We were both seemingly deeply moved by the presence of this image in the room.

Session 3 – Reaching

At the beginning of our third session, I left a blanket and a hot water bottle on a chair and, without making a fuss, offered it gently to Amardi. It was quickly taken and became a mainstay of our work together during the colder months perhaps serving as a bridge between the coldness Amardi had previously experienced to

Figure 7.1 The Faceless Face.

the tangible warmth of the room and our joint therapeutic endeavour. Amardi's internal reality and external life betwixt by an intermediate area of experiencing, together with me, in the room.

Amardi had suffered a huge blow to their sense of self when publicly shamed by the other step-parent in a most intrusive and cruel way. Although this happened prior to our therapeutic work together it was a contributing factor for Amardi beginning arts-based counselling. So powerful was my sense of Amardi's shame-filled suffering I often felt pangs of anger towards their perpetrator, experienced viscerally as if a lightning bolt was piercing my heart. Although unspoken between us the lasting impact of this shaming on Armardi was evident in their demeanour and created images.

We settled into the regularity of weekly meetings and the familiarity of the room appeared to help Amardi settle more readily. However, Amardi's demeanour changed little during these early sessions. Whilst Amardi sat somewhat awkwardly on the stool at the table, typically hands together on their lap, I would ask what they might like to use for their image creation that day. At the beginning, Amardi did experiment with collage, montage, sand-tray and clay, only returning to them on rare occasions.

Amardi soon settled into a pattern of almost ritualistic use of the art materials that included brown or white paper, paint, pens or pencils, and items for collage or montage. The image creation would begin with Amardi purposefully selecting the paint required and squirting tiny amounts onto a paper plate. Then, paper ready, Amardi would quickly draw an image outline before completing it, typically with paint. The process of paint selection, paper being cut and being ready to create, was quickly turning into a collaborative event. It felt to me that we were co-creating the necessary conditions for change together with a kind of practical communication emerging. Few words passed between us yet there was a strong sense of coming together to facilitate the flow of Amardi's psychic expression without fear of criticism or shaming.

Another important element to the work began in one particular session several weeks into Armardi's therapy; the cutting out of the previous week's work and sticking it into a large scrapbook (although it certainly wasn't scrap!). Once a book was finished Amardi would take it home and, with permission, I would take photos of some of the created images that, also later permitted by Amardi, I could use in any future writing.

Session 6 – Duality

Amardi was not talkative. Any discussion was always brief and felt slightly awkward, although it seemed apparent we had a deepening mutual respect and trust developing. I tentatively explored with Amardi what today's image (see Figure 7.2) might mean to them. Amardi offered only that it was a person with red hair. Based on my own response to the image before me, I offered that I sensed a certain strength and vitality to the image; I wondered if the character may perhaps be overcoming something difficult? Staying within the metaphor I did not want to name 'shame' at this stage, conscious not to risk closing Amardi down. In this image, the hair appears to be blown gently back perhaps from the confident strides forwards. A deliberate turn of the head, somehow dignified with piercing green eyes and striking red hair, a combination typically denoted as mysterious due to its rarity. As if Amardi is saying "I am unique and will not own the shame you try to impose upon me". Yet Amardi sat in silence with head bowed and shoulders hunched. A wave of shame engulfed me as I admonished myself for being clumsy. Then, all of a sudden, a slight smile appeared on Amardi's face as they nodded their head in recognition of my wonderings. The relief was palpable but more importantly, in that moment, I felt, very tentatively that I had perhaps, in this moment, begun to reach Amardi. I sensed I had seen them and they had felt witnessed.

Reflecting on the image, I wondered to myself if this was Amardi's anima and animus transcending their psyche as they perhaps unconsciously processed the cruel and shameful injustices experienced in childhood – leading to the

Figure 7.2 I See You.

development of a more coherent sense of self. I also began to wonder how Jung's theory of these two primary and binary anthro-pomorphic archetypes applied to a non-binary gendered person (Jung, 1969)?

Session 10 – Breakthrough

Amardi arrives promptly for our regular weekly session. I hear Amardi walking on the stones outside towards my therapy room. I check in with myself and take a few deep breaths. Amardi knocks on the door. As I open it I notice their head tilted slightly to the ground bearing a smile. I welcome Amardi in as they nod and make their way to the green leather chair. Amardi is not in their usual oversized uniform of the strict Catholic school they attend but, instead, dressed resemblant of the Dandy fashion of the early 19th century. I remark that their clothes suit them well as the smile broadens across their pale face. I'm struck that I'm starting to see more of Amardi and less of the chair. Shoulders are less hunched than is typical but their shame is never far away. Amardi sits, their hands together in front of their body. I feel uncomfortable and we exchange what I can only really call pleasantries. I ask how they are, how their week has been and as usual Amardi nods, their face turning a shade of darkish pink as they tell me it's been "okay". I know already to leave it there but I offer that their new haircut suits them; they appear pleased and say "thank you" with a smile which lights up their face and for a few moments eye contact is made. This feels significant: Amardi's clothes and new haircut appear to signify a shift. I had previously wondered if Amardi avoided looking at me in case I might see deep inside their soul by looking into their eyes.

Feeling less anxious I ask Amardi if they would like to move to the table. Amardi begins the session, as usual, by cutting and sticking last week's images into their book (unless creating a collage/montage – for which I would produce a photograph to use instead). This feels like a ritualistic yet collaborative event marking the beginning of our session; setting the scene for the creativity that will inevitably ensue. I ask Amardi what they would like to do and again briefly engaging my eye, they say: "I'd like to paint" to which I suggest that they get the things that they need ready – this in itself is significant movement. It may seem unremarkable but whereas Amardi barely uttered a word before they now speak from the I, indicating their developing sense of self.

I get the scissors and tape to stick the paper down. Amardi chooses brown paper and begins to sketch what looks like a horse (although I never assume anything). I know that Amardi likes to ride horses. A fleeting thought crosses my mind – our mutual desire to connect to the strong steadfast resilient beast before us, powerful and knowing. A creature without shame. I am again struck by the speed with which Amardi's image takes shape. Amardi has chosen black, brown white and yellow paint. Suddenly Amardi stops, turns to me, engages eye contact again and asks for a paper plate – I usually provide this as part of the preparation but, in my anxiety, I had forgotten – I noted my own shame-based somatic response. The French existential philosopher Sartre describes the affective embodied response to shame as: "… an immediate shudder which runs through me from head to foot without any discursive preparation" (Sartre, 2003).

Historically having to ask for anything would seem to trigger Amardi's shame response as if their shame traversed the space between us, my purpose being to swallow and contain it. I have had to work hard in attending to my own counter-transferential material so it hasn't unwittingly interfered with our work – i.e. the triggering of my own shame response and need to be the 'good therapist'. I reflect on the significant change in Amardi's confidence; subtle but very much there. I note that mine has shifted too.

As Amardi begins to paint, I'm aware of their breath calming. Often Amardi will take a gulp of air during the beginning phase of the image creation. I note my response is to mirror this as our co-regulation kicks in. As Amardi works, I become aware of what appears to be their emotionality joining their physical presence in the room. I notice a brightness in Amardi's eyes, a smile upon their face. Their body is still engaging with their task, but they appear to be relaxed and at one with their creation. It is 'as if' the creating of the image facilitates a joining of Amardi's 'parts' and I am witnessing their integration. I sense Amardi is now lost for a few moments within the richness and diversity of their inner world, a place where, if enabled, Amardi is able to access their innate creativity.

I am also careful not to over-collude with Amardi's shame. It is theirs and not mine although I feel a tension between us that has a numinous quality, as if reaching a depth of understanding that shame has touched us both. Shame continues to permeate our being when we keep it secret; it needs secrecy to survive. Yet, through the creation of imagery as a metaphor for their life, Amardi's shame is being reached, seen and accepted within the safety of our therapeutic relationship.

Amardi takes more of the brown paint and again a tiny amount is used on the plate. Something strikes me about the paint but presently I am not sure what. A metaphor for Amardi's life perhaps? Small, seemingly insignificant amounts of paint, that when applied to a (secure) base, will transform into something that holds the creator's narrative. I am aware of my continued anxiety although it has reduced to a more manageable degree. I sense I am holding Amardi's shame for a while whilst they are free to be with the image they are creating. I am questioning my purpose and conclude at this moment it is as a container, a safe held space which enables Amardi's freedom for psychic expression. I hold their shame whilst they are free to explore their psychic world, for the moment at least, uninhibited (see Figure 7.3).

I find myself mesmerised by the image that has arrived in the room today. The eyes are focused forward; they want to be seen as if the horse is saying: "You can see me, I will allow you to". The horse archetype has long been linked to our primal drives. The horse may evoke wild intense feelings which, for Jung, meant being out of control. I wondered how little control Amardi, at times, felt they had. It has been said that horses have enabled people to connect to feelings deep within their shadow self, vulnerability shown as a strength. The horse is strong, powerful, with a sense of embodiment and sensitivity.

Amardi finishes the image and we spend a few minutes looking at it together. From Amardi, I sense a strong affinity for this horse and wonder how this horse might relate to them. It feels like an opportune moment to gently enquire – aware always that for Amardi talking about themselves is anxiety and shame-provoking. I wonder out loud about the character of this horse. Without prompting, Amardi tells me that the horse is nervous and shy and has to get to know the rider before it is able to respond and respect them. I am immediately drawn to the metaphor through which I am offered insight into Amardi's world. I inquire whether the horse likes to be in a group or prefers to be solitary? "Solitary". Again I am afforded more insight into Amardi's world. I thank Amardi for sharing this beautiful strong horse with me. Amardi engages eye contact and smiles a knowing smile. Although I have seen this image for the first time, I sense for Amardi it is an old faithful friend, one that they have allowed me to see to help me reach them in the session.

As Holliday explains, by externalising feelings into a created image a young person can achieve a less shaming distance from them (Holliday, 2014). Using the

Figure 7.3 The Power of the Horse.

creative-arts in therapy enables painful feelings to be contained within the metaphor which is typically much less shaming. The image may be talked about or dialogued with and thus removes the focus from the young person whilst helping them gain insight and understanding. Malchiodi suggests that when using creative approaches, we are bypassing, rather than actively confronting, well-practised defences (Malchiodi, 2012). Amardi's defences have been crucial to their survival. As a therapist, my work is not to try and break down these defences and risk leaving Amardi feeling unsafe and exposed. But instead, through an attachment-informed arts-based approach, help Amardi's issues become accessible for therapeutic intervention in a way that verbal psychotherapy alone would not be likely to achieve. I cannot help but be struck by the metaphoric richness I'm privileged to witness and Amardi's willingness to let me begin to reach them in their world. A world where, through their use of imagery and their innate artistic talent, they can begin to feel good enough and acceptable not only to others but most importantly to themselves.

Figure 7.4 Ork 1 and Ork 2.

I remind Amardi that we have ten minutes left of the session and ask if they would like to talk or create another image. Choosing to create an image Amardi uses white paper and fine-tip pens. Characteristically quick, Amardi now appears more relaxed and sketches two characters in five minutes (see Figure 7.4). I am prepared for the last five minutes to feel conversationally awkward but something unusual happens. Suddenly Amardi comes alive and through the use of metaphor helps me reach deeper into their psyche. Amardi tells me that the images are Orks, inspired by the video games that enable Armardi to escape to a fantasy world.

Ork 1 Amardi tells me depicts a character who is withdrawn, preferring to relate to animals than humans; humans can be difficult and judgemental. Ork 2 Amardi continues is educated, confident and quite arrogant depending on who they are relating to. Ork 2 has empathy for people and will talk to anyone. I am struck by the polarity in these two characters and wonder to myself if Ork 1 represents Amardi's shame whilst Ork 2 perhaps signifies shame as the flipside of narcissism and thus Amardi's desire to be acceptable to themselves is exaggerated as a defence against their shame.

Although discussing existential verbal therapy, I find May's words are analogous to witnessing the young person creating an image: "It is the experience of the instantaneous encounter with another person who comes alive to us on a very different level from what we *know* about him" (May, 1986). In other words, we may have an appreciation of the young person and their situation already but until we *experience* them phenomenologically in a certain moment we cannot *know* them. Through their created image, I sense Amardi *shows* me what it feels like to be them, what it *means* to inhabit their world and lets me reach their shameful parts thus far hidden to the world.

Session 10 – The Vigilant Crow

Crows hold great meaning for Amardi and appeared a few times in our work together. Painted black on brown paper, the crow has a beady eye as if looking out for any threat to their safety. Crows feature often in books and games that Armardi engages with. Armardi likes the mystical and ethereal qualities of the crow, often seen as dark and mysterious. I wonder if Amardi is showing me their shadow aspect or, as depicted in Celtic mythology, they identify with Morrigan the crow, goddess of battle and war? Perhaps the crow represents a transition between the 'real' world which can feel hostile and shaming and Amardi's fantasy world where their omnipotence is given freedom to be expressed. Again this snapshot into Amardi's inner world helped us both reach the parts of Amardi's being that they were too ashamed to express in daily life. I was aware of the enormous privilege in bearing witness to the sanctity of Amardi's inner and very private world (see Figure 7.5).

Figure 7.5 The Vigilant Crow.

Session 21 – Shame Becomes Visible

In this final glimpse of being in the therapy room with Armardi, I will illustrate the session in which I felt we had reached the core of Amardi's shame. It was through the somewhat unexpected creation of the most powerful and haunting image. I sensed that if ever a piece of art represented someone's shameful sense of self it was perhaps this one. More flustered than usual Amardi arrived to this session with an air of discomfort. Without elaborating they were able to verbally acknowledge that it had been a difficult day. Amardi chose chalk pastels and brown paper and began to create with a sense of urgency, exuding a strong sense of purpose. There was a strange atmosphere in the room, difficult to put into words, some-what volcanic, as if something was about to blow. I felt this session would be important.

Amardi was very focused with strong determined gestures as they connected the chalk to its substrate. It was as if the fragile pale embryo had matured into a stronger more assertive young adult. The image, created in chalk pastel, appeared to be the embodiment of Amardi's shame. I felt profoundly moved at the intensity of the dark pink/red totality of the neck, face and ear; the bright green cat-like eyes, the blackest of hair and the strikingly non-human presence. Utterly spell-bound I was on tenterhooks as the image unfolded, shocked almost at its rawness and prevailing offering (see Figure 7.6). The image was painful to apprehend. Not only did I recognise the embodiment of my own shame manifest before me but

Figure 7.6 Shame Arrives.

more importantly I sensed we had arrived at the point of Amardi being able to *show* me, through the profoundness of the image, their deepest and most vulnerable shame in the most evocative manner.

As Amardi gazed at the image I noticed a serene calmness, as if they were purging their shame and possibly anger from not only their difficult day but their unjust and challenging life experiences. We momentarily made eye contact and simultaneously took a deep breath. Amardi had let me in; their shame had been reached. Their demeanour appeared calmer and they had moved not only from the flustered beginning of the session but significantly, I imagined, towards a less shameful future. There were no words necessary and none shared between us. I think the image speaks for itself.

Discussion

Whilst our work continued for some time, it was the first six months or so that were crucial in reaching Amardi's shame and so freeing them up to explore, through the creative arts, themselves more fully. Amardi had started therapy as a painfully shy, cold and frail-looking young person with significant trauma in their background and shame at their core. Yet by the time we ended the therapy, Amardi had a stronger stature and was noticeably more confident and colourful.

Typically I work in a pluralistic or integrative manner yet my work with Amardi demanded of me that I be able to meet their needs in a truly creative way. I knew from the outset I would find the work challenging both personally and professionally. Whilst supervision helped me explore my own perceived feelings of inadequacy, I found attempting to interpret the images to be almost invasive at times. It felt unnecessary in the session and therefore also in supervision. In trying to understand the images Amardi had created I realised that all I could do, without their verbal input, was make a series of hypotheses with my supervisor about what they might mean. The images were so powerful it felt more congruent to trust in the process of being in the room with Amardi and their creations; no interpretation necessary, instead an acceptance that sometimes hypotheses have to remain just that. They just were and we just were.

There was also something about the image as the 'other' and the metaphor it held being powerful enough to elicit and process Amardi's deeply held shame. It had been quickly apparent that 'talking therapies' would not reach Amardi's shame and therefore arts-based therapy provided a valuable resource for discovery. Whilst any therapy is part of a client's journey through life and not the whole answer, I am left with no doubt that without the use of the creative arts within the context of a developing therapeutic relationship, Amardi's shame would still be as concealed today as it was at the beginning of the therapy.

References

Holliday, C. (2014). Working with Thinking, Feeling and the Importance of the Body. In Colleen McLaughlin and Carol Holliday (Eds.), *Therapy with Children and Young People: Integrative Counselling in Schools and Other Settings* (pp. 118–129). SAGE.

Holmes, J. (1993). *John Bowlby and Attachment Theory*. Routledge.

Jung, C. G. (1969). *The Structure and Dynamics of The Psyche* (H. Read, M. Fordham, & G. Adler, Eds.; 2nd ed., Vol. 8). Routledge & Kegan Paul.

Malchiodi, C. A. (Ed.). (2012). *Handbook of Art Therapy*. Guilford Press.

May, R. (1986). *The Discovery of Being*. W.W. Norton & Company.

Sartre, J.-P. (2003). *Being and Nothingness* (2nd ed.). Routledge Classics.

Souter-Anderson, L. (2010). *Touching Clay, Touching What?* Archive.

Wampold, B. E., & Imel, Z. E. (2015). *The Great Psychotherapy Debate: The Evidence for What Makes Psychotherapy Work* (2nd ed.). Routledge.

Chapter 8

The Locust on the Platter

Aileen Webber

Snapshot 1: Revealing and Concealing

Hattie sidles into my room self-consciously. Her jacket hood is up and her long dark hair is draped across her pale face. I'm surprised she can see to negotiate around the materials in my private practice room. It flits into my mind that it's as if she wants to hide. What has happened to make her want to hide? I try to pull myself back into the present and indicate the floor cushion across from mine and she sits down and hunches even further into her hood. I wonder if the hood is protecting her from the whole world or from me in particular. I feel she will go to a defensive place if I ask questions so I wait. But when the silence is beginning to feel oppressive, I eventually ask: "What's bothering you that you decided to come and see me today?" A prolonged silence follows: "Nothing" she says eventually accompanied by a shrug of the shoulders.

"Okay. How about you show me your family with some of these animals then?" I'm hoping that this will introduce the fun of using play and art materials which might ensure the work does not become too overwhelming too soon for Hattie. I am feeling deeply curious about this 12-year-old girl who seems to be too timid to make full contact with me or indeed herself. I think perhaps I'm premature in my suggestion to use the art materials as she looks as though she might run out of the room. But my intuitive feeling that the arts will lead the way for Hattie is confirmed a few seconds later, when I bring out a series of baskets of sheep, cats, dogs, elephants and Russian dolls and she looks sideways around her hair and her hood as though she is intrigued despite herself. I decide to try to mobilise her from her frozen state (of what I guess is anxiety: anxiety about being here now with me I wonder or what she might reveal despite her strong desire not to show anything), and I place on the floor between us a mat with a picture of a sunset over water with grasses in the foreground. How about you show me your family? I'm surprised when after a short pause, she places two large elephants and two smaller elephants onto the scene. Then she looks up directly at me for the first time and says:

"I watched a YouTube video of elephants and the mummy elephant pushed the baby elephant under her legs with her trunk... but this one won't fit!" While she is saying this, she is trying to push one of the smaller elephants under the legs of one of the bigger ones (see Figure 8.1). I'm wondering if this is about keeping the

DOI: 10.4324/9781003163015-8

Figure 8.1 The Elephant Family.

baby elephant safe, protected and defended by its mother, when she starts to get really agitated and push the elephant really hard. She is pushing and muttering: "It won't fit… Get in there…" She reaches for the other small elephant and pushes hard with it, but the little elephant still won't fit under the mother's legs and falls over. Now Hattie is getting really distressed and this is only her first session. I experience an overwhelming yearning to reach her and enable her to show me in the metaphor what she seems to be trying so hard not to tell me. This leads me to make a suggestion: "How about using the Russian Doll Elephant set?" This seems to shift the angry spell without breaking it.

She unscrews the elephant set and discovers that the third smallest of the nestled elephants will fit under the mummy elephant's legs (see Figure 8.2). "There now it's hidden." She seems mightily relieved. I wonder if I've rescued her and not let her struggle enough – but for a first session, this felt a necessary containment. Strangely, however, she continues to push the baby elephant under the mother's legs with the other baby elephant's trunk. So much so, that she is bashing the baby elephant and the mother's legs. I find myself speaking as the baby elephant: "Ow you're hurting me" I say.

A look flits over Hattie's face that seems to be a mixture of delight, disgust, horror and embarrassment, alongside the previous angry feelings, but then she suddenly sits back in her seat, hiding behind the hood of her coat. I wait a while

Figure 8.2 Hiding the Baby Elephant.

and then say: "Okay. So you really showed me the elephant family today. Thank you. I hope you'll come back next week and we can find out more about them and about you."

Hattie looks non-committal, but she seems to have a little bit more colour in her face and to be less inert as she makes her way out of my room. I'm left feeling intrigued. There is clearly much she has shown me through her Elephant Family but what exactly? I just feel that although she seems to be trying hard to hide what is troubling her, I intuitively believe she is also hoping I will reach her.

Context

After this first session, I'm wondering about whether Hattie was trying to hide from showing me what she demonstrated all too clearly – that she felt "bad." I know from the referral by the school that Hattie gets into rages towards other children in the classroom. She clearly demonstrates her anger towards the baby elephant and the mother elephant. I guess that she has angry feelings that she is not permitted (by others or herself) to show and she ends up feeling "bad."

I have decided to make suggestions to Hattie at her next session. I want to find a way to allow her to own her defences and not seem as though I'm trying to knock them down. In order to ensure that the therapy is contained in this next session, I have decided that I will be more directive than I usually am and suggest that she makes a Pause Button and imagines a Safe Place. I am hoping to help her to feel that she can dip in and out of difficult material in this way as I'm conscious that I want to avoid her tipping into feeling "bad" (shame) as it is my belief that this is the very situation I am trying to help her to overcome.

Snapshot 2: Keeping Safe

I'm delighted when Hattie comes in and flops down opposite me on the other large floor cushion the following week. She seems slightly less apprehensive than at her first session. I launch straight in with what I've decided to introduce in this session:

> Hello Hattie. I was thinking that perhaps we could make a "Safe Place" and a "Pause Button" today. That way you could press the button and stop things if they feel too much for you and take yourself to a safe place in your mind to help you can feel calmer.

Hattie looks bemused but somewhat curious: "I don't know what you mean?"

"Well it's natural to want to protect yourself against difficult feelings. I wonder how you imagine *your* protection? It could be something like: a wall, or a locked box, or a cellar?" I can see that Hattie is thinking about this. There is a long silence that feels productive not oppressive. "I think it's an empty shed." "Okay I'm picturing an empty shed. Can you tell me anything more about it?" Hattie looks more alive than I have seen her so far.

"It's at the bottom of the garden and I stuff the feelings in there and padlock the door and take the key with me so that no-one can get in and the feelings can't get out!" "Right. So you shove the feelings you don't want into the shed at the bottom of the garden and padlock the door. Is there anything else I should know so I can imagine this shed even more clearly?" I feel sure she is picturing it in her mind, and she confirms this when she says: "Well sometimes even I can't get in! And sometimes the feelings seem to burst out and charge up the garden path and take over..."

This is such a helpful metaphor that I decide to stay with this and suggest she draws a picture. She draws the shed with a huge padlock and shows the feelings pushing out the walls of the shed so they are round instead of straight and then she draws some feelings with legs escaping. The feelings are cartoon drawings using a mixture of stick people and manga faces with speech bubbles. I can see that she is quite pleased with what she has drawn and that she has surprised herself. She has now clearly shown me that she has some very difficult feelings that can burst out unbidden. It is too early to find out what the feelings are and what events or circumstances might have caused them. I decide to remain openly curious without probing too obviously.

The following week Hattie thinks of a "Safe Place" that she can go to if she needs to press the "Pause Button" in the therapy session. We have fun making both these safety measures and I can feel Hattie warming to the therapeutic process and being with me. The safe place she chooses is "a tree house at the very top of a very high tree that no-one else is able to climb."

★★★★★★★★★★★

The therapy continues over several weeks and Hattie makes many angry, sad, black and red paintings full of expressions of difficult feelings. I still don't know what the feelings are exactly, although there is a lot of red that appears to be about anger. She follows these with a series of predominantly green paintings of eyes, monsters and floating green bits. Eventually, she uses chalks of different shades of green and creates a picture that seems to be of a virus or alien threat of some kind (see Figure 8.3).

I wonder aloud if Hattie feels like a green-eyed monster sometimes and she says "Yes" and then she adds: "And sometimes I think I'll contaminate the whole world with my greenness!"

Figure 8.3 Alien Threat.

"How frightening that must feel" I say: "To feel you could infect the whole world with your green envious feelings." She looks affirmed whilst also looking ashamed. She turns away and mutters almost inaudibly: "You're lucky you don't have to have my younger sister in your therapy room – she'd mess up everything! Everyone thinks she's the little cute one but they don't have to put up with her." I sense that it's important that she has "brought her sister into the room" ironically by saying it's lucky she doesn't come into the room. I believe she wants me to know that her sister messes things up (and I extrapolate therefore that this might be deeply annoying to Hattie and she has to "put up with her"). But it feels important not to make too much of it, so she doesn't feel overwhelmed by the shameful feelings this provokes. But now we have both acknowledged that her feelings of anger are about, or include, feelings of jealousy and she's mentioned that she feels that her family prefer her little sister to her. Several weeks later a breakthrough session occurs:

Snapshot 3: The Locust on the Platter

Hattie seems more upbeat than I have ever seen her today and I feel delighted about this, noticing that she seems less fidgety and she's not hiding in her coat. "Can we play with the squidgy, plastic, insects?" she says as she rummages across the baskets on my shelves looking for the container she is after. "Oh yes of course. It's on the second shelf." She pulls the basket down, spilling out one or two of the smaller plastic spiders and snakes in her haste and places it at the side of the brown furry rug that I have spread out on the floor to provide an outline and edge to her play. I'm intrigued as I have no idea what today's session is going to be about but Hattie seems to have a plan in mind. Her enthusiasm is infectious and I feel full of attentive energy. She goes back to the shelves and starts hunting around. I leave her to it for a while and then she says:

"What can I use as a plate for a banquet?" I hand her a plate and she beams with delight. "Oh this is perfect. It's a silver platter" she says. And thus she sets the scene.

She proceeds to tip out the basket of insects and seizes upon a rubber locust and places it on the plate. It is so large that some of its limbs spill over the edge of the plate. She places it down outside the brown rug and hunts around in other baskets, and other places in the room, lining up large and small dolls, teddies and puppets around the edge of the rug. She asks me to sit alongside them. "You are all the guests at the banquet," she says solemnly as I silently move across to join the other guests. Then Hattie turns herself around and when she turns back she has a white square of material draped over her arm and she is holding the platter up aloft with one hand. She walks ceremoniously around the edge of the rug and up to the middle and places the dish on the floor in the centre.

"The locust is served." She says to the gathered company in a mock formal voice. At this point in the proceedings, she catches my eye and laughs. What passes between us feels like a pivotal moment in her therapy. The look contains within it a mutual knowing that the guests are all members of her close and extended family and friends. We also both know, without anything needing to be said out loud, that the locust on the platter is her annoying little sister. Hattie is serving her sister

Figure 8.4 The Locust on the Platter.

up as a meal to be devoured by all those she feels see her little sister as the "cute one" (see Figure 8.4). It feels very important that I allow this knowing to remain unspoken to avoid her tipping into feeling shame about what she is enacting. The drama continues for some time whilst the locust is "carved" and "served" to various guests until, in a sleight of hand that takes my breath away, Hattie makes the locust vanish. After a short pause, Hattie acts out the gathered group saying how enjoyable the meal has been and gradually leaving the banquet. As they leave they are put back into the baskets and corners of the room from whence they came.

I watch with awe until finally Hattie and I are left sitting alone on either side of the rug gazing at the middle. The banquet is over. The guests have gone.

Only the empty platter remains.

Reflections

After this session, I am left astonished at how powerful it has been to witness this imaginary cannibal feast. Even when she muttered that it was lucky that I didn't have to have her sister in my therapy room, no explicit link had been made by either of us that this could provoke jealous feelings or murderous rage. However, somehow she seemed to know that I knew when she caught my eye and smiled her knowing smile and laughed. Her feelings were unacceptable to her and she could not state them out loud, but in acting them out in her story of "The Locust on the Platter" I believe she could begin to loosen some of their powerful hold on her.

Snapshot 4: The Hero's Journey

After the breakthrough session (Webber, 2017) of the week before, Hattie sets about creating a journey – by laying out a series of silk scarves that stretch around my Practice Room and also extends out into the passage outside the room. She creates it spontaneously having as the main protagonist one of the baby elephants. I assume the baby elephant is her (not least because her younger sister was "eaten" in the previous session) but I keep my thoughts to myself. This is Hattie's story of one of the Baby Elephant's journeys. In keeping with Joseph Campbell's Hero's Journey and Carl Jung's archetypal characters (Jung, 1952), her story includes obstacles, helpers, enemies, and the unknown. At each new stretch or turn of the scarves, she collects objects from my baskets and shelves and describes the obstacle or enemy that the baby elephant has to confront. These dangers include meeting a three-headed monster, having to get through a locked gate, and meeting a transformer that changes from enemy to friend. At times she asks me for help and at other times she calls for support from objects in my room by putting them beside the baby elephant.

My role seems to be to witness the unfolding journey making occasional comments on the elephant's struggles and triumphs. Hattie smiles when I say things like this and that guides me to understand what she is wanting from me as she undertakes this adventure. At the end of each session, we take photographs and the following week set up the play from the previous photograph and continue from where she left off. Somewhat shockingly at the end of one session, Hattie creates a chasm between two of the scarves in the passage outside the Practice Room and all the characters fall into the abyss, and she covers them over with the scarves. I peer round into the passage to see what has transpired and say: "Oh good gracious, have they all fallen in?" I feel shocked and appalled as up to this point the story has been such a balance between trauma and survival, good and evil. But now, in a similar way to the disappearance of the locust, we seem to be left with nothing, as though the journey itself had never taken place. "That is the end of the story" Hattie states matter of factly as she leaves my therapy room for the end of the session. I feel bereft and almost on the verge of tears. I wonder if this might be a foreshadowing of the sudden ending of Hattie's therapy.

Snapshot 5: The Sally Spoon Puppet Story

The next week, Hattie bounds into the room and asks if she can make up a story. I show her the 6-Part Story Structure and she chooses a title of "The Girl Who Always Felt Bad." She draws in each of the boxes filling in the outline of the story of Sally Spoon who lived in a house with The Spoon family: mother and father and a younger sister. The quest she said was to stop feeling "bad." The obstacle was little Sister Spoon, who kept messing up Sally Spoon's games and who everyone preferred. Then what happens next shows the family saying Sally Spoon should let her sister play: "She's only little!" This enrages Sally Spoon and she hits her sister and then feels so "bad" she runs away and climbs up a tree. The final part of the story shows a Mr Wizard character, who is encouraging Sally Spoon to come down from the tree, saying it must be so difficult having a sister messing up her games. Sally Spoon comes down from the tree. At this point, Hattie says to me: "I don't think the story ends there, that's too tidy for real life. "Of course I say, how do you want to "not end" your story then?" She replies immediately, I want Sally Spoon to say "goodbye" to the Wizard and end the story with her still up the tree, so that we can imagine or act out different possible endings.

We spent the next few weeks using paint and bits of material to make the scenes and by putting them onto two pieces of A4 stiff card, joined in the middle, we got them to stand up. We dressed the wooden spoons with bits of material with eyes and hair stuck on and acted out the story. Hattie loved it and we laughed a lot especially when things would go wrong when we acted out her story (like scenes falling over and puppets' hair falling off and getting caught up in the trees we had made). When Mr Wizard was standing at the bottom of the tree calling up "Goodbye" to Sally Spoon who was still up the tree, I had a lump in my throat – it felt like the end of Hattie's therapeutic journey and our relationship.

The alternative endings idea seemed to signify that what happened next would depend on how Sally Spoon was able to use Mr Wizard's supportive comments that she wasn't "bad" for being frustrated with Sister Spoon. I felt as though the story was a summary of Hattie's own Therapeutic Journey and how Hattie had found a way (at least sometimes) not to feel "bad" and ashamed of her powerfully jealous and angry feelings towards her sister.

From this work with Hattie using scenes and puppet characters and leaving the end of the story open, the seed of our idea for Therapeutic Story StartUps (Amos, Cunningham, Webber, 2020) was planted.

Reflections on the Art Approaches Used in Hattie's Therapy

Painting and Drawing

Malchiodi makes the general point that when using arts approaches in therapy, there is the opportunity for "transforming troublesome emotions, behaviours, and experiences through authentic expression" as opposed to attempting to eliminate or cure them (Malchiodi, 2005). This is a helpful summary of why encouraging children to paint and draw can be so powerful.

In Hattie's therapy, I am pleased when she decides to use paint, as I feel intuitively that this may help her to express some of the feelings that are troubling her which she cannot just tell me as they make her feel "bad." It is also an opportunity to visit and re-visit these feelings in different versions with coloured pencils, charcoal, paint, wax crayons and chalks. In allowing her jealous, angry, hurt feelings some outlet, I am hoping that she can find a way to integrate them into her understanding of herself. I hypothesise that these unwanted feelings have become split off as they are considered by others (and so ultimately by Hattie herself) to be "bad" and make her believe she is a "bad person" for feeling them. Gestalt Therapy (Perls, 1973) and Internal Family Systems Therapy (Spiegel, 2017) look to find ways for the client to befriend these unwanted parts. By putting the repressed feelings "out there" onto the paper, this can be the first stage of the client being able to acknowledge these feelings and separate from them to some extent.

I feel that Hattie's pictures hold her unwanted feelings that are too painful to be expressed verbally. Schaverien speaks about "the scapegoat and the talisman" (Schaverien, 1999). The image can be diagrammatic and more left-brain, or it can be an embodied image, which I believe is the case with Hattie's Elephant sand tray, and her story of the Locust on the Platter and within her red, angry pictures and her green, envy pictures. Scapegoating can be thought of as "the ritualised disposal of unwanted or evil aspects via transference to objects or people" (Ibid). Within therapy, or cultural rituals, "painful feelings, physical and/or psychological" can be transferred to animate and inanimate objects" (Ibid). The talisman carries the transferred feelings and through its disposal purifies the tribe, individual or group. Hattie appears to be wanting to dispose of her jealous feelings about her sister and deposit them into the picture and thereby gain some distance from them.

The art image, and in Hattie's case also the image of the Elephant Family and the story of "The Locust on the Platter", hold some of her unspeakable and possibly unknowable pain and unbearable feelings of shame and in this way act as a container. Interestingly, I believe her art creations also helped to serve as a container for *my* pain in beginning to have access to Hattie's story that she could not tell me.

Play

It is now widely accepted that play can be useful in therapy with young children. It is less clear why this should be the case. So the question becomes *why* is play helpful in therapy? In Theresa Kestly's seminal work, "The Interpersonal Neurobiology of Play" (2014), she researched into scientific evidence, for what therapists had been discovering for some time, that for children and adolescents play can be deeply powerful. It can be a way to work through difficult and troubling feelings and thus help the client reduce dysfunctional ways of trying to cope with them and to help them to find positive ways of managing them. She particularly wanted to be able to explain to parents and teachers *why* play worked in their child's therapy sessions.

It would seem that Hattie was stuck with feeling "bad" about her feelings of extreme envy and anger at her sister (and her parents and extended family). Cornered in this way, she was isolated and defensive. There was no way she could tell me how she felt until we began to build a bridge between us with the play and art materials. By placing the elephants on the picture, she showed me her family dynamics, and then despite herself, she began to play out her extreme feelings of anger towards the other baby elephant and the mother elephant. This can be pertinently encapsulated by Fred Rogers when he says:

> Play allows us a safe distance as we work on what's close to our hearts.
>
> (Rogers, 1994)

In this way, Hattie was able to experience the feelings of what mattered to her without telling me in words anything about them, a version of what Dayton describes "as if" (Dayton, 1994). To start with it remained safely contained within the metaphor of the "Elephant Family." Later in her therapy after doing much expressive work through drawing and painting, she arrived one day and enacted her story of "The Locust on the Platter." In this dramatic play, her murderous feelings remained couched within the play and the story, but this time she knew that we both knew the Locust was her little sister being offered up to be devoured at the banquet by all her friends and family. Hattie was able to feel it was "just play" and coupled with the gentle support of me as her therapist, she experienced the safety and courage to play out her difficult feelings and avoid too much of the shame that usually accompanied them. The symbolic language of play gave her some distance and concealed the difficult feelings whilst simultaneously revealing them to me and to herself. This enabled her to "experience them directly enough to arrange and rearrange them playfully in different patterns" (Kestly, 2014). I believe the fact that providing a banquet to devour her sister was so shocking was an important part of its powerfulness. Her laughter and knowing smile I believe showed that she was both appalled and delighted with what she was playing out.

Metaphor through Story and Drama

I looked in the literature for some discussion as to when and why the therapist should support the client to remain in the metaphor of their play or made up stories and when they should encourage them to voice the parallels to their own life story. I couldn't find anything that fully satisfied me, so I devised the following table that creates a continuum around this. The client may be working at more than one level simultaneously even within one session (see Table 8.1).

In thinking about Hattie's therapy, the Metaphor Continuum was a useful framework with which to analyse different moments and phases of the work. In the first snapshot, Hattie seemed to be *showing* me how she felt within the dynamics of her own family by **staying entirely within the metaphor** (Level 1). However, she then began to show, seemingly outside of her conscious control, how angry she felt towards the bigger elephant and the other smaller elephant. Was this perhaps her **acting out in a manner that was analogous** to how she experienced her family? (Level 1b). In fact with all Hattie's work leading up to The Locust on the Platter, she didn't explicitly state her annoyance with her younger sister apart from when she made a throwaway statement just as she was leaving the session: "You're lucky you don't have to have my younger sister in your therapy

Table 8.1 The Metaphor Continuum

Continuum of staying in or out of metaphor in therapy working through play, story and art materials
These are not linear stages, the work may dip in and out within a session, along the therapeutic journey, or by the end of the therapy. The work may move along the continuum and these serve only as a helpful reference for thinking about the therapy.

1. Therapist and client **both stay entirely in the metaphor** (within a session or throughout the therapy) *never* making it explicit why this story/play situation/art making is so resonant for this client at this time.
   1b. The client **acts out/behaves in a way that is analogous to their traumatic experience**, (through the transference and countertransference) but it is not acknowledged to be a metaphor by the client or the therapist.
2. Both therapist and client **know that the other knows** (why it is so resonant for the client) but it is not made explicit by either of them.
3. Gradually gently, the **therapist lets the client know that they both know** how it is resonant to the child's story. The client ignores it (or seems to ignore it).
4. The **therapist lets the client know how it resonates with the client's story and the client nods or acknowledges** this in some way.
5. The **client slips in and out of the character and themselves** as they play/act out/ tell the story.
6. The **client makes it very clear how this is relevant to their story** at the beginning of the work, or further along the line. The therapist empathises with the feelings this experience brings up now and in the past for the client.

Source: Aileen Webber (2021).

room – she'd mess up everything!" I said nothing in reply to this deeply significant casual remark but I definitely mentally "clocked it" and filed it away. I also believe that Hattie noticed that I had seen it as important, as she looked back after saying it when she had almost reached the door (a classic therapy "door handle moment") and caught my eye. We held each other's gaze for longer than usual and both smiled with our eyes. Perhaps this was touching on both therapist and client **knowing that the other knows** (Level 2) without making it explicit.

This important moment foreshadowed the Locust on the Platter which seemed to be carried out **entirely within the metaphor** (Level 1). Although she did in fact **act out a story analogous to the trauma** she was experiencing in her own family (Level 1b), it felt really important for Hattie that it should remain shrouded within the story as otherwise the extreme shame she had demonstrated in Snapshot 1, could have prevented her from acting out her true feelings of extreme jealousy and rage later on in the therapy.

The Metaphor Continuum was very useful in analysing The Locust session as I believe it didn't in fact stay totally within the metaphor (Level 1) or at Level 1b. Within the setting of the scene of her story, there was a deeply significant

Breakthrough Moment (Webber, 2017), when we met eyes and **I knew that she knew that I knew** (Level 2) that the locust was her little sister and that the banquet guests were her family who she imagined preferred her "cute little sister" to her. Kept safely within the metaphor she could act out the depth of her banished feelings, that she wanted everyone (including me) to devour her sister and have her gone! It didn't feel appropriate to try, even gently, to tell Hattie more explicitly that I knew this (which would have taken it to Level 3). It felt right for it to remain at Level 2, acknowledged non-verbally, but not brought out of the metaphor where it would have the potential to shame her and would have meant I was admitting to "eating" her sister.

The Metaphor Continuum can also help to demonstrate that the therapy can be multi-levelled and multi-layered, working on many different levels simultaneously. Even though it appeared that The Locust on the Platter stayed firmly **in the metaphor** (Level 1) in reality the moment where **we both knew that the other knew** (Level 2) what we were acting out, took it to a very deep level in terms of my relationship with Hattie and in revealing what the work was about. With The Hero's Journey work, although the story was the journey of one of the small Elephants, Hattie did not make any mention of this being her, she **stayed entirely in the metaphor** (Level 1) although again I believe **we both knew that the other knows** (Level 2).

In her Sally Spoon Puppet Story, Hattie makes the **story very similar to her own** and although neither of us ever put it into words, I feel we did in fact go to Level 6, whilst honouring that this did not need to be said in words. Additionally to acknowledge this would have been to be implying I was cast in the role of The Wizard and I felt Hattie needed some distance from admitting how important the magic of the therapy had been for her or indeed how much she felt towards The Wizard. Having Sally Spoon as her character rather than the little Elephant also made it seem as though she was revealing a little bit about how she was identifying with the character.

When Hattie Returned for Therapy

Unexpectedly Hattie came back for a few more therapy sessions two years after her therapy with me had ended. She told me that her Dad had taken her for an assessment with a Psychologist and the therapist had said she would probably have been diagnosed as Asperger's (or as it has now been re-named: High Functioning Autism), if she hadn't undertaken the therapeutic work with me. I asked Hattie about her experience of the assessment session and she said: "It was a bit like what we did together but less fun!"

References

Amos, A., Cunningham, A., Webber, A. (2020). *Therapeutic Story StartUps*. London: Routledge. Companion website: www.Routledge.com/cow/Speechmark

Campbell, J. (2008). *The Hero with a Thousand Faces*. New York: Joseph Campbell Foundation.

Dayton, T. (1994). *The Drama within: Psychodrama and Experiential Therapy*. Deerfield Beach, FL: Health Communications.

Jung, C.G. (1952). Symbols of transformation (R.F.C. Hull, Trans.). In H. Read et al. (Series Eds. Trans.), *The Collected Works of C.G. Jung* (Vol. 5). Princeton, NJ: Princeton University Press. (Original work published 1911).

Kestly, T. (2014). *The Interpersonal Neurobiology of Play: Brain-Building Interventions for Emotional Well-Being*. New York/London: W.W. Norton.

Malchiodi, C.A. (2005). *Expressive Therapies*. New York: Guildford Press.

Perls, F. (1973). *The Gestalt Approach & Eye Witness to Therapy*. Palo Alto, CA: Science & Behaviour.

Rogers, F. (1994). *You Are Special*. New York: Viking (Penguin Group).

Schaverien, J. (1999). *The Revealing Image*. London: Jessica Kingsley.

Spiegel, L. (2017). *Internal Family Systems Therapy with Children*. London: Routledge.

Webber, A. (2017). *Breakthrough Moments in Arts-Based Psychotherapy*. London: Karnac.

Webber, A. (2021). *Art Resources for Therapists Working with Children and Adolescents*. Cambridge: Self-Published.

Chapter 9

The Boy in the Orange Tent

Suzanne Little

Martin has arrived in his wheelchair. He is shouting with loud vocalisations and deep cries that clearly suggest great discomfort and anger. He is biting the covers on his hands, which I know are there to protect his skin, but he is biting with real viciousness. It is so upsetting to see. This feels really alarming and disconcerting. I am focusing my mind now on how I might reach out to him. My plans within this first meeting were to observe and assess Martin's sensory needs in class, but this will not work today. I am reassuring and calming myself that I will find a way of using my intuition and 20 years' experience of working with students with complex needs. I remember that many of these children found a sensory connection with their immediate world through a reduction in sensory stimulus, but will it work for Martin? I tell myself that my belief in reaching out to Martin, needs to start with finding a bridge of calmness. I am not sure yet how that will work, or what will be the best form of connection in this moment. I am feeling somewhat disturbed, but Martin is more so, as he is now trying to self-harm, banging his head with his fists and with louder cries of distress. I know that I need calmness to hopefully soothe some of his agitation.

I can see my feeling is shared by Martin's support worker, who is looking very confused as she is trying to console Martin. She is beginning to express stress now in her voice and this is leading to more intense negative reactions from Martin. She tells me that she has checked his comfort and adjusted his positioning in his wheelchair to maximise his physical comfort and feels at a loss of how to help. The atmosphere of the classroom is changing as Martin's loud cries are affecting and agitating the other students and the staff. I feel that as the support specialist teacher I need to step in now. I need to see if I can possibly connect with Martin and help him to release some of the apparent emotional disturbance raging through him uncontrollably. I am putting my whole focus now on deep and slow breathing to try and create calm energy around myself and hopefully Martin.

I am meeting Martin today for the first time and recalling the latest information that has been given to me. Martin is a new pupil within this residential special school, and like the other eight students in this class, he is immobile and non-verbal. Martin's teacher has given me new information that Martin has a rare neurotransmission disorder, which has only recently been diagnosed, after 16 years of misdiagnosis and confusion. I feel the pain and frustration that his family must

DOI: 10.4324/9781003163015-9

have suffered for so many years without a means of communication with Martin. My plan today had been to observe how Martin connects with his senses to this new world of support workers and a noisy classroom environment; however, his cries are upsetting the other students, who also have profound and multiple learning difficulties. Now my attention is on finding a calm space to try and find a way of reaching some self-awareness for Martin.

Thoughts flash through my mind, as I move forward towards Martin, concerning his severe brain injury at birth and the distinct possibility that he has severe Cerebral Visual Impairment (CVI). I know that it often remains undiagnosed when it is a part of complex health issues. I think of my studies, "CVI refers to disordered vision or vision perception of any type or severity as a result of damage or disorder to the visual pathways or centers of the brain" (Lueck & Dutton, 2015). I feel this could be a major factor of why Martin is experiencing such difficulty in connecting to his new environment. I am thinking and pulling on my experience for reassurance and understanding and realising that this unfamiliar classroom also creates auditory difficulties, with all the strange new noises and unrelated chatter. I suspect that this is likely causing sensory clutter and overload as Martin is expressing confusion and fear.

I know in this moment that my plans to observe and gradually become a familiar voice in this classroom setting and to find an appropriate sensory stimulus for connection with Martin are now on hold. Martin is totally out of control flinging his arms around and screaming. I am cautious with my movements towards Martin so as not to alarm him further, or cause harm to myself. He may not be able to hear my voice through his distress and I sense that it is not possible or appropriate to use a calming method of firm, but gentle touch communication on Martin's shoulders. Martin is not listening to my voice gently singing his name and the touch communication is not possible as he is pushing me away as I get closer to him. I cannot connect with Martin, as he is increasing his banging to his face and biting his hands. I hope that I am right, that the best solution now for Martin and everyone else in the room, which is now charged with negative and fearful emotion, is to leave the room and find a quiet clutter-free space.

I am slowly moving Martin away, with help from his support worker and going into to my small, uncluttered assessment room. I do not want to leave Martin lost in his distress, but I don't know yet what will work to reach him. Will this uncluttered room create a new energy of calmness and quiet? I feel an enormous sense of relief, as after a few minutes, Martin appears to be aware of this different environment, as he is moving his head around with some apparent awareness however, his eyes have erratic and fast movements, and his screams are not lessening yet. I hope that with more time the distress will settle. I have decided it is not wise to add any sensory stimulus by singing his name or use touch to try to connect to Martin, I am just using this quietness to watch and wait for the emotional storm to calm a little. I feel the calmness of this quiet space is helping me as much as it is Martin and his support worker. I am relieved that coming into this small quiet space has broken the distress by a crack, that is good, and I am allowing time and the calm atmosphere to soothe us all.

Maybe there will be a chance to reach out to Martin, as this environment has no demands upon him, and he has stopped his flailing arm movements and the hand biting is slowing down. I find I am really feeling a sense of relief and gratitude for this quietness after experiencing Martin's deep distress and he appears to be feeling the same. The biting of the gloves on his hands is a different response now, as it is not a vicious biting, but a bite that appears to be giving Martin some strong sensory feedback of connection with his body. I sense that in the classroom he was overwhelmed and possibly his brain activity of intense stress had triggered some of his apparent involuntary arm movements, but now the quiet room is helping to calm the storm of emotions.

While I sit and wait with Martin in this room, I am reflecting on the overload of sensory clutter that may have affected Martin's distress. In class, he appeared disconnected from everyone and everything around him and reacting in an apparent flight and fear mode. Nothing in that new environment gave him any form of a sensory cue or meaning. I recall my reading about the latest brain and attachment research, by Daniel Siegel (Siegel, 2020), and the importance of letting children know that at least one adult in their life is present and understands their emotions. The "four S's" keep running through my mind of: "safe, seen, soothed and secure." I understand that Martin needed to feel safe in the first instance in order to be able to respond rather than react in fear, he needs to feel seen and understood at his own level of perception to feel soothed and secure (Siegel, 2020) that is what I am trying to offer him by reaching out to him with my full attention and presence by sitting quietly with him at his sitting level. Martin's support worker is rightly seeking his physical comfort and ease but to reach a point of communication with Martin, time and understanding needs to be given to how sensory information is being processed, even more so because of his brain injury complexities.

> The processing of sound is fundamental and fast chatter at a normal pace means the information is inaccessible for most young people with learning disabilities. Time is rarely given to make the space for differences in brain processing of information and this leads to no connection.
>
> (Dutton, 2018)

I believe this might explain Martin's extreme distress and now I need to find a way to begin to achieve the "four S's" for Martin.

In this quiet room, I have time to realise that Martin was taken from his home area and straight to school with no time to adjust to the environment and no sensory cues to match his level of understanding, - he was fitting into the system and place rather than experiencing a slow-paced introduction. "We all perceive through our senses, the information in the space around us, if there is a lack of attention of perception in specific areas of our surroundings, then access is limited" (Lueck & Dutton, 2015). The sensory overload of sound with people speaking fast and maybe with anxiety creates distress for people who need more time to process temporal incoming information. All minds work within their own specific time constraints (Dutton, 2018) and Martin has had no time to adjust to this new experience of moving from one new place to another. He had no one and no sensory input to connect with to feel safe.

It has been 20 minutes now since coming into this room and I am feeling quite encouraged that I may soon have an opportunity to reach out to Martin with the sound of his name and maybe even shoulder touch. It is a huge sense of relief to me that Martin appears to be letting go of screaming continuously and is now just giving a shout every now and again. I can observe that his erratic eye movement is calming. I want to let him feel safe in this quiet room after his apparent fear and confusion in this unfamiliar school building. Now after another few minutes, I am feeling more confident that this quiet space is calming Martin, as he has now completely stopped biting his hands and banging his face. I am going to gently test Martin's response to see if he might feel safe and secure enough for me to enter his space. I am thinking I will employ the "Kiss Principle" with Martin which works by "Keeping it Slow and Simple" (Dutton, 2018) to avoid the distressing experience of sensory overload. Children like Martin with severe brain injury and communication difficulties, need to have slow and simple spoken language at a level that they can understand, and this may mean one or two words in context. They need, "the environment to provide an appropriate quantity of the right quality of input" to enable connection with experiences (Ward, 2004). Lack of stimulation and/or over-stimulation can have devastating effects on communication and learning for all children and especially young people with brain injury and sensory processing difficulties.

I am carefully and slowly reaching out to Martin now bearing this information in mind. I am using three main words only in context saying: "Hello Martin," this is "Suzanne." Happily, Martin turns his head towards me and is listening calmly. It is wonderful to feel this first connection and I sense that I might also gently reach out with a shoulder touch. He is relaxing and so I feel hopeful, as I gently hold one shoulder, while saying "Hello Martin" slowly to allow him time to respond through his body language. Martin is much more relaxed now and so am I, as I use the gentle shoulder and arm massage, while sitting quietly beside him. Hopefully, he is now feeling seen and soothed. I feel calmer by using this pattern of shoulder touch and using repetitive slow and simple speech, by emphasising a few words only in context. This will be the beginning of our communication programme for each time we meet. I feel hopeful and soothed too, as I now have a plan in mind, and I will also try to introduce an uncluttered visual space to assess Martin's vision responses as the eye movement has also calmed a little. Martin's support worker and I agree that in keeping with the "Kiss" principle of slow and simple today, Martin can return to his room in his residential flat to continue with this calmness, before taking more time and ease in going back to the classroom for the afternoon session.

I am now sitting at my desk and reflecting on the positive outcome after the 30 minutes of quiet time. The apparent success of the shoulder touch communication and using just a few words has given me hope. I am excited as I reflect on what has just taken place as I write my notes and think about our next meeting. I write that my plan is to use a calm voice and an uncluttered, quiet space. I will begin with using the sensory level of touch which can be built into a form of communication, as the skin has thousands of touch receptors. The shoulders (if it is possible and if allowed to step closely into someone's personal space) can be a starting point for reassurance and a calm connection especially when a person is distressed. Martin calmed enough to accept this first connection. I am considering that it could provide a basis for repetition of "touch and sensory plasticity" (Doidge, 2007) as a touch programme which can be accepted and consistently repeated. This could open the door to Martin learning a new sensory cue and perceive a seen, safe and secure experience.

I pause to reflect on my readings about neuroplasticity and the quote "Neurons that fire together, wire together" (Doidge, 2007), and how I feel this gives hope for children with brain injury. I have observed how the uncluttered environment has helped many of the children I have worked with. I am thinking carefully about this. As I look at new information about Martin's medical history, I discover that he has a rare neurological disorder (which was detected via electrode analysis) and that he has a history of frequent periods of distress related to extensive periods of erratic brain activity. I wonder if the programme of a quiet space and touch communication with a few words only will also have an effect in other settings after repetition of this sensory programme. I hope that some neurons will eventually connect to form a new brain map (Doidge, 2007) through maybe weeks, months or even years of a repetition of a sensory approach that Martin liked and responded to today. I have just read that Martin has been given a visual diagnosis of Cerebral Visual Impairment (CVI), which was to be expected with such severe brain injury. I am pleased that this has been recognised as often this damage to the visual pathways through brain injury is overlooked. This impairment means that Martin has difficulty processing visual information. "Visual limitations caused by injury to the brain in children include difficulties with impaired primary processing of the image" (Lueck & Dutton, 2015). A child's ability to discern shapes and details of the things they can see and contrast and colour vision can also be affected as well as fields of vision and perception of movement, this might be Martin's experience. I have also taken note that the erratic eye movements have been diagnosed as Nystagmus. It is very clear to me that Martin was experiencing complete sensory overload and the quiet space of the uncluttered room relieved that distress. I feel reassured and now I need to plan how best to try to reach Martin with this information in mind.

I am waiting in the small room for the second weekly meeting with Martin, with hope and anticipation for a calmer time with him today. I can hear Martin's cries as his support worker brings his wheelchair into the room. She tells me that Martin did not sleep well and woke up distressed. It is now mid-morning, and he appears to still be locked into his distress. Martin's body language is calmer than the last time we met, but I can see his eye and arm movements are still very erratic. He does not appear to be connecting with anything visually, or through touch, or sound. It feels to me that he is lost in a space with no sensory connection other than the sense of biting his hands. I feel focused and hopeful to try my touch and sound programme as planned, by softly and slowly singing his name and using touch pressure gently on his shoulders. I am slowly moving towards his wheelchair saying his name and my name. In anticipation, I wait for a while to observe if he is listening to me. I am controlling my thoughts with positive intentions which focuses my calmness and Martin is also calmer now. After some time of repeating these few words and gently touching his shoulder, I feel happy as I can feel that Martin is releasing some of his tension and the erratic movement of his arms and head are reducing.

I am taking time in reaching out to Martin and feeling his response improve from the loud sounds of distress and his hand biting is slowing down. I begin with a gentle hold on the top of his right shoulder while saying his name with the hope he might feel "Yes! I am here" and take this as a communication cue that Suzanne is here, and she is coming to find you. Martin is relaxing his body tension, so I am now holding both his shoulders and I feel Martin relax a little more. I am using calming stroking movements, beginning with one hand to stroke from his shoulder and down his right arm and my left hand to stroke the left arm. To my delight, this appears to be giving Martin a sense of connection with me as he has relaxed enough to allow me to take my hands to his hands, and he has turned his head towards me to listen to his name.

I am applying the "Kiss" principle as I am slowing my words down, prolonging consonants, vowels and syllables, as well as gaps between words. When I speak, I just say his name or my name and wait. I sing his name as in my experience songs and poems work well as they prolong articulation of words. This feels like a massive step forward as Martin's eyes have fewer erratic movements. He is not looking towards me, just his head turned towards the sound of my voice. This is a joyful and unexpected experience for both of us, but after some minutes, Martin has regressed back to distress and erratic movements and loud cries. We are sitting together in the quiet room with occasional moments of calm and connection again and then return to distress. I can see the erratic eye movements are beginning to increase and I sense the buildup of tension in him, which I am focusing on not feeling too. The touch and sound programme is helping, but still erratic movements are dominating. I did not expect an immediate change as the process of "neurons that fire together, wire together" takes time, but Martin has responded positively to touch and sound today in between his erratic movements and vocalisations. This is a beginning.

I am following my intuition now, which tells me that a smaller enclosed uncluttered space may help to eliminate sensory input even more so than this room. I take a piece of material of a bright fluorescent orange and hold it around Martin's head to see if this aids Martin to keep calm for longer. I feel a great surge of joy as Martin immediately looks up and to the sides and after a few moments' smiles. Why is this I wonder? Why has his erratic eye movement and restless body movement calmed? Why has he seemed to find such joy and peace? I realise as I stand here with this tent dome around Martin (holding my breath with joy as this extended calmness is continuing longer than the touch and sound sensory programme), that Martin's dramatically changed behaviour can perhaps be understood further. Perhaps the fact that I am presenting one single sense stimulus using the orange tent surrounding Martin has provided a way to reach him. I remember Gordon Dutton's theoretical explanation: "Children with simultanagnostic visual dysfunction have an inability to see more than one thing at a time and they may have an inability to know where sound is coming from" (Dutton, 2018). Martin has erratic eye movements and CVI, so the colour tent I am using appears to be giving him an opportunity to find one thing and engage with his visual awareness and attention. I feel a smile come to my face as I observe Martin's smiles. This new approach to reach out to Martin will mean I will erect a tent in this room to use as part of the hope for longer periods of sensory connection.

While writing up my notes from this last session. I am feeling positive and intend to use a colour tent with Martin in our next meeting as it is: "a single sense stimulus cutting out extraneous sensory clutter" (Little & Dutton, 2015). I am reflecting on the way I have used the colour tent approach for several years with children with CVI and complex needs and how it began with the same approach I used with Martin of holding up a piece of fabric to create a simple space with no clutter. Over the years, the Colour Tent Therapy has developed to be used by many teachers across the country and has enabled many children to engage with their visual awareness often for the first time. I am smiling with pleasure as I write my notes. I am reflecting upon my plan to produce colour tents with an assessment framework for babies and children with complex needs, alongside the possibility of promoting future research into tent therapy. My thoughts go back to Martin as I write that I have found that fluorescent orange is the optimal colour choice for children with severe and complex needs. It seems to provide a warm intensity of colour which calms as well as offers a visual stimulus. I will observe if the warm fluorescent orange colour continues to help Martin to calm and use any visual awareness he may have.

I am reflecting that this tent space could enable Martin to feel a connection with himself and his immediate environment, as in the short experience in his last session, it appeared to give him the opportunity to experience a sense of self as described in the "four S's" of: "Safety, Seen, Soothe, Security"(Siegel, 2020). The tent session may open a door for Martin to feel "safe" as the tent creates a totally enclosed calm space and helps with the sense of being "seen." This has been described as "feeling felt" (Siegel, 2020) through the connection of sharing and seeing by a parent or significant other giving their full attention. It appears to me that through Martin's increased moments of calmness, he may be connecting with me, by listening quietly to his name and relaxing from the touch sensory cues. Martin appears so far to be "soothed" for a longer period while in the tent, which could enable an experience of regulation of his overwhelmed senses. I am writing my notes with optimism. I am hoping that this tent experience could help Martin (as it has many other children with complex needs) through this calm and meaningful routine, cultivating within him a knowing of being.

It is now ten minutes into the next weekly tent session, and I am thrilled to see Martin is smiling every now and again and even giggling already. I am anxiously holding my breath wondering if he will respond well today. I am stepping back slowly and quietly to observe without using any sounds or interruptions to disturb him. Martin is sitting inside the tent in the distraction-free space with the sides surrounding and bathing him in an orange glow. To my delight, his rapid eye movements have slowed down and he is gazing for several minutes at a time from one side to another. Martin's vocalisations are much quieter, and he is biting his hands less often. This is wonderful to observe. The calmness is slowly helping Martin's visual awareness and enabling visual attention of his environment. Martin's responses are much calmer and happier now, rather than his previous reactions of agitation. A different Martin is now emerging and between his scanning of the tent he is just sitting and giggling to himself off and on. It feels to me like a: "Here I am" response, and I am beginning to be able to find and reach Martin with the same sense of joy as Martin is experiencing the joy of just "being" in this present calm moment. This is a great response and I find myself giggling too. I feel I am witnessing Martin's new-found connection with his visual sense which is allowing him attention to his immediate environment.

I am video-recording this calmness and joy of Martin's newly acquired visual awareness and attention to a single-sense stimulus with no distractions. He now appears to show in his body language a sense of consciousness of self by sitting in the glow of the orange tent. I am so excited and pleased that Martin is calm, smiling, gazing and scanning for several minutes at a time. I am so absorbed in this experience alongside Martin and have just realised that we have both been in this session for 30 minutes. I slowly enter the tent to bring Martin and his wheelchair away from the space. I am using touch and my voice to simply say his name, the word "tent" and my name, as I am working on building upon using a few words in context over each of our sessions together. I feel excitement at the connection of Martin with visual awareness while he is in the tent and his calm response of relaxation with my use of touch and sound cues.

Now I am taking Martin back to the noisy classroom and I am wondering how he will respond after leaving the quietness of the tent and if this experience has any generalised affect in different settings. I am rather anxious about what may happen. I find to my surprise and delight that Martin is accepting the change of a different space and sensory experience. I am now feeling confident in planning to do weekly tent sessions over a three-month period, to observe whether Martin's calmness and willingness to connect with other people while outside of the tent continues. Martin is now being moved from his wheelchair to his standing frame for a change of position and he is co-operating with his helper by accepting this movement and change. His helper turns to me and says this is a new experience for her as usually Martin becomes stressed at being moved in this way. She is delighted. Martin is relaxed and so am I. I record my intention to check if this response continues in the weeks ahead.

We are now in the sixth weekly session of colour tent work, and I am full of anticipation as today I am going to share the experience of witnessing Martin's calm responses with his key worker. Later today I will show the video to Martin's mum. I am excited waiting to see Martin who has had six sessions in which he has calmed and is beginning to use his visual awareness and attention to scan light movements in the tent. I am continuing with reaching out to Martin with the increase of a few words in repetition: "Hello its Suzanne here" and the touch from shoulder to arms while singing his name. This time Martin has turned his head towards me, and he has stilled as I say my name. I haven't experienced this response before and I feel really encouraged by this, as Martin turns his head and stops biting his hand to listen. I think that the routine, repetition and use of a few simple words in context is enabling him to make a new connection in his mind. I am even more thrilled today as when I say the word "tent" (which I have always used while placing Martin in the tent) he holds his body still. Oh, how I hope this is in anticipation of the tent experience. He immediately begins to gaze and scan from side to side, and he is smiling as he is wheeled into the orange tent. He is giggling and turning his head in a controlled way – with the whole of his body relaxed and holding his hands together rather than biting them. I feel a sense of delight. This feels like the beginning of a breakthrough for Martin being able to connect with himself and feel happy, which he has rarely shown in other situations. I feel I have the building block to start to expand our connecting – a few words at a time.

I am following the concept of "Neuroplasticity," that when an experience is motivating and repeated, there is a possibility to create new neural pathways. I feel this is hopeful for Martin as through our tent sessions he is becoming calmer and more visually aware. I am reflecting again upon the well-known phrase of: "Neurons that fire together wire together" and can thus create change (Doidge, 2007). This appears to be the case, as the connection Martin and I are having now is different to when we began with the tent sessions. Martin is showing anticipation by body language of stillness and attention to my voice and the few words I am using, and I am observing his increased and consistent visual attention to being in the tent. He is happier, and so am I, with this way of reaching out through a calm space. It appears to me that the overload of sensory stimulus prior to the tent sessions prevented any new connections being made.

I am feeling positive as the calm responses from Martin have been consistent in his weekly tent time. It is now two months since we began working together and today, I feel it might be possible to see if Martin will connect with a new experience. I can again hear his cries and loud vocalisations coming towards the room and I wonder if he will continue to show recognition and anticipation of the tent time. Martin and his helper are here, and I move forwards to greet him in the same way as always, saying his name, use of touch contact and my own name. Is it going to relax him today as he is madly biting his hands? With relief and delight, I still see a calmer response from Martin, as he is turning his head towards me and stilling. I feel I can use a few more words to explain what is going to happen today. I am showing a small hand light-effect projector to Martin and turning it on, hoping he may be aware of the light moving. Happily, he is still, and he is looking towards the light effects on my hand for a few seconds at a time. I tell Martin we are going to the tent to look for the light. He is still calm and not shouting although some hand-biting continues. After settling Martin and his wheelchair within the colour tent, I am waiting for him to enjoy scanning the tent for several minutes at a time before I add the light movement. I am increasing my plan of the use of a few words at a time in context by saying "light" before I begin to introduce the light movement. I am beginning with the light moving from his favourite right side and feel thrilled at his response, as he is now tracking the light from side to side. He looks tired though, so I am stopping and leaving him to just "be" in this space.

In the following weekly sessions, I am using the light movement as a small part of the tent time, and Martin is responding by smiling and tracking the light movement from side to side and above. I can see he is totally calm now and smiling on occasions, so I am going to try introducing "more" as a chance for increased communication, maybe from body language or a vocalisation. I am moving the wheelchair slowly out of the tent and asking Martin if he wants "More?" "More tent?" He is still and appears to be listening to the word "more." After a few minutes, I am moving Martin back into the tent and he smiles using his vision to locate the tent. I use the word "lights" and begin to move the slow light movement slowly up and to his left side. Martin locates this movement with full concentration for several minutes at a time, then he stops to hold his hands together and giggle a little.

I am feeling confident that he will trust me if I try moving him out again, as he is so calm. I am slowly moving Martin out of the tent with my hand on his shoulder and just saying my name and "moving out of the tent." Martin is calm and accepting this move. I am repeating the use of "More?" and then "More tent?". Martin is quiet and still. It's five minutes later now and I repeat "More?". Martin has not made a sound or moved. He is just sitting, very still with his head up. I am not going to be tempted to stop this yet or move back into the tent, as he is still, so it could be that his brain is processing the question. It is eight minutes. Sheer rejoicing. I asked again and Martin makes a clear vocalisation. His key worker who is present and videoing this activity says that Martin has never communicated in this way before. I am thrilled as this seems to be the beginning of communication that enables Martin to initiate an action, as when Martin is taken back into the tent he immediately smiles.

I am again reflecting on the continued developments that Martin is making based upon the enjoyment he is experiencing through these tent sessions. It appears that a door has been opened to his mind and is giving him the opportunity to learn through a further sensory experience related to his engagement and at his level of perception. Martin has used a vocalisation in direct response to a question for the first time in his 16 years. This fits with the new science of neuroplasticity and how the brain changes. Neuroplastician Merzenich has claimed, "… plasticity exists from the cradle to the grave; and (that) radical improvements in cognitive functioning – how we learn, think, perceive, and remember – are possible even in the elderly" (Merzenich in Doidge, 2007). He argues that practicing a new skill, under the right conditions, can change hundreds of millions and possibly billions of the connections between the nerve cells in our brain maps. "The brain can grow and change itself with proper nourishment and exercise" (Doidge, 2007). I am reflecting that this appears to be the case for Martin over this period, as the tent experience has been shown to be an appropriate learning environment.

After three months of these tent sessions, I am thrilled to witness the benefit it has given to Martin in his ability to calm and use his vocalisation to communicate and how these sessions have enabled him to find calmness in other settings. I am interested and wondering with concern that Martin's tent time today may not be so calming for him, as I have not seen him for three weeks and he has not had his tent sessions in the intervening period. His key worker is bringing him to his session today and I will talk to her about creating a tent in his room for relaxation and a break from moments of distress. I do feel concern that the break in our regular sessions may have meant he has lost the impact and maybe the neuroplasticity of: "Neurons that fire together, wire together," will not be evident, and maybe he will be starting these sessions afresh with no memory of our previous times together with the orange tent.

I can hear Martin's cries as he is brought towards the room. When he arrives, his key worker says she is really pleased he is coming for his tent session and hopes it will help him to calm down. She tells me that he has had some quiet times, and these do allow him to enjoy some activities; she wants to create a tent space in his room so he can relax away from the noisy flat, which he shares with other students. We both agree that we are interested to discover if Martin remembers the tent sessions and if it may be possible to engage with the communication response to "More?" "More tent?" from our last session. The question I have in my mind is, will we continue to build on and develop this communication today?

I am greeting Martin using the same sensory cues and I am delighted that he is stilling his arm and head movements to turn towards me, and he seems to be remembering, as he is giving a quick smile. This is wonderfully hopeful. I am moving him into the tent with the word "tent" as he is visually scanning the tent with a giggle that seems to be of recognition. My concerns have left me now and I am thrilled to see his immediate response: his eye movements and body movements have calmed, and he is visually attending to the tent and scanning from side to side and above. He seems to be understanding that he is in the tent and carrying on with his attending to the experience and being calmed by the experience once more. It is now ten minutes that he has been in the tent happily scanning and then just sitting with his hands together with a giggle now and then. I am saying his name and mine as the sensory cues, so I can slowly and gently take the wheelchair from the tent and try to use "more?".

I am pleased to see Martin still has his head up and is turning towards the sound of my voice, hopefully in anticipation of what comes next. I say "More?" and wait. No response. I repeat this and wait but still no response. Martin is very still and has his head up. I repeat the question and this time add "More tent"? I am waiting to see if Martin will respond. He has used a soft vocalisation, not as loud as last time, but it is a vocalisation. I feel joy bubbling up at this response and return Martin to the tent. His carer and I are thrilled and Martin is smiling intermittently. I realise that these sessions really do seem to have begun "opening the door" of attention to being in the tent and leading to periods of a new awareness for Martin while he is in the tent and when he is in different settings. Moreover the new neural pathways seem to have formed a lasting memory in his brain.

Martin has complex sensory impairments, and he needed the appropriate stimulus of the tent which matched his level of sensory response and visual-processing capacity (Little & Dutton, 2015). He increased his visual and sensory awareness through the removal of sensory clutter and the sensory experience of introducing one thing at a time through the Colour Tent Therapy. Allowing time for sensory processing appears to help with sensory integration in the brain. This view is consistent with exciting findings at the cutting edge of contemplative neuroscience that studies the impact of meditation on neural function, as well as the perspectives of integrated information and the consciousness of the social brain (Siegel, 2018). Martin's responses showed over time that as Viktor Frankl's work on meaning describes, "the bodily sensations of feeling at ease, calm and whole, when one lives with meaning and purpose directing actions creates a new sense of presence" (Siegel, 2018). Martin and other children who are experiencing a different sensory world experience need to be given the opportunity to engage in learning in their own individual way and to be seen and valued for their differences. In this way, they can be reached.

I recall a statement by Taylor, a brain scientist who suffered a stroke. She writes about her experience while in her brain-damaged state and how she longed for people to reach out to her saying so poignantly:

> Yelling louder does not help me understand you any better! Don't be afraid of me. Bring your gentle spirit. Speak more slowly. Enunciate more clearly. Again! Please try again! S-l-o-w down. Be kind to me. See that I am a wounded animal, not a stupid animal. I am vulnerable and confused. Whatever my age, whatever my credentials, Reach for me. Respect me. I am in here. Come and find me.
>
> (Taylor, 2009)

References

Doidge, N. & Merzenich (2007). *The Brain That Changes Itself.* London: Penguin.

Dutton, G.N. (2018). *Power Point, Understanding Children with Multiple Disabilities and Cerebral Visual Impairment.* CVI Conference, UK.

Little, S. & Dutton, G.N. (2015). Some children with multiple disabilities and cerebral visual impairment can engage by a 'tent': Is this due to Balint syndrome? *British Journal of Visual Impairment*, 33(1), 66–73.

Lueck, A.H. & Dutton, G.N. (2015). *Vision and the brain. Understanding Cerebral Visual Impairment in Children* (pp. 9 and 537–549). Arlington County: American Foundation for the Blind (AFB Press).

Taylor, J.B. (2009). *My Stroke of Insight, A Brain Scientist's Personal Journey.* London: Hodder.

Siegel, D. (2018). *Aware, the Science and Practice of Presence* (pp. 182 and 329). London: Scribe.

Siegel, D. (2020). *The Power of Showing Up: How Parental Presence Shapes Who Our Kids Become and How Their Brains Get Wired.* London: Scribe.

Ward, S. (2004). *Baby Talk, Maximise Your Child's Potential in Just 30 Minutes a Day.* London: My Arrow Books.

Chapter 10

Lost in Lockdown

Carole Rawley

Introduction

Lockdown took us all by surprise; within weeks of hearing about the strange new virus detected in Wuhan, we had been enveloped. I moved all my counselling online within two weeks. Up until then, I had only ever worked with clients for face-to-face sessions. It was a steep learning curve. It was in those early days of online counselling that I was contacted by a mother who was concerned about her daughter.

Mia, aged ten, lived with her parents and one younger sister. Both parents were working from home during lockdown. The most pressing problem was with Mia's sleeping. Her parents were having to stay with her until she fell asleep and when she woke in the night, would have to stay with her again until she fell back to sleep. Mia was terrified. She was also having regular headaches diagnosed by her GP as migraine.

The family home had been burgled some weeks before and Mia's parents traced the start of her sleep problems back to this event. The burglars had robbed the house during the day when the family was out. Mia and her dad had arrived home to find the patio door broken open and glass scattered everywhere. The burglars had been through the house including all the bedrooms. Mia observed the destruction first-hand.

From this time on, Mia had found it difficult to sleep. She heard noises upstairs and became extremely distressed if her parents tried to go downstairs once they had said goodnight. In order to help, her parents had developed a plan of checking on her every ten minutes through the evening until she fell asleep. Then they took it in turns to be "on duty" to answer Mia's calls for help when she woke in the night. When I was contacted, they were all exhausted, having experienced many weeks of this relentless routine.

At first glance, this case history was a familiar one. I had experience of working with clients who had been burgled and seen first-hand the fear in their eyes when they talked about going to sleep. But this felt very different. I was unable to meet Mia in person or have her come and sit in my therapy room where she could express her fears using a range of easily accessible art materials. My mind was filling up with concerns.

DOI: 10.4324/9781003163015-10

- Gone was the neutral therapeutic space with me present, replaced by therapy at a distance with me on Zoom, in the location of the trauma.
- Gone was the guaranteed confidentiality, replaced by the potential of being overheard by family members.
- Gone was working person-to-person in the therapeutic space replaced by working through a flat screen with only head and shoulders visible.
- Gone was my full range of art materials replaced by what was available in Mia's home.
- Gone was the familiar in-person session, replaced by a dependency on the unfamiliar technology of Zoom.
- Gone was the safe world she used to live in invaded firstly by a burglar and then by Covid-19.

As I mulled this all over, I was trying to work out how I could reach Mia and in particular reach the anxious and fearful parts of her that were dominating her life.

I knew I had to approach this work in a different way to my face-to-face work. I love being in my counselling room surrounded by shelves of figures, sand trays, puppets and a variety of arts materials. Over the previous weeks, I had determined that the computer screen was to be my friend rather than seen as an impersonal barrier to counselling. That might seem a strange thing to say, but in those early days of lockdown when everything was being transferred online, I'd experienced a deep sense of loss at not being able to see my clients in person. As with everyone else, I was having to face my own feelings of separation from family and friends, work colleagues and yes, clients too. This loss of embodiment was very real. I was wondering if Mia might also be feeling loss of physical contact with her friends, teachers and family. And now she was not going to meet me either. Somehow we needed to make this new way of communicating work for us. Kronengold asks a good question: "Can we use the very medium that we often see as isolating, to help us to connect to people who may have been previously out of reach perhaps because they live far away?" (Kronengold, 2019).

Weinberg and Rolnick (2020) talk about the change from full-bodied three-dimensional communication to a flat screen, two-dimensional experience. They encourage therapists to be more intentional in asking what physical sensations a client is feeling in their body at different moments in the therapeutic process.

Practical Changes

I had already written new guidance for parents about working online which covered technological issues, provision of physical space and privacy, proximity of a parent after the session in case their child needed comforting and provision of arts materials. In my initial phone conversation with Mia's mother, she had stated that she thought working through the arts would suit Mia as she loved drawing and storytelling. What follows is the story of Mia's therapy told in a few selected snapshots along with my reflections.

Snapshot 1: From the Therapy Room: Mia and Her Mother

Mia's mother sets up their laptop so we can start our session. She has also provided some art resources so that Mia has some choice of what she might like to use. Her mother stays on the call as I introduce myself and talk about confidentiality. I am so aware that these first impressions are important and wonder how Mia is feeling about meeting me. All her other online interactions to this point, whether with her teacher, her grandparents or her friends, were with people with whom she already had an established relationship. This is the first time where she herself is being introduced to a stranger. As her mum gets ready to leave, she reassures Mia that she will be in the house if she needs her. Mia nods.

I begin, "Tell me about your family and what you like to do." She says: "I like playing football." She tells me about her friends, her pets and her teacher. She is both excited about moving to secondary school and worried that new children might not like her. I am very conscious that I can only gauge how she's feeling from seeing her face and shoulders. With what I can see, Mia seems relaxed as she chats and it feels like a familiar "getting to know you" interaction. We start to talk about feelings and I ask her to pick four that she has experienced over this past week. She chooses sad, worried, scared and happy. We talk about the things that make her sad, worried, scared and happy. She begins to talk about the burglary, coronavirus, not being able to go to school and her sadness that all the Year 6 leaving events have been cancelled.

"I wonder if there are any images that come to your mind when we talk about these feelings?" I say. She searches through images online and shows me some. I go on to suggest that in the following week, we both make mood boards from these images and bring them to the next session. "Yes I'd like that" she says. One of my aims in doing this is for her to know that I will be keeping her in mind in the days ahead.

Reflections

Firstly, it was immediately apparent that there were parallel processes going on in Mia's experience; invasion of the world by coronavirus and the invasion of her home by an intruder. She had to leave the school environment, leave her class-mates and leave her teacher and stay at home where the burglary took place.

Secondly, I was concerned about the lack of embodied experience between myself and Mia. Eppel, Charlebois and Blaire (2020) talk about the limitations in gauging affect by what's visible on the screen. Without seeing the lower body's posture or movement, we can't fully know how comfortable or uncomfortable a client may feel.

I made note of Snyder's (2021) recommendation that therapists increase their use of physical and facial gestures so that the client on the other side of the screen can sense their presence and attunement.

In the following week, Mia's mother emailed the images Mia had chosen. As I cut out and placed the images, I could feel her fear and sadness, her sense of

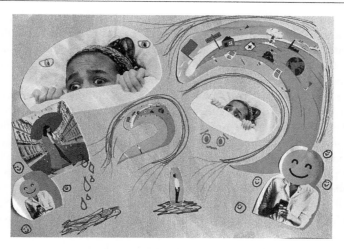

Figure 10.1 Therapist's Empathy Drawing.

smallness in the face of overwhelming anxiety along with the moments that made her smile. We shared our mood boards at the next session (see Figure 10.1).

Snapshot 2: The Following Session

As we take it in turn to hold our pictures up to our separate computers, there is an immediate difference. Mia's includes newspaper cuttings of devastation and violence, such as people who have been murdered in their homes, stabbed to death in their beds.

The sense of overwhelm returns to me as she speaks and I am suddenly aware of the distance between us. Being online is not comfortable. I feel deep frustration that Covid-19 has put us in this situation. I have to consciously focus on what she is saying and put my feelings aside. Mia continues: "Some people have been killed. I am scared the burglar will come back and kill me too." Quietly I ask: "Do you think this is what's making you frightened to go to sleep?" Mia nods.

Reflections

Over the next few sessions, we talked about how the brain works and what happens when triggered by fear, sadness and anxiety. I taught her some breathing exercises to start using when she felt anxious. We then made a "sensory first-aid box" of things that would help calm her brain when she woke in the night. They included a soft scarf sprayed with her mother's perfume, a squishy toy and photos of her best friend and a family holiday which triggered happy memories.

With a bit of ingenuity, these were all relatively simple things to do online. She really enjoyed collecting the items to put in her box and she practised the breathing techniques as I suggested. She told me how all these things helped her to get to sleep, but she was still waking in the night, feeling very scared and needed her mum or dad to help calm her.

I knew she needed something more. I was finding it hard to access the intense feelings of fear and anxiety that we'd begun to touch on when making the mood boards with her images. As I thought about how we might do this, I wondered if her love of drawing and storytelling might help her engage with a therapeutic way of working that I had recently started to incorporate into my practice.

Two years previously I had completed training in the basics of Internal Family Systems (IFS) Therapy and since then had included it in my practice with children and adolescents. One of the attractions of IFS for me was that it builds on the foundation of child-centred play therapy. Developed by Richard Schwartz, he recognised that the internal world is made up of a series of relationships between different parts led by the Self. "The Self is defined as an active, compassionate inner leader containing the perspective, confidence and vision necessary to lead an individual's internal and external lives harmoniously and sensitively" (Schwartz, 1995). This is echoed by Van der Kolk: "All systems – families, organisations or nations – can operate effectively only if they have clearly defined and competent leadership. The internal family is no different" (Van der Kolk, 2014).

In using this approach, I had already seen positive changes in children surprisingly quickly. However, that had been working with children in my practice room. There, we could make, draw and then interact with different "parts" of the child's internal world. "The goal of IFS, now an evidence based treatment, is to embody the Self and heal our injured parts so we can live with confidence, guided by curiosity and compassion" (Anderson et al., 2017).

I was not feeling confident that this embodied way of working could transfer online. I was also aware of Mia's young age and wondered if I could adequately explain the process without being physically present. Would she get bored or distracted? It was with some trepidation that I decided to give it a go.

Snapshot 3: Body Mapping

Mia talks about the burglary in great detail: the broken door, the smashed glass strewn over the living room floor, the cupboards open, belongings scattered around the bedroom. The details pour out of her, like water being released from behind a dam. As she talks, she begins to cry and shake with emotion. I gently reassure her that I'm listening carefully and can totally understand why she's so upset. At this point, I am concerned that not being in the room with her will cause her distress and become completely overwhelming for her. I am conflicted – one part of me knows I need to keep her safe, but another part of me knows that we need to gently access the injured parts so healing can begin to take place. How can I do both from this distance? Mia continues, "I feel worried and scared that the burglar will come back." "So there's a part of you that is **Worried** and a part of you that is **Scared**" I reflect back. "Yes" she whispers.

She starts talking about her school and her best friend and her family.

> I am happy when I get to play with my best friend in the park... I feel sad when my teacher tells me off ... I am really sad when my sister and I argue... I'm sad the burglar took stuff from my house...

Once again I name the parts she's expressing, "So there's a part of you that is **Sad** and a part of you that is **Happy** too." "Yes," she says.

> I wonder if we could get to know these parts more and see how we can help them. These parts are really clever and let us know where they live in our bodies. We could find them if you like?

Mia nods. "Which part would you like to start with?"

Over the rest of the session, I lead Mia in the mapping of different Parts on a body outline. She takes one part at a time, closes her eyes, focuses inside and locates it. IFS guides a client to shift from thinking and talking *about* a part to moving their attention internally to directly connect *with* that part. I then ask her what colour it is. She chooses a colour and draws it onto the body outline on her side of the computer connection. I also complete a body map that matches what she is saying.

"When you look at the body-map Mia, what do you see?" "There's a lot of stuff in my head. So much, it gives me headaches." "Yes I can see that." We carry on talking about the parts and the way they make her body feel.

Reflections

Spiegel states: "Mapping is a great way to externalise parts. It gives the child a comfortable distance from the issue, making it safer to address the conflicts at hand" (Spiegel, 2017). Mia added to her map throughout the weeks as we met different parts. Once located, I asked her to describe how each one felt, such as: pressure, shape, heat, tightness or emptiness. Thus began the process of reconnecting Mia with her bodily sensations. Understanding that her headaches were connected to the worried feelings inside and her stomachaches connected to feeling scared, helped her begin to make sense of the distressing pains. Van der Kolk says: "Trauma victims cannot recover until they become familiar with and befriend the sensations in their bodies. Being frightened means that you live in a body that is always on guard" (Van der Kolk, 2014).

This is what I saw in Mia. In those first few weeks, her hyper-vigilance was palpable. She would jump at any sudden noise near the room where she sat at the computer. She would swing around to see if there was anything behind her, or even have to open the door to check if someone was outside the room. As we began to map her parts, I saw her body begin to relax.

Snapshot 4: Externalising a Part

Mia is keen to tell me that she's been practising the breathing techniques when she feels scared. "When I lie down, I do my breathing and I feel a bit more peaceful." "So is there a part of you that's **Peaceful**?" Mia nods in agreement. When I ask her which part she would like to focus on today, she chooses this **Peaceful** part. I wonder aloud what this part of her might look like. She takes her coloured pencils and starts to draw a picture. She tips the screen down so I can see what she is

Figure 10.2 Mia's Drawing of Her **Peaceful** Part.

drawing (see Figure 10.2). As she looks at her image, she uses words like graceful, peaceful, mindful, calm, elaborate and colourful to describe it. Together we take the words and she begins to put them together into a poem:

> Peaceful image
> Graceful imagination in a mindful sea
> Calm sea with little ripples
> Elaborate colours across the page.

"How do you feel about this part of you?" "I love it." As she says this, I can sense her love of it. Together we are caught up in wonder as we observe the picture she has drawn.

Reflections

When children find it hard to locate parts inside or see an image of them or listen to their words, externalising them may be easier. Externalisation of parts is an important part of the process in IFS. This can be done using drawing, figures, clay models or objects. In doing this, the part is moved from the child's inner world to the exterior world of play. Here we see Mia externalising her **Peaceful** part by creating an image of it.

> In IFS therapy, therapists are, of course, paying attention to what is going on in the external world of the child: parents, siblings, school and peers. But the therapeutic work itself is focussed on creating more harmony for the parts in the child's internal family system.
>
> (Spiegel, 2017)

As we will see, drawing becomes an integral part of Mia's therapy. It helps her connect with those hard-to-reach parts but in a way that is familiar and comfortable for her. Although we had been able to access some parts fairly easily, I sensed it was harder for Mia to access the **Scared** part of her. I thought I'd gently try and help Mia find and listen to the Scared part in the next session.

Snapshot 5: Finding a "Hard to Reach" Part

I begin, "I've been wondering how **Scared** is doing?" Mia immediately answers, "She doesn't like the night when I wake up and she's on her own." I ask: "If **Scared** could speak now what would she say?" Mia shuts her eyes and focuses inside. She opens her eyes, which reveal how scared she is even thinking about it, and says: "I'm scared of robbers and I want Mum and Dad." "Where is **Scared** when you go to bed?" "She's lying down in bed awake," "Shall we ask **Scared** how we can help her?"

Mia shuts her eyes again. She opens them and reports: "**Scared** says she doesn't want to be on her own." "Is anyone else around?" I ask.

"Yes, **Peaceful**." "Where is **Peaceful** at nighttime?" "She goes to sleep." "What would you like to say to her?" I ask. "Wake up, we need you." "Could you ask **Peaceful** if she's got any ideas about how we can help **Scared**?" Mia pauses and then says: "She says maybe she could stay up a tiny bit." "I wonder if you could ask **Peaceful** to find **Scared** and talk with her." After another pause, Mia whispers: "She says she really wants to help **Scared**."

Mia draws a picture of **Peaceful** and **Scared** together (see Figure 10.3).

Figure 10.3 **Peaceful** and **Scared** Together.

Figure 10.4 **Worry, Scared** and **Peaceful's** Sleepover.

The interaction between the **Peaceful** and **Scared** parts continues with the organisation of a sleepover between them. When I ask where **Worry** is, Mia says she is feeling left out as she usually hangs out with **Scared** when Mum and Dad aren't there. When I ask what **Peaceful** thinks about this Mia tells me that **Peaceful** wants to invite **Worry** to join them, giving her a spare pillow and PJs. This session ends with **Peaceful** talking to **Scared** and **Worry** and reassuring them that they are now safe with her. Mia draws a picture of this (see Figure 10.4).

Reflections

This is the first time Mia's "hard to reach" parts have started to interact. It felt significant to me. Up until now, these **Scared** and **Worry** parts had needed the external physical presence of Mum and Dad for them to be reached and to calm down. Now Mia is beginning to access her own internal Peaceful part to reach and calm **Scared** and **Worry**. Finding and befriending each of these parts in turn was the beginning of a turning point in Mia's therapy. IFS therapy introduces the idea of being "detectives together" and learning all about the worried parts so we can help them. It is a concept children connect with readily.

I am beginning to notice a change not only in Mia being able to access her more scary parts, but also in myself. As I connect to Mia on the computer, I find myself caught up in the story. I am curious to find out more about the parts and how they interact and am wondering how they might be able to support each other. In the next session, I am interested to see if **Peaceful** helped **Scared** and **Worried** in the night.

Snapshot 6: Mia Reports Back

Mia excitedly reports: "When I woke up in the night, **Peaceful** stayed awake to help me." I was intrigued. "Do you mean she helped **Scared** and **Worry**?" "Yes," she stayed awake to comfort them," Mia replies. "Can you find **Peaceful** inside and say thank you to her?" Mia closes her eyes and focuses inside. She opens her eyes after a moment, "She's says: 'You're welcome.'"

Reflections

At this point, Mia's mother reported that Mia was still waking but wasn't taking as long to go back to sleep. Over the next few sessions, we continue getting to know other parts: **Sad**, **Scared**, **Worry**, **Happy**, **Tired** and **Angry**. IFS teaches that rather than banishing more challenging parts, all parts are welcome, need to be heard and have a role to play even if it's not working that well. In the example of Mia's **Angry** part, rather than trying to get rid of it, we want to find out what we can do to help **Angry**. Working in this way helps the internal system to settle and parts to work more harmoniously together. As we did so, Mia reported that her headaches had stopped.

Mia seemed fully engaged with her storytelling now. It felt like a door had opened into her inner world and we were now working with the parts of her that had been hard to reach, even though it had to be through a computer screen.

Snapshot 7: Three Tribes

Mia describes three tribes of sisters made up of her different parts. They each have their own teepees in their own camps. Mia talks as she draws …" In **Happy**, **Angry** and **Sad**'s camp, **Happy** always takes charge. They roam in woods and forests. They own bows and arrows and swords, which they need for fighting other tribes and for catching animals.' Our conversation flows and we laugh and wonder at the different characters. She describes each part of them in minute detail; hair colour, clothes and ages (see Figure 10.5).

Mia continues: "…in **Scared** and **Worry**'s camp, there's no campfire; the grass is dead and black. The camp is cold and mysterious. They are dressed in black cloaks with black hoods pulled over their heads. No one can see their faces. In one teepee, there are shelves of potions. There is a cauldron on a fire where they make their potions. As Mia begins to describe and draw **Scared** and **Worry**, I am conscious of holding my breath. The contrast between the other parts and these two is quite startling. With the other parts, our conversation flowed as I took an interest in the details of their clothes, hair and teepees. Once she starts to draw **Scared** and **Worry**, we both grow quiet (see Figure 10.6). I am fascinated by the complete change of tempo and affect. At last, these harder-to-reach parts are making themselves known. It feels like a breakthrough moment.

Figure 10.5 **Happy**, **Angry** and **Sad's** camp.

Snapshot 8: Sad Gets Lost

Mia wants to tell Sad's story today. She draws three different camps. Mia begins: "**Sad** leaves camp to visit **Peaceful** and **Tired**. She walks along but soon gets lost." I wonder aloud if **Sad** has anything to help her find her way. Mia explains: "**Sad** did have a compass but it got stolen." I wonder if this reference to an item being stolen links to the burglary and Mia feeling lost and sad. Mia continues: "She can see some glowing lights in the distance and two black cloaks that make her scared. She climbs to the top of a tree to hide from them. She thinks it's **Peaceful** and **Tired's** camp (see Figure 10.7) that has been destroyed. **Sad** thinks they've all been captured."

Scared

Sisters

Worried

18

19

No fire, grass dead + black, cold, mysterious

Figure 10.6 **Scared** and **Worry's** camp.

I wonder if Mia might be referring to the moment she and her Dad found their house "destroyed" by the burglars. She goes on:

> **Scared** and **Worry** are sort of evil. They make good potions that make people see in the dark and evil potions that are poisons. **Sad** climbs down and sees the glow coming from a tent. She creeps in and takes some potions including Deadly Nightshade. It slips out of her hand and the glass smashes everywhere. She climbs back up a tree to hide. **Scared** and **Worry** rush over and sweep up the potion and glass with their capes and put the potion into a new bottle.

As I listen to this, I can't help wondering if **Sad, Scared** and **Worry** are acting out Mia's own feelings generated from being robbed. It feels as if these parts are locked in the tussle of stealing and retrieving, breaking and mending. It's significant to me that it's these specific parts that have been so adversely affected by the burglary.

Figure 10.7 **Peaceful** and **Tired's** camp.

Mia goes on:

> They hear **Sad's** breathing and climb up the tree to find her. **Sad** quickly drinks a potion, which makes her invisible. **Scared** and **Worry** then make a potion that will make them see her. **Sad** runs back to her camp with **Scared** and **Worry** chasing her. The others are sitting around the campfire thinking about how they will find **Sad**. Suddenly they see **Sad** running towards them and they grab her. She is being chased by **Scared** and **Worried** who want to attack them all with their deadly potions.

At this point, Mia pauses for what seems an age. Her face slowly relaxes and she gives out a big sigh. She continues in a softer, quieter voice: "…in the end, they all decide to make friends and go and have a sleepover at **Happy**, **Angry** and **Sad's** camp."

This pause feels significant to me. Mia herself helps the different parts connect and make peace with each other.

Reflections

One of Mia's great fears was that she and her family would be attacked and killed by the burglar coming back in the night when they were asleep. This picture of **Scared** and **Worry** chasing **Sad** brings all those distressed parts of her together. The other parts protected **Sad** and I was on the edge of my seat wondering if another fight would begin. But then Mia's compassionate Self stepped in. Harmony was restored. From this moment on life changed for Mia. Once the wounded parts are listened to and cared for by the Self, a deep transformation of those parts is possible. Once again Spiegel aptly states: "One of the main goals of IFS therapy is to heal wounded and vulnerable parts. In order to heal them, the client's Self must be able to connect and develop a relationship with these exiled parts" (Spiegel, 2017).

Mia is now sleeping through the night with undisturbed sleep. If she does wake up for something, she can go back to sleep herself without her parents' help. Her move to secondary school has gone well and she is making new friends.

Snapshot 9: The Final Session

Happy, **Angry** and **Sad** have a nice camp now. **Peaceful** and **Tired** have meat and weapons. **Scared** and **Worry** make lots of good potions like berry juice and weave mats out of leaves. Suddenly there's an invasion from another camp of new people. They want to own as much land as they can and steal things.

I notice that Mia is really animated as she speaks. She continues:

Tropical Tribe capture them all. They tie them all to trees with rope and roast some of their meat on their fire. At night when **Tropical Tribe** have gone to sleep, **Angry** breaks the rope and gets free. **Angry** then frees everyone else and gets their stuff back. They all creep back to **Scared** and **Worry's** camp to make potions and set traps for **Tropical Tribe**. They cover a trapdoor with moss. **Tropical Tribe** see they've gone and go looking for them. When they get to **Scared** and **Worry's** camp they fall through the trapdoor and are shot at with arrows from **Peaceful and Tired**. They pull **Tropical Tribe** out of the trap and get ready to send them back to their own land. But **Tropical Tribe** steal a jar of fireflies as they leave. **Sad** notices the fireflies are missing and says that if **Tropical Tribe** give them back, she will give them a pearl necklace in exchange. **Tropical Tribe** agree and say sorry. They all make friends. They are glad they've made new friends and **Tropical Tribe** sail back to their land.

Reflections

One of the things I love about working with children is that they can always surprise us! I was not expecting the entrance of **Tropical Tribe**! There had been the
very real "invasion" of Coronavirus into our world during this time, as well as the
actual invasion of Mia's home by the burglars. Mia had also started her new school
and was meeting lots of different people.

I was fascinated by the exchange of fireflies for a necklace as the final interaction
between tribes. Mia's parents had just bought Mia a new bike with the insurance
money, which was given for the loss of the jewellery. I was wondering if this was
reflected in the exchange especially because it was necklaces that were taken in the
robbery.

Mia's parts worked together and made peace with the **Tropical Tribe** in the
end. This statement of Van der Kolk seems to apply to Mia: "…the resolution of
the trauma was the result of her ability to access her imagination and rework the
scenes in which she had become frozen…Helpless passivity was replaced by determined Self-led action" (Van der Kolk, 2014).

Final Thoughts

Mia ended her therapy sessions here. I am aware that these few snapshots from
the therapy only illustrate some of the steps used in IFS therapy but hopefully
they will stimulate your interest. Working with young children online and in the
middle of a worldwide pandemic is difficult. For the first time perhaps, we find
ourselves needing to attend to our own **Sad**, **Scared** and **Worried** parts whilst we
work with those of our clients. As I said, the learning curve for me was steep! As
we continue to access our own compassionate selves, it is possible that our young
clients can also access theirs. But in case you are wondering how Mia's parts are
doing now, let me give them the last word as reported by Mia:

> **Scared** and **Worry** parts are much calmer now.
> **Sad** is quiet.
> **Happy** is doing really well.
> **Angry** is quiet.
> **Tired** is tired because she's going to bed late.
> **Peaceful** is doing well playing online games with her best friend.

References

Anderson, F. et al. (2017) *Internal Family Systems, Skills Training Manual*. Eau Claire, WI:
PESI.
Eppel, A. et al. (2020) Out of the Frame: Boundaries in Online Psychotherapy. *Journal of
Psychiatry Reform* 8:2.
Kronengold, H. (2019) *The Screen Door. In Thinking about Technology in Psychotherapy in
Integrating Technology into Modern Therapies* (J. Stone, Eds.). London: Routledge.
Schwartz, R. (1995) *Internal Family Systems Therapy*. New York: Guildford Press.

Snyder, K. (2021) The digital art therapy frame: creating a 'magic circle' in teletherapy. *International Journal of Art Therapy*, 26:3, 104–110.

Spiegel, L. (2017) *Internal Family Systems Therapy with Children*. London: Routledge.

Van der Kolk, B. (2014) *The Body Keeps the Score*. London: Penguin.

Weinberg, H. and Rolnick, A. (2020) *Theory and Practice of Online Therapy: Internet-delivered Interventions for Individuals, Groups, Families and Organisations*. New York: Routledge.

Chapter 11

Magical Horses
Equine Therapy

Lucy Jayne

Introduction

As an integrative arts psychotherapist, much of my work with children and young people, both in schools and in private practice, involves using art and play to facilitate communication and process a wide range of emotional and psychological difficulties. These can include: behavioral problems, Attention Deficit Hyperactivity Disorder (ADHD), anxiety, attachment issues, friendship difficulties and bullying. I also have experience of working with adopted and 'looked after children'.

My approach is gentle and non-directive and most clients are able to engage well with this way of working: using the arts materials to explore and process their difficulties with my support. However, there are some children and young people, who find it difficult to engage, even with this gentle and indirect approach. Those children, whose experiences of relationships with caregivers involve abuse and neglect, may not be able to trust any adult sufficiently to engage in a therapeutic relationship. For these "hard-to-reach" children and young people, Equine Assisted Psychotherapy (EAP) may be a valuable alternative.

Equine Assisted Psychotherapy

EAP is suitable for a wide variety of clients, but may be particularly valuable for children and young people, who are "hard-to-reach" through more conventional therapeutic interventions, or where their experiences have left them deeply distrustful of adults. The experience of being *attuned* to and understood by a horse provides children and young people with experiences of relationship, not previously available to them, and this, together with the repetitive and consistent nature of interactions with and feedback from the horses, has been found to assist in emotional regulation. Developing secure relationships and the ability to regulate emotional arousal leads to improvements in other areas, including trust and empathy and an improved sense of self. For some, it may be their first positive experience of being able to give and receive nurture and physical affection.

In this chapter, I will describe my experience of using EAP in work with children, young people and families. Some of them had already proved to be

DOI: 10.4324/9781003163015-11

"hard-to-reach" through more conventional psychotherapeutic methods. As some readers may not be familiar with EAP, I will provide a series of *vignettes* from casework, providing a flavor of the actual sessions. I will intersperse these with some explanation of the EAGALA (Equine Assisted Growth & Learning Association) model, how I became interested in using horses with clients and how it may work.

The Children and Young People

To protect their confidentiality, I have used pseudonyms for everybody and although the *vignettes* are based on real clients, details have been changed. I have attempted to select examples from their equine therapy in order to illustrate particular client issues.

Ace (13 Years)

When we met Ace, he was on the point of being permanently excluded from school for persistent, disruptive behaviour and intimidation of staff and other pupils. Ace had been taken into care, at the age of five, after a traumatic early childhood. It seemed that he had little understanding of his own feelings, or those of others and he demonstrated many other attachment-based difficulties. His carer described him as having "no empathy" and was concerned for his future. Ace's emotional age seemed almost infantile. He had little sense of self, no memory of his life before being taken into care and little memory of anything beyond the recent past.

Despite his imposing appearance, Ace presented as friendly and eager to please and immediately engaged with Toffee (the yard terrier), who takes responsibility for greeting all clients as they get out of the car. Ace seemed uncertain about how to connect with the horses and seemed to find them quite imposing, commenting on their size and asking whether they might bite him.

In the first few sessions, Ace struggled with simple exercises, such as leading a small pony from one space to another. He found it difficult to focus and, although kind and gentle towards the horses, he seemed to lack any sense of purpose, or even of who he was, which resulted in the horses ignoring him.

Reflections

Developing Assertiveness

Ace experimented with head collars, whips and food bribes but his efforts remained ineffectual: He kept trying to move the horses, but the horses dug their feet firmly into the ground and kept eating grass. Eventually Ace became frustrated and, as he started to be able to reflect on his frustration, he began to embody and channel the feelings to connect with the horses. It seemed that connecting with his own feelings, Ace could begin connecting with the horses. At first, we supported Ace, to maintain the connection by getting him to imagine himself as an army general, marching them from the field to the arena. Gradually, as Ace became more self-aware and in touch with how he was feeling, he was able to maintain his focus and the connection with the horses for longer periods. He was able to get them to move with him, change pace and even negotiate obstacle courses, without physical connection and sometimes without words or bribes.

Developing Empathy

Ace formed a strong attachment with a large bay mare, who he called Big Horse, choosing to work with her in preference to the geldings. He enjoyed spending time playing with her, grooming her and finding her treats, such as apples and dandelions. On one occasion, Big Horse was unable to participate after being bitten by a snake and was in considerable pain, with a swollen leg. Ace was very attentive to her, grooming and caressing her. Whilst doing this, he started to talk about his own experiences (soon after being in care) of being in hospital. Following this session, Ace's carer reported that he was beginning to talk about early memories and was also starting to be more considerate to other members of the family.

What Is Equine Assisted Psychotherapy?

EAP is a relatively new approach, where horses are used to work therapeutically with clients, who are experiencing mental distress, to facilitate psychological and emotional healing. Counsellors, psychotherapists and other mental health professionals work with horses and clients, using a variety of models according to their training and theoretical orientation. There is variation in the amount of structure provided and some models involve riding the horse, whilst others involve only "groundwork". These specialties are expanding in the UK and are attracting cautious interest from the establishment, although there remains a need for further evaluation. Browne's *Therapy Today* editorial (2012, p. 3) begins: "Up and down the country horses are being used to work therapeutically with a range of conditions – addiction, depression, Post Traumatic Stress Disorder (PTSD) and even autism." It continues:

> Some of the best results reported for equine assisted psychotherapy have been with teenagers with serious behavioural problems; for the first time these young clients have felt an authentic relationship with another being… a relationship about contact and connection instead of manipulation and abuse.
>
> (Ibid)

The initial task in EAP usually involves observing the herd and reflecting on the feelings and sensations which emerge, and possible parallels for clients. For trauma sufferers (particularly children who have suffered abuse) boundaries and physical contact are likely to be central to the therapy. The behaviour of the horses in the first session provides important information about the scope of the work.

Kara (14 Years)

Kara was part of a small group of young people. During the first session, a fight broke out within the group, which resulted in one of the geldings galloping around the arena, with his penis extended, apparently in pursuit of a smaller female pony. Several members of the group, including Kara, expressed concern that the female pony was receiving unwanted sexual advances. It seemed that the horses might be picking up on multiple individual and group issues.

Leaving the other two young people to work together, Kara left the arena and sat on the other side of the fence complaining "this is boring" and worrying about her new trainers getting dirty. A pony in a field next to where she was sitting approached her and she began, absent-mindedly, to stroke it through the fence. When it started to lick her, she complained loudly that it was "disgusting", but continued to pet the pony and allowed it to nuzzle her, but not lick her, whilst expressing concern about the behaviour of the gelding towards the mare in the arena.

In the next session, Kara chose to work with the pony from the field, although still expressing disgust about the smell. She started gently grooming her and making occasional clicking noises and the pony moved away, but gradually the pony turned towards her and started nuzzling Kara and eventually licking her hands, which Kara accepted. Over the course of three sessions, Kara seemed to change from a sulky, disenchanted adolescent to a self-confident enthusiastic young person, who was able to give advice to other members of the group about the horses.

Reflections

We noticed that, when Kara left the arena, she seemed to want everyone to hear her loud protestations. We wondered if this was an attempt to mask her discomfort about the horses' display of sexuality and uncertainty about engaging in something unfamiliar. Erikson describes how the adolescent stage of development involves searching for a new more mature sense of self, or identity, together with the "integration of the identity elements ascribed in the forgoing to the childhood stages" (Erikson, 1968). He suggests that there is a need for trust in self and others and that the adolescent "looks most fervently for men and ideas to have *faith* in", whilst at the same time "fears a foolish, all too trusting commitment, and will, paradoxically express his need for faith in loud cynical mistrust" (Ibid).

When the pony from the field chose to approach her, Kara did not push her away and allowed herself to form a connection. Although we wondered about Kara's feelings of concern for the female pony, in the first session, and her disgust about smell and the pony licking her hands, Kara hardly engaged with us and spoke mostly to the pony. It appeared that she was able to regulate and process difficult feelings, through the *attuned* and nurturing relationship with the pony and our role was merely to facilitate.

Personal Experience

I became interested in the therapeutic potential of horses whilst training as a therapist. I was already aware of a sense of increased wellbeing and spiritual refreshment from riding and caring for horses and of the importance of my daughter's relationship with her horse, during the turmoil of adolescence. As well as attending several workshops during my training, I was able to undertake a small ethnographic qualitative research study, as part of my M.Ed. degree: (Children's and young people's experiences of relationship and affect regulation in Equine Assisted Psychotherapy 2013) based on my observations of EAP sessions with a group of young people. My motivation for this was to find out whether it might be an effective therapy for children, who had suffered relational trauma, in infancy, resulting in *disorganised attachment*. For such children, the effectiveness of conventional psychotherapeutic interventions may be limited.

The study enabled me to gather insight into the young people's experiences of engagement in relationship in EAP, involving: identification of the issues, negotiation of boundaries and mutual calming. The process involved features of the attachment relationship and many instances of affect regulation. The extraordinary power of these young peoples' experiences inspired me to undertake the EAGALA training as a *Mental Health Professional* and I have now been working as part of a small team, with an *Equine Specialist*, Sam, and different groups of horses for almost ten years.

The EAGALA Model (www.eagala.org)

The EAGALA (2018) model, which is widely used within the UK and worldwide, provides certification and training and a framework for practice. The model is ground-based, rather than involving riding, and is described as "solution-oriented", which is founded in the belief that their "clients have the best solutions for themselves". The model is experiential and non-directive and involves clients working directly with the horses. Through connection with the horses, they begin to process traumas and effect change.

Sessions involving one to five horses and either an individual client, or a small group of clients, take place in the ménage, a round pen, or in the field or stable. Equipment is made available, including: halters, grooming brushes, poles and cones. Clients may work individually, or with others in a team, depending on the issues to be addressed. Sessions are experiential, in nature, and last one to two hours. Clients engage in un-mounted horse-related activities. Once a connection has been established, subsequent tasks are chosen according to the needs of the client/s. These may be quite simple, such as entering a space containing a loose horse, or catching, haltering, leading or grooming a horse. More complex tasks may be designed to elicit particular issues, such as assertiveness, problem solving, relationships or teamwork.

Although our practice is based on the EAGALA model, in planning our sessions and in thinking about the clients and reflecting on our sessions, we draw from other models including Shambo's HEAL Model™ to broaden our understanding, as well as considering models of child development and other theoretical ideas that are particularly relevant. We reflect, independently and in supervision, on our own feelings, to shed light on what is happening in the therapeutic relationships both with the horses and with the human members of the therapy team.

Horses have been present in the human psyche and closely involved with them, in more practical ways, throughout history. The Ancient Greeks believed that horses were both messengers of the gods and concerned with healing. The Celts worshipped a white mare, Epona, believed to transport the human soul. McCormick and McCormick describe them as "faithfully" accompanying people on "journeys external and internal" and "willingly [carrying] us to faraway places, to enchanted castles, to and from battle, and even to the grave" (McCormick & McCormick, 1997).

In considering what makes horses suitable for psychotherapeutic work, the research literature suggests that the answers lie both in the history of man's relationship with horses and in the unique combination of characteristics, possessed by horses, including their vulnerability as *prey* animals, their highly social and inquisitive nature as *herd* members and their *power and physical presence*.

Power and Physical Presence

Descriptions of horses often refer to their "power", "size", "grace" and "regal presence" and it seems they often inspire feelings in humans including wonder, awe or sometimes fear, which may lead to a desire to find out more.

Tyro (14 Years)

When we met Tyro, his foster placement was at breaking point and he was frequently suspended from school for aggressive behavior, particularly towards black female teachers. There were concerns that Tyro was becoming involved in gang culture and he was reported to be struggling with feelings about his racial identity, as a mixed-race young person. As an infant, Tyro had suffered multiple severe beatings from his black grandmother, before being taken into care aged three years old.

We wondered whether the horses would find Tyro's size, appearance and self-confident manner intimidating, but in fact, Tyro seemed in awe of the horses, commenting on how large and strong they were. Initially, Tyro was drawn to working with a grey (white) gelding, which was quite aloof and disinterested in working with him. The gelding was rapidly replaced by a very assertive bay (dark brown) mare, which shared a field with the gelding. The mare engaged with him and followed him "like a shadow", taking every opportunity to engage with him, nuzzle him and give and receive affection. It seemed to us that she was providing him with the experience of a caring black mother figure, who had been lacking in his early childhood. Towards the end of his sessions, he spent time with a younger "Paint" (brown and white) gelding, about whom Tyro exclaimed on first seeing him: "He's mad, really cool!"

Reflections

As with Kara, there was little conversation and our role was to observe what was happening, without interpretation. The horses seemed to pick up on Tyro's issues and he was able to accept what might have been perceived as "rejection" by the white horse and engage in an *attuned* and nurturing relationship with the bay mare. It seemed that, this enabled Tyro to process his early trauma and integrate a positive internal representation of a black mother figure, resulting in his becoming more accepting of his own dual heritage. Leigh Shambo suggests that "wounded, mistrustful people and horses often really 'get' each other", which she believes is due to the neurophysiological effects of trauma, causing humans to "become like prey animals", ready to run, or in a constant state of hyper-vigilance or mistrust (Shambo, 2013).

Prey Animal

Karol describes how the horse is "a vulnerable creature" and therefore "serves as an apt companion for a child overwhelmed by his or her own sense of vulnerability and imperfections" (Karol, 2007).

Hari (15 Years)

Hari had complex health issues and had been the victim of severe bullying over a sustained period. When we first met him, he seemed young for his age, his affect was flat and he was very "scared" of any contact with even the smallest pony. The pony respected his need to take things gradually, but gently persisted in engaging him, drawing him into a playful relationship, mirroring his movements and eventually culminating in a joyful dance. As Hari's confidence visibly increased, he became quite jokey: "Come on pony, you need some counselling". Over his three sessions, he allowed the pony into his space and into his heart (see Figure 11.1).

Figure 11.1 Mirroring Dance.

Hari expressed his delight and he talked about how there was: "Something magical about horses", which drew him in and made him want to continue and gave him courage to conquer the fear.

Irwin and Weber (2001) believe that horses' "exceptional powers of intuition" have evolved over thousands of years, due to their being *prey* animals. Their awareness of potential predators has resulted in an acute sensitivity both to their surroundings and to the moods and mental states of humans. Kohanov suggests that:

> In their dealings with the human race over the past six thousand years, horses have become even more sophisticated in the non-verbal language of feeling … even the most secure horse knows that any two-legged creature conveying the gestures of one emotion in order to hide another is either up to no good or delusional enough to be dangerous to herself and others.
>
> (Kohanov, 2007)

It seems that horses are able to assess both the level of arousal and the mood of a human, interpreting subtle physiological signs, from a distance. They can decide how to respond, by allowing them to approach, or choosing fight or flight. Having decided that it is safe to approach, horses' sensitivity to humans enables them to adapt the manner and speed of their approach, so as not to frighten or endanger a child or young person, who is vulnerable or fearful, thereby maximizing the likelihood of making a connection (see Figure 11.2).

For many young people meeting horses for the first time can be daunting and some horses, due to their sensitivity, are cautious about being approached. Other clients are overconfident and approach the horse too quickly, resulting in the horse running away, or sometimes becoming intimidating by coming too close and invading the young person's personal space. *Negotiating boundaries* between clients and horses, where horses are comfortable being approached and clients don't feel intimidated, is often the first part of the work and maybe central, where the young person has a particular issue with boundaries. Clients become aware that horses are highly sensitive to mood and that to be able to connect with the horse, they need to become aware of their own mood and be able to moderate their behavior. As Hari puts it: "When I'm scared, the horse is scared; when I'm calm the horse is calm".

Having overcome his fear and established a connection with the pony, it seems that Hari is able to engage playfully with the pony, which he experiences as having a "magical" quality. According to the McCormicks & McCormick (1997), Jung believed that wild horses represent both "the uncontrollable instinctual urges that erupt from our unconscious, even though we try to repress them" and, at the same time, "the magical side of us, the mother within us, who is intuitive and understanding" (McCormick & McCormick, 1997).

Shambo suggests that once a "limbic connection" has been established through this stage of "mutual regulation", involving grooming and close physical contact with the horse, clients will be able to work in partnership with the horse to engage in more "action-oriented" tasks (Shambo, 2013).

Figure 11.2 Large Brown Mare Connecting with Small Child.

Billy (11 Years)

Billy had been out of school for more than a year and was refusing to attend medical appointments, despite complex health and emotional issues. At the time that we saw him, he was undergoing an assessment by CAMHS but was struggling to engage and his mother was distrustful of any form of medical and psychological intervention.

Billy was initially hesitant about leaving the car, but was persuaded by Toffee and came into the arena to meet the horse. He had problems with mobility and struggled to walk, so there was concern about him being in the arena with loose horses. However, both ponies seemed instinctively aware of Billy's needs and planted their feet in the sand, a safe distance from Billy, stretching out to enable him to touch their faces and necks. We attempted to reflect with Billy on both his own experience and how he imagined the ponies' sensory experiences, asking him what stroking and brushing felt like for him, or might feel like for the pony. Although Billy did not respond to us, as soon as he entered the arena with the ponies, his demeanor changed and he seemed to grow in confidence and become fully focused on finding out about the small "grey" pony, preferring him to the larger "scary" one. His walking appeared less impaired and when he moved the pony followed him close by.

Reflections

Billy did not speak or engage with us, except to indicate the pony he preferred to work with, choosing only to interact with the ponies and Toffee, who followed him everywhere. It seemed that Billy rapidly formed a strong connection with the pony, brushing him and talking to him. Somehow, by connecting with Billy and communicating an understanding of his needs, Billy was empowered to explore his abilities (rather than his disabilities), in a way that was unusual for him. By refusing to put this experience into words, we wondered whether Billy might be protecting the experience from scrutiny by his mother, although sadly she withdrew Billy after only two sessions.

Karol (2007, p. 81) describes the sense of empowerment, when a child is on a horse and can "look down onto an adult" and "experience the power of the body of the horse as the horse moves under him or her and so is given an enhanced sense of his or her own body and, thus, his or her sense of 'self'".

Observing the Herd

The initial task in EAP often involves observing the herd and reflecting on the feelings and sensations, which may emerge and any possible parallels for clients. Occasionally, clients are asked to stand amongst the horses and allow a horse to choose whether to work with a particular client. Choosing horses to work with, or being chosen, often elicits strong feelings about being wanted or rejected.

Jess (26 Years)

Jess was suffering from anxiety and depression when we met her. She had three young children, an unsupportive partner and felt suffocated by the relentless burdens of keeping house and caring for the children. She had also had a difficult childhood and felt that some of her own unresolved difficulties from childhood had been triggered by the current circumstance.

Initially, Jess felt the horses: "Don't care about me" and they seemed to her to be playing out the "squabbles" of her children, in a way that she found stressful. Jess felt that the smallest grey pony represented her youngest child. The first few sessions focused on working with the horses (symbolizing her children), experimenting with boundaries and finding more positive ways of interacting. Fascinatingly this rapidly translated into change with Jess's real children within the family. There followed a period where Jess worked with the bay mare, involving lots of grooming and connecting with her in a mutually nurturing way, which seemed to enable Jess to process some of her unresolved feelings.

Around the fourth session, the mare came into the arena and, instead of engaging with Jess, walked into the center and spent several minutes rolling on the ground with her legs in the air, snorting and moaning and apparently taking great pleasure in it. Jess became very animated and described her as "demonstrating real freedom". As we wondered with her about what rolling on the ground might be like for a horse, Jess was reminded of a time when she last felt "truly happy" and experienced similar freedom, whilst swimming in the ocean.

In the following session, we asked Jess to build a space to represent her life. The space she built was small, cluttered and chaotic. The mare trampled through it knocking it over and even partly removing walls. Without thinking, Jess tidied it up and reconstructed it and the mare again destroyed it. Jess gasped in amazement, as she understood the message. We then asked her to build a space she would like, whereupon the horse went and stood with its head on her shoulder while Jess petted her and tears streamed down Jess' cheeks. It seemed that with the help of the bay mare, Jess was able to rediscover her own needs for nurturing and self-care.

Reflections

The horses' apparent disinterest during the observation, resulted in strong feelings of rejection for Jess, which made it hard for her to connect with them. It seemed that the horses were picking up on her issues with her children. Once Jess found ways of interacting with the ponies in a more playful and caring way, she was able to form a strong nurturing bond with the bay mare. This appeared to enable her to process some of her unresolved feelings from childhood and understand her own needs.

Herd Animal

Bachi et al. suggest that: "Horses are highly suitable for therapeutic work due to their being herd animals, for which cooperation is as important as competition, and the bonding among members is very strong" (Bachi et al., 2012). Shambo describes the complex structure of the herd and the role of "dominant mares", in caring for the young. She considers that horses have a natural herd instinct to regulate other herd members and that "the stabilising matrix of bonding and regulating behaviours", within the herd, has an "important role in keeping the herd together, alive and in balance" (Shambo, 2013).

Mutually calming behavior between horses, which involves vigorous, simultaneous grooming of manes and withers, using teeth and lips, is frequently seen when horses have been startled by something, such as a loud noise, triggering their *fight/flight* response. Such mutual grooming behavior amongst the horses results in visible calming and restoration of normal breathing and heartbeat rhythms, with accompanying biochemical effects, including endorphin release (see Figure 11.3). The McCormicks suggest that horses are motivated to offer this type of mutual calming to humans, particularly young ones, perhaps because they are seen as honorary members of the herd, as a result of the long relationship between the species.

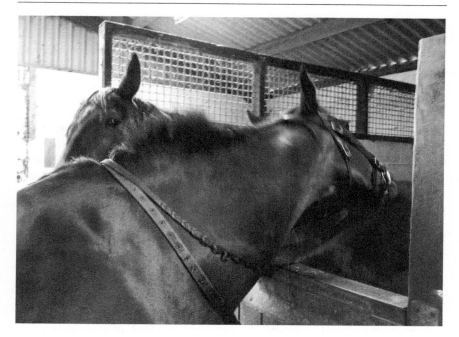

Figure 11.3 Mutual Calming.

Reading Non-Verbal Communication and Mirroring

Horses have an exceptional ability to read non-verbal communication and mirror behavior, which provides immediate, direct and honest feedback. Participants are able to try out alternative actions, thinking and behavior, based on the responses they receive from the horse. By trampling through the chaotic space to show Jess what she needed to change, the mare demonstrated not only extraordinary powers of intuition and connection with Jess, but also the extraordinary power of EAP itself.

Zoe (19 Years)

Zoe struggled to get out of bed to come to the first session. She had become severely depressed after being bullied and sexually harassed at work. The large bay mare chose to work with her. Her first few sessions involved grooming and leading, during which time the mare remained very quiet, attentive and affectionate. When Zoe arrived for her third session, her demeanor had changed and she was smiling and seemed more energetic. The mare sensed the change and responded with enthusiasm and the session involved much more playfulness and fun.

With Zoe, as with many of the other children and young people we have worked with, the mare immediately sensed Zoe's low mood and made a connection with her which was sufficient to motivate Zoe to return for the next session.

Shambo suggests that once a "limbic connection" has been established through this stage of "mutual regulation", involving grooming and close physical contact with the horse, clients will be able to work in partnership with the horse to engage in more "action-oriented" tasks (Shambo, 2013).

Discussion

In these examples from practice, I have sought to describe how the initial sessions work. They usually involve identifying issues and in negotiating comfortable boundaries, for both clients and horses. This is followed by a process of mutual calming, which results in the formation of an *attuned* connection with the horse. Once the connection is established, the client and horse can engage in activities, designed to elucidate the client's issues. Through this connection, the horse can reflect back the client's behavior and the associated feeling, conveying an understanding of the client's experience. This process is similar to "marked mirroring" in the infant-mother dyad (Gergely & Watson, 1996), which gradually enables the client to regulate their feeling states and at the same time to develop a sense of self, which is similar to Winnicott's idea of the baby finding himself, or herself, reflected in the mother's face (Winnicott, 1967).

For young people, like Ace and Tyro, whose early encounters of relationship have been abusive and traumatic, the bay mare provided an experience of an attuned and nurturing relationship. This seemed to enable them to give and receive physical affection, regulate their feeling states and begin to develop a sense of themselves and others. This in turn meant they could see themselves reflected in the eyes of another living being, perhaps for the first time.

Many of our clients have reached adolescence by the time we start working with them. Erikson describes how, although unsuccessful navigation of adolescence may result in mental health difficulties, often it is young people's "resourcefulness" which enables them to find a path through this turbulent period. He gives the example of an adolescent girl, who overcomes adolescent difficulties, including an eating disorder, by caring for young horses and developing a sense of identity (Erikson, 1968).

Frequently during equine therapy sessions, it appears that nothing is happening and the horses are just interested in eating grass, or interacting with each other – such as during the early sessions with Ace, when he struggled to form a connection. Then there is sometimes a moment when something extraordinary seems to happen and the horse is suddenly fully involved and provides a glimpse of clarity. In these moments, there seems to be justification for, Hari's observation, that: "there is something magical about horses".

References

Bachi, K., Terkel, J., & Teichman, M. (2012). Equine-facilitated psychotherapy for at-risk adolescents: The influence on self-image, self-control and trust. *Clinical Child Psychology and Psychiatry, 17*(2), 298–312.

Browne, Sarah. (2012). Editorial. *Therapy Today*, *23*(2). Retrieved from http://www. therapytoday.net.

EAGALA. (2018). *EAGALA (Equine Assisted Psychotherapy and Equine Assisted Learning) Primary Site*. Retrieved from https://www.eagala.org/.

Erikson, E.H. (1968). *Identity: Youth and Crisis*. New York: Norton.

Gergely, G., & Watson, J. S. (1996). The social biofeedback theory of parental affect-mirroring: The development of emotional self-awareness and self-control in infancy. *The International Journal of Psychoanalysis*, *77*(6), 1181–1212.

Irwin, C. & Weber B. (2001). Horses Don't Lie, *What Horses Teach Us About Our Natural Capacity for Awareness, Confidence, Courage and trust* (First British edition). London: Souvenir Press Ltd.

Karol, J. (2007). Applying a traditional individual psychotherapy model to equine-facilitated psychotherapy (EFP): Theory and method. *Clinical Child Psychology and Psychiatry*, *12*(1), 77–90.

Kohanov, L. (2007). *The Tao of Equus: A Woman's Journey of Healing and Transformation Through the Way of the Horse (annotated edition.)*. New World Library.

McCormick, A., & McCormick, M. (1997). *Horse Sense and the Human Heart: What Horses Can Teach Us About Trust, Bonding, Creativity and Spirituality* (1st ed.). Deerfield Beach, Florida: HCI.

Shambo, L. (2013). *The Listening Heart. The Limbic Path Beyond Office Therapy* (1st ed.). Chehalis, WA: Human-Equine Alliance for Learning (HEAL).

Winnicott, D. (1967). *Mirror-Role of the Mother and Family in Child Development in the Predicament of the Family: A Psycho-Analytical Symposium ed. P. Lomas*. London: Hogarth Press.

Chapter 12

The Silent Voice

Aileen Webber

Snapshot 1: First Meeting

With some difficulty, Samuel manoeuvres his electric wheelchair along the awkward passage leading to my practice room. He enters and stops in front of my chair, with just a coffee table between us. We meet eyes and I smile. He glances away. I get up and close the door, symbolising the privacy and confidentiality of our time together. I'm aware of my sense of excitement and hope that I will be able to reach him. Samuel's eyes convey that he is a bit nervous, and I wonder if he's thinking this won't be any better than his previous counselling (that I have been told took place the year before) or conversely he might be imbuing me with powers I do not possess. This is the first time I have tried to communicate with Samuel. I remind myself, he is really no different to any other client and I have worked with many. "So you can speak about anything you want in here and it's totally confidential." My voice sounds really loud in the quiet space. Samuel indicates a word on his alphabet keyboard that says: "Yes." I feel a childish rush of gratification. I'm aware that Samuel and I are both covering new ground. I'm pulled back from my musings to the here and now when Samuel starts to spell out what feels like a carefully considered reply:

i space **w-a-n-t** space **t-o** space **t-e-l-l** space **y-o-u** space **h-o-w** space i space **f** ... At this point, he pauses, looks directly at me and bends over his keyboard once more pointing to the symbol that denotes a question mark. I take this to mean: "You can guess." I didn't expect Samuel to be happy if I predicted what he was going to say, but I'm prepared to give it a shot, so I repeat the whole sentence back to him with what I guess he was going to say: "I want to tell you how I feel?" He jerks a little in his chair and I wonder if this is to show me that I am right in my guesswork. My repetition of what he spelt out has the additional effect of allowing his words to hang in the air, as if I had used the therapist's technique of "reflecting back" to a client.

My mind is spinning at the felt empathy of what it must be like to need so much physical support just to exist. How can a bright, independent-minded young person cope with the level of dependency he is forced to accept? Suddenly I'm hit by the irony of what he is wanting from therapy – to tell me how he feels. How on earth can he tell me even remotely what it feels like to be unable to speak in words,

DOI: 10.4324/9781003163015-12

without being able to speak in words? The only thing I can think to say next is to ask a question – but I'm remembering that we were warned against asking too many questions in training. My head is filled with Gestalt techniques and experiments that form part of the training I have recently completed but I have no idea how to use any of them with Samuel as he has no words and all the techniques I have learnt involve the use of words.

So in the absence of anything more constructive that I can think of to say, I ask him: "Do you think you would like to come and see me at this time for fifty minutes every week?"

His reply is as instant as it can be for Samuel. "Yes." I feel a rush of pleasure and anticipation. I like and respect Samuel already. I sense he has something important to say to me that it would perhaps be difficult for him to tell me even if his way of communicating was more straightforward. Before he has wheeled himself out of my room, my mind is whirring trying to think of creative ways to reach him.

Context: Samuel communicated to a teaching assistant at his school that he would like to talk to the school therapist. He had seen another counsellor for a short while in the past, but I knew he had chosen not to continue seeing her. Samuel was living at a residential home at this time. I knew him to be an exceptionally intelligent 12-year-old boy with a vivacious personality and a quirky sense of humour, who had cerebral palsy quadriplegia. Samuel had limited movement and mostly used an electric wheelchair to move around, although sometimes he would be pushed in a manual wheelchair. He had no intelligible speech but used low-tech *Alternative Augmentative Communication* (AAC). This comprises a cardboard, printed "keyboard," that was attached to an arm of his wheelchair and he would point to the relevant letters to spell out words, indicating the space bar to end a word (see Figure 12.1). I had not conversed with him before and in truth I didn't feel particularly confident to do so in this first session, but I hadn't taken into

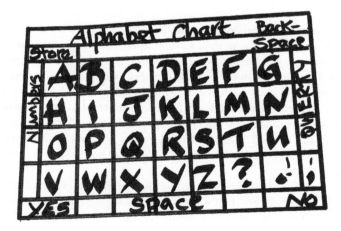

Figure 12.1 Communication Board.

account that Samuel was an exceptionally bright young person who was well experienced in helping new people to communicate with him.

Reflections After Snapshot I

After this first session with Samuel, my thoughts keep returning to the same questions going round and round. How can he express himself in words without being able to speak? We seem to have already found a passable way to communicate with each other about everyday things but my Gestalt training had presented me with ways of working experientially and phenomenologically (Mann, 2010). In terms of how to use these approaches with Samuel, I felt out of my depth. It was as though we were two pioneers in a rudimentary boat, setting off on a long journey together, far away from familiar land. This made me think of Yalom's suggestion that therapist and client can be seen as "fellow travellers" and that "we are all in this together and there is no therapist and no person immune to the inherent tragedies of existence" (Yalom, 2001). This feels particularly apt with regard to Samuel. Without the use of Gestalt experiential techniques and approaches (Perls, 1973), I am wondering how I am ever going to enable him to let me know how he feels (his self-professed goal for coming to see me). The moment in the session when I'm hit by the ironic thought that Samuel doesn't have the words to express how he feels as he doesn't have spoken words, nearly knocks me off balance. I'm wondering if it will ever be possible for him to express how he is feeling.

I presented Samuel's therapeutic work to date to my Gestalt supervision group, but neither the group leader nor any of the group members had any experience of working with young people like Samuel. They were as perplexed as I was as to how I might reach him. During the week that followed, I saw my usual number of clients at the school but my mind kept returning to the conundrum of Samuel. Then a few days later, one of my colleagues from the supervision group kindly rang me and suggested that I obtain a book titled Inscapes of the Child's World by John Alan (1988) that included using practical arts-based approaches with children with serious illnesses and other special needs. I obtained the book from the library and hungrily devoured many of the ideas and stored them away for future use. But still I had nothing to use the following week with Samuel. Then synchronistically, whilst providing supervision for a drama therapist (who had been referred to me because of my experience with clients with special needs), she mentioned how working with postcards had been really helpful with one of her clients who due to a hearing impairment had little intelligible speech. I gathered together all the picture postcards that I could find and blanked out the reverse side. That weekend, I scoured the shops and obtained some packs of picture postcards to add to my new collection.

Now I was really keen to see if this would enable me to reach him. I was hopeful that this approach might give him some protection through the "embodied image" (Schaverien, 1999), so he could *show* me his feelings, which might be very difficult for him to *tell* me, especially if they were uncomfortable feelings or might make him feel embarrassed in some way. I also wondered if part of the reason this felt like a good way to work with him, was that it might provide some protection for *myself* from hearing too directly about his experience – which I was already finding painful to imagine. How to reach the different parts of this independent adolescent that must surely be caught in a conflict between wanting to be independent and push away the care, whilst also needing that very same care for survival? (Webber, 1991, Book 1). It seemed totally inadequate but armed with my picture postcards I felt almost ready to meet Samuel for his next session.

Snapshot 2: Trapped Octopus

Samuel comes into my room and immediately spells out the word "Hi" on his communication board. I smile and say: "Hello" and he meets my eyes solemnly. "Would you like to show me some of your feelings using chosen postcard images?" I say, probably rather too eagerly.

"Yes," he hits the word sitting on the bottom left-hand corner of his cardboard keyboard. Again I feel a rush of delight. I feel affirmed. He wants to use the picture postcards. When we look at each other this time, we both smile, and I feel more hopeful that I might be able to work with him this way. I suggest he selects a card from a pack (Dixit Harmonies Expansion Cards 2017) as I hold them up. Although I think if he has to hit the "Yes" or "No" on his keyboard every time, this will take longer than the 30 minutes we have left. A very long time ensues while Samuel sits there seemingly unresponsive as I turn over card after card feeling hopeless and disappointed. My emotion switches to alertness as he moves suddenly in his chair when a particular image appears and this jolts his head a fraction and he smiles. I feel elated and thus he chooses (see Figure 12.2). I say: "That makes me think of how many different forms of life there are and how quirky they can be." Samuel smiles.

Then I look more closely at his choice, and realise that the octopus is tangled up in a chain as well as being tossed around by the huge sea waves. This feels so apt for Samuel's situation in so many ways. I don't yet know if he chose the card because of the chains, so I say: "Oh goodness, look he's all caught up in a chain." Samuel jumps expressively in his chair – whether he chose the card for this reason or not, it appears he is relating to this aspect of the image now. In order to find out more, I ask him if he has any words to add to the picture. He indicates "No" on his board. So I find myself saying: "Well the image speaks without words, but for my part it makes me feel like the octopus is desperate to be saved from being trapped by chains in an unsafe world." Samuel jumps so much in his chair at this, that I feel I may just inadvertently have hit on something that he might want to communicate to me.

"Wow!" I say totally unoriginally and rather un-therapeutically. But it seems to be received as authentic by Samuel, as his expression now mirrors the delight that I felt earlier. Already he has shown me so much about his life, and how he feels; and already I feel deeply impacted by him. So Samuel was able to *show* me something about himself with his chosen card. But there was still much to discover about how I could enable him to communicate on a deeper level.

Figure 12.2 Octopus in Trouble.

Reflections After Snapshot 2

When I first meet Samuel, *he* is able to communicate efficiently using his communication board, but as I am still relatively new at the school, (that provides additional support for children with physical disabilities so they can be included in a mainstream school), I have yet to learn how to "hear" him effectively. Although Samuel spells out that he would like to tell me how he feels, I realise this could be very difficult as we don't yet have a relationship. I also realise we will have to learn together how best for Samuel to use art materials as neither of us has done this before. The suggestion from the drama therapist of using postcards was very helpful and it feels as though we have made a start in working experientially – a key component of my Gestalt training.

While reading the book by John Allan, I keep thinking, how could Samuel make his own pictures like some of the clients mentioned in this book? It must be frustrating enough that Samuel cannot speak, but equally how can he express himself through art, when he doesn't have the physical ability to freely move? This leads me to thinking that Samuel could perhaps use pictures that already exist to create a collage. So I gather together some pictures torn out of magazines and sitting inside my doubts I make a decision to try it. After all my Gestalt training emphasises the use of experimentation (Perls, 1973). Samuel is more confident with me now and he will surely let me know if he doesn't want to do what I'm suggesting.

Snapshot 3: Samuel's First Art Creation

Samuel is sitting opposite me. I'm full of anticipation about trying out collage. Laid out on the coffee table between us are some pictures. He looks at them and back at me and because he can't rifle through them independently, he raises his eyebrows and slightly moves his head. I receive the message as him questioning what is going on. Now that I can interpret his gestures and facial expressions more easily, I have to be careful not to anticipate too quickly what he might be feeling, and instead wait for him to express himself in his own way.

"I wondered if you'd like to make a collage of some of your feelings?" This feels somewhat directive but neither Samuel nor I have any experience of how using the art materials is going to work. Samuel hits the "Yes" square on his cardboard keyboard. I am so gratified at his enthusiasm about making art. I suggest that I hold up different pictures and he selects those he would like to choose. He doesn't select any pictures though and he doesn't hit his communication board once. I feel so disappointed. He doesn't want to make a collage of his choices. Then suddenly he moves jerkily in his chair – almost as though he is in spasm – and indicates his first affirmative choice. I hold up the magazine image I have arrived at which is an advertisement depicting a bleak scene, from which I've cut out the product writing that was at the top. I lay it flat on the coffee table. He turns to his keyboard that is fixed to the arm of his chair, and spells out:

h-a-v-e space y-o-u space g-o-t space b-l-a-c-k space p-a-i-n-t?

"Yes I've got some black paint and brushes." I pour some runny black paint into a palette and as I'm reaching for a brush, Samuel starts to move around in his chair. As a therapist, I'm used to thinking at many levels simultaneously, but with Samuel, I have to be able to switch from one action to another equally fast. Almost spilling the paint, I decipher that he is indicating that instead of a brush I should use the piece of sponge that is alongside the brushes. "Do you mean I should put this sponge into the black paint and *print* with it?" He affirms my prediction of his communication and I feel a glow of satisfaction.

Samuel is looking full of anticipation and I have a wonderful rush of not knowing what's about to happen alongside a feeling that we are co-creating something totally new here. Samuel has chosen a bleak landscape that depicts a path through some fields within a large expanse of sky. I stick the image in the middle of a large sheet of white paper. Now I ask him where I should put the black paint sponge prints.

m–o–v–e space **t–h–e** space **s–p–o–n–g–e** space **o–v–e–r** space **t–h–e** space **p–i–c …**

"Ah right – you want me to hover the sponge over the picture until you indicate and then print there!" I feel really excited. Partly because I have understood him, but mainly because it's such a great idea of his and will mean he can actually create the picture himself, under my direction. I tell my mind to quieten its overdrive thinking that this would have so much applicability for Samuel (and others in his situation) with regards to creative work. Samuel is totally focussing on this picture in this moment and I need to be equally in the present with him.

I do what he has suggested and move the sponge carefully over the landscape image occasionally dripping bits of black paint by mistake. He squirms suddenly in his chair and in response, I lower the sponge onto the picture and gently make a sponge print. He smiles and I smile too. I move the sponge across the picture and he indicates where I should make a print. I smudge some sideways in the sky and he smiles, so I do it again. He then turns towards his board and I ask if he thinks that's enough and he smiles. I hold up the picture and we both sit and look at the extraordinarily atmospheric scene he has created. We sit for a long while taking in his first ever piece of art (see Figure 12.3).

Figure 12.3 Lost in an Empty World.

Eventually, I say: "Does it have a title?" He pauses for so long that I wonder if he can't think of one and then he begins to spell out:

l-o-s-t space **i-n** space **a-n** space **e-m-p-t-y** space **w-o** ....

"Lost in an empty world" I say out loud, as we both gaze at what he has produced. I dare to take a risk and name some of the momentousness of this session.

"You chose a picture of an empty landscape with a path through an open field. But together we found a way for you to *show* me how you feel." I think this naming of what just happened is more for my benefit than his, but he graciously acknowledges my comment with a hesitant smile. I'm left feeling elated that Samuel made his very first piece of art today. On the other hand, I still have a very strong sense that he hasn't yet expressed the main reason why he wanted to see me.

Reflections After Snapshot 3

I feel that now we have found a way to communicate and Samuel has learnt to direct me to create the art he wants to make, perhaps now is the time to go deeper. I feel he could be ready, but I have no idea how to reach the depths of his hidden feelings or experiences that he can't yet reveal. Now that the art is forming a bridge between us maybe I just need to "Trust the Process" (McNiff, 1998) and believe that continuing with the art making will mean I can reach him and his hidden depths will be revealed.

★★★★★★★★★★★★★★★★★★★★★

Around three months later, when Samuel had completed myriad variations of pictures of his feelings of being lost in a world where he felt he did not fit in, the following session takes place:

Snapshot 4: Breakthrough Moment

Samuel wheels himself into my room. I have been trying to help him to *show* me, what I sense he cannot *tell* me and based on the reading I have been doing about when to be client-centred and wait and when to be more directive, I have decided to make a suggestion today. I have also been reading about the power of using metaphor (Siegelman, 1990) to reach a client, who might be feeling they are not ready to state in words what is happening in their internal or external worlds (Sunderland, 2000). So I ask:

Remember how you said about that first picture you made that you felt 'lost in an empty world?' And how you also picked a postcard that showed an octopus tangled up and trapped by a chain seeming to be desperate for help in an unsafe world of huge waves?

Samuel leans towards his alphabet board and hits the "Yes" square.

"Well I'm wondering what landscape you would choose for how you are feeling today?" I'm aware that I'm hoping he will think of a metaphor that shows that the therapy has helped him to move into a more positive place and that he won't be feeling so stuck and alone. So I'm not at all prepared for what he actually spells out:

I space **f-e-e-l** space **I'm** space **i-n** space **a** space **P-i-t** space **o-f** space **D-e-s-p-a-I-r.**

I'm totally caught off guard by the wave of desperation that instantly encompasses me. I have to force myself to breathe. I remind myself that this is about Samuel not me, and gather myself as best I can and ask him: "Could you tell me more about this pit?" I'm staying with the metaphor rather than asking him about the despair directly. Without any hesitation, as fast as his communication system allows, he spells out:

"**I-t-s** space **b-i-g** space **b-l-a-c-k** space **a-n-d** space **b-l-e-a-k.**" He pauses and looks up at me. I swallow and remain silent and attentive.

"**I'm** space **t-r-a-p-p-e-d** space **i-n** space **i-t** space **f-o-r-e-v-e-r.**" I'm caught in a powerful vortex of my own feelings and am completely immobilised. I try to push aside the feelings of self-doubt that are flooding my mind that the therapy has not helped him at all and force myself to think that he needed this time to reach a place of trust. Then Samuel breaks the spell of my frozen state by spelling out:

"**W-i-l-l** space **y-o-u** space **d-r-a-w** space **i-t** space **f-o-r** space **m-e** space **p-l——?**" Oh the relief of being released from my unyielding state. I gather everything ready and draw a rough outline of a pit with boulders and stones to his directions.

With the Pit of Despair between us on the coffee table, we sit like this until almost the end of the session. I feel I can no longer reach him, but I do feel as though I am quite literally sitting alongside him at the bottom of his Pit of Despair. It feels as though his desperation is like a fog pervading the therapy room. Towards the end of the session, I find myself saying:

"We can sit together in your Pit of Despair as long as you need to…" I am still sensing that Samuel has something he wants to tell me but he is frozen by the despair of not being able to tell me. I feel it is important for now that he knows that I'll wait with him for as long as it takes.

Reflections After Snapshot 4

By this time, we have been working in a client-centred way for many weeks. Samuel was also finding ways to feel a sense of agency and autonomy emerging out of his previous sense of helplessness and experience a stronger sense of self (Mollon, 1977) by showing me how he was feeling through his newly acquired ability to create art. I have been empathising at a deep, bodily level how it feels to be Samuel. But now he is not on his own as I am there alongside him. I speak about him in supervision and my wise supervisor says I will know when it is time for change. Kottler reminds us that what brings about change is frequently not something the therapist has said or done, but rather: "a cascade of events that occurred indirectly or tangentially from" the client's experience (Kottler, 2014). I am hopeful that Samuel will show me or tell me when the time is right and he will at last feel able to reveal what he has been hiding. When Samuel arrives for his next session, I look across at him and something about his demeanour leads me to intuitively feel that now is the moment to suggest a change...

Snapshot 5: Climbing Out of the Pit of Despair

Samuel wheels himself into my room. I say: "I said I would sit with you in your Pit of Despair as long as you needed but if you feel you could imagine a change, what might that look like?" Samuel looks suddenly flushed and moves around in his chair in an agitated way and I wonder if this is too directive or too soon for him, but then he says something that I was not at all expecting: **I** space **a–m** space **j–u–s–t** space **b–e–g–i–n–n–i–n–g** space **t–o** space **c–l–i–m–b** space **o–u–t** space **o–f** space **t–h–e** space **p–i–t**.

We exchange tentative smiles. Something deeply important has just happened. All my reading about using metaphor in therapy suggests that the therapist encourages the client to stay within the metaphor until they might feel ready to make a more literal statement. So I ask him what kind of shoes he is wearing as he climbs out of the Pit of Despair. He says he has on climbing boots and will I please draw him climbing out of the Pit. I draw an approximation of a climbing boot, cut it out and am just sticking it onto his original Pit of Despair drawing when Samuel colours up and it feels as though something pivotal is hanging in the air. Perhaps he is starting to move out of the impasse. So I'm knocked completely off balance when he shakily points to letters on his alphabet board and spells out:

M–y space **k–e–y –w–o–r–k–e–r** space **h–i–t–s** space **m–e...**

Figure 12.4 Climbing Out of the Pit of Despair.

I feel as though *I* have been hit. My mind is blank. I am frozen in silence. Then after what seems like an eternity, my mind starts whirring. What should I do? What can I say? I swallow to keep the pressing tears at bay. Of course, I know what my training's Code of Ethics says I must do. It's totally clear what has to happen now. But I keep imagining how Samuel is dependent for his personal care on the very same person that is abusing him. I can't just follow the rules, that feels too cruel. I look at him with his head bowed over his alphabet board. I sense he is struggling to hold back the tears. I'm not managing to hold back mine. I instinctively reach out to touch his arm, whilst completely inadequately saying:

> Oh Samuel. That is terrible. It shouldn't be happening. We have to tell someone today and we have to stop it ever happening again.

On hearing this, he points out his reply through the tears that he can no longer contain:

> **B–u–t** space **h–e** space **i–s** space **m–y** space **b–e–s–t** space **f–r–i–e–n–d** …

I feel so sad. My chest hurts. I feel torn in two. Surely this is a microcosm of what Samuel might be feeling? Here is this person who looks after him, sees to his personal needs, who has been hitting him. And yet Samuel sees him as his best friend in all the world. No doubt they sometimes have fun and know each other well but I *have* to tell the Named Person for safeguarding at the school and they will *have* to contact his Residential Home. What happens then is out of our hands. I feel the weight of responsibility in this moment, as I can clearly see that for Samuel, life will never be the same again. What is more will Samuel cease to trust me? It has taken so long to reach him but he may blame me forever for turning his world upside down.

★★★★★★★★★★★★★★★★★★★

I send a message to the teacher of his next lesson, and as I have a space in my schedule, Samuel and I spend the next hour speaking about what has to happen next. Samuel is distraught, but I can see that a part of him knows he had to tell someone. I believe working through the art enabled him to *show* me what he couldn't *tell* me. I say some of this to him and he indicates his "Yes" square. So we talk about these two parts of him (Spiegel, 2017) – and he tells me the hitting has got worse recently and a part of him knows it has to stop and yet another part of him doesn't want to get his beloved Key Worker into trouble and doesn't want to lose him as a friend. By the end of the next hour, he agrees to come with me to tell the deputy head what he has told me. He understands that it has to be him that says it. "This is you exercising your human right to say 'yes' or 'no' for yourself" I explain to him (quoted in Webber, 1991, book 4). I assure him that I *know* that what he is telling me is true and that it has happened more than once – he jerks affirmatively in his chair. I tell him that I feel as though I'm being torn in two by the dilemma he finds himself in and what I know we have to do. He jumps in his chair, and almost bashes the Yes on his chart. At last he reluctantly but decisively wheels himself out of the therapy room, with me trailing behind. We make our way to the Deputy Head's room.

Samuel spells out what he has told me for the Deputy Head. She clearly has difficulty keeping the distress out of her voice. She too reassures Samuel that it will never happen again and after some further reassurances, he goes back to class escorted by his favourite support assistant. It feels unreal but I am extremely proud that Samuel has found a way to give voice to his horrific secret.

That very same day an emergency multidisciplinary meeting is called. Ten professionals meet to go over the facts as we know them. As if in a dream I attend whilst the hardest joint decision this group of professionals has ever had to make is arrived at: that Samuel will never go back to that residential home and the key-worker in question will be dealt with according to the policies and procedures of the residential home. His social worker manages to find Samuel temporary accommodation with his respite carers, whilst a new residential home is sought. On top of everything else, Samuel has to be moved away from the area and the school. In one moment Samuel thus loses his home, his school, his therapist, his beloved key worker, and his best friend. There was no opportunity for a series of therapeutic "ending" sessions. By the next day Samuel had gone.

Reflections After Snapshot 5

The impact that this had on me was profound. I felt as though I had been punched in the stomach and I continued to feel desperate for and about Samuel whilst having to go through the all-important procedure of ensuring that from now on Samuel was physically safe. He had already been emotionally hurt and I couldn't prevent him from feeling even more pain. A few weeks later supervision helped me to understand cognitively why I was impacted so profoundly both bodily and emotionally. My natural empathy, compassion and liking for Samuel, would most probably have combined with reactive counter-transference (Clarkson, 1995) – feeling many of Samuel's feelings – alongside proactive countertransference – activating feelings for my own "inner child" (Bradshaw, 1999) and the lack of safety in my own childhood.

Reflections on the Multidisciplinary Meeting

The multidisciplinary meeting of ten professionals was deeply disturbing to attend but at least it meant there was a shared decision, so that no *one* person had to carry the responsibility on their own. The decision the team faced concerned either Samuel having a different Key Worker at his residential home and thus being able to stay on at our school, or removing him from the home. Eventually, after several hours of harrowing discussion, the latter was chosen. I found this deeply disturbing not least because my work with Samuel had been all about giving him a voice and I believe he did indeed find a way to speak up and speak out. However, the outcome of this was that his whole life was upturned. I was no longer empowering him to give voice to what he wanted. In truth, what I imagined he wanted was impossible; to stay on at the home with the same key worker and not be abused any more.

The British Association for Counselling and Psychotherapy (BACP) Ethical framework for the Counselling Professions (2018), states as one of its principles, the importance of "justice: the fair and impartial treatment of all clients...." Was what happened to Samuel fair and just? It also outlines another ethical principle for therapists to have "autonomy: respect for the client's right to be self-governing." In this instance, Samuel was deemed to be at risk and he did not even have his views represented at this meeting. Was this right? He was only 12 years old and we professionals made decisions about his immediate future. Was that respecting his right to be "self-governing." What are the rights of children in these circumstances? The Children Act (1989) was in existence at this time, but I believe we were faced with an example of an unresolvable "Ethical Dilemma." An occasion where it was "impossible to reconcile all the applicable principles" and it was necessary to choose between them. It helped to be reminded in supervision that "a course of action does not necessarily become unethical merely because it is contentious or because other practitioners might have reached different conclusions in a similar situation" (BACP Ethical Framework).

I'm still unsure if this was in fact the best decision, but it was felt to be the safest for Samuel and would provide him with a context that didn't continually remind him of the trauma. To be abused by a care provider has the potential to create a deep fissure within a person's sense of self. The person can become stuck in crisis or turmoil, or "terminal ambivalence" (Fisher, 2017).

The power of the work with Samuel has never left me. It shaped the importance of such moments in my thinking as a therapist from that moment forward. It led me to train as an Integrative Arts Psychotherapist and later to research into breakthrough moments and present my findings in a book titled Breakthrough Moments in Arts-Based Psycho therapy (2017).

I think Samuel was hard to reach in three main ways. Firstly, he was hard to communicate with as he was pointing at letters on a keyboard to spell out words as his mode of communication in his therapy sessions and this was something with which I was unfamiliar. Secondly, he was not independently physically able to paint, draw, cut up pictures, or make his own art. Thirdly, it was hard to reach him in the sense that he had something he desperately wanted to tell me whilst simultaneously being strongly defended against telling me. However, I feel that together we did in fact reach each other, with art, metaphor and symbol as the bridge between us and Samuel found a way to tell me what he couldn't tell me.

References

Alan, J. (1988). *Inscapes of the Child's World: Jungian Counselling in Schools and Clinics*. US: Spring Publications.

Bradshaw, J. (1999). *Home Coming: Reclaiming and Championing Your Inner Child*. London: Piatkus.

British Association for Counselling and Psychotherapy (BACP). (2018). *Ethical Framework for Good Practice.*

Clarkson, P. (1995). *The Therapeutic Relationship.* London: Whurr.

Dixit Harmonies Expansion Cards. (2017). *Libellud ASMDIX10EN.*

Fisher, J. (2017). *Healing the Fragmented Selves of Trauma Survivors: Overcoming Internal Self-Alienation.* London: Routledge.

Kottler, J.A. (2014). *Change.* New York: Oxford University Press.

Mann, D. (2010). *Gestalt Therapy: 100 Key Points & Techniques.* London: Routledge.

McNiff, S. (1998). *Trust the Process.* Boston, MA: Shambhala.

Mollon, P. (1977). *The Fragile Self: The Structure of Narcissistic Disturbance.* London: Whurr Publishers Ltd.

Perls, F. (1973). *The Gestalt Approach & Eye Witness to Therapy.* New York: US Science & Behaviour Books.

Schaverien, J. (1999). *The Revealing Image.* London: Jessica Kingsley.

Siegelman, E.Y. (1990). *Metaphor & Meaning in Psychotherapy.* New York & London: The Guildford Press.

Spiegel, L. (2017). *Internal Family Systems Therapy with Children.* New York & London: Routledge.

Sunderland, M. (2000). *Using Story Telling as a Therapeutic Tool with Children.* Milton Keynes: Speechmark.

The Children Act (1989). Known as the Children's Charter. An Act for the Prevention of Cruelty to, and better protection of, children. Establishes the legislative framework for the current child protection system in England and Wales. Followed by The Children Act 2004.

Webber, A. (1991). Book 1. In Association with RADAR. *Independence and Integration: Dunstable: Folens.* (1) Living Skills for students with physical disabilities. (2) Pre-vocational skills for students with physical disabilities. (3) Sport & mobility for students with physical disabilities. (4) Inservice: practical approaches, attitudes and equipment for staff working alongside students with physical disabilities.

Webber, A. (2017). *Breakthrough Moments in Arts-Based Psychotherapy.* London: Karnac.

Yalom, I.D. (2001). *The Gift of Therapy: Reflections on Being a Therapist.* London: Piatkus.

Chapter 13

Why Can't You Reach Me?

Amy McInerny

Introduction

This chapter presents the findings taken from research undertaken within my psychotherapeutic counselling. The study explored the meanings young people with cancer attach to seeking, accepting and declining psychological support through counselling. The young people I interviewed for my research spoke eloquently and movingly about their cancer experiences and whether the counselling they were offered did or did not help them. In this chapter, I have presented a synopsis of their experiences incorporating some of their actual words and how their opinions and different themes arising link with my experience of young people with cancer and with the literature.

Buddy

Buddy was upbeat, chatty and immediately struck me as particularly resilient. His account demonstrated an almost impenetrable capacity to remain positive through his diagnosis and treatment with little suggestion of defences. He was an 18-year-old university student when diagnosed with Hodgkin's lymphoma – a disease curable through multiple intensive rounds of chemotherapy. Three years on, Buddy's life is pretty much back on track, yet I was still struck by the calm and thoughtful way he recollected his cancer treatment. Buddy talked much more about the gains of the experience – a phenomenon now referenced in Teenagers and Young Adults with Cancer (TYAC) literature as "post traumatic growth" (Zebrack et al., 2015). He reported having a greater appreciation of life and his cherished family relationships. Buddy's adaptive coping style and positive mindset meant counselling did not feel needed, he was able to process, assimilate and cope with the shock of diagnosis and unavoidable disruption to his daily life through an internal process of positive self-talk, reinforced by his family and treatment team.

Penny

Similarly, Penny chose not to accept frequent offers of structured counselling sessions. Unlike Buddy, she was in a precarious clinical position when interviewed

DOI: 10.4324/9781003163015-13

(being recently informed that Acute Lymphoblastic Leukemia, diagnosed three years previously, had spread to her brain). Despite this, Penny genuinely appeared to be coping well, being supported by her devoted family to manage the highs and lows of treatment. She was funny, cheery even, with what seemed a naturally mindful outlook, enabling her to surrender to the uncertainty. Perhaps there were bigger, darker feelings lurking, but I never felt these were being fought against. If they were, then they seemed certainly not to be winning. There were moments of sadness yes, particularly around lost opportunities to be a "normal" teen, doing "normal" things. For years, her life had revolved around the hospital. Penny felt no need to accept a counselling offer, although appreciated all the ad-hoc support offered to her on the ward as it offered an outlet, familiarity and distraction. Penny told me "there is nothing that I can do in terms of my treatment or whatever, there is no way of changing what happens. I feel like what happens, happens."

Buddy and Penny displayed remarkable levels of resilience, instantly challenging what I imagine are widely held assumptions about young people with cancer. They confirmed that many young people can cope and overcome adversity without needing or wanting formal professional help. They reminded me about the dangers of pity – the risks of underestimating the inner strength of those faced with even the biggest challenges. Both spoke of a need for support during treatment but not the intense, therapeutic intervention you might expect. Portnoy et al. writing specifically about Teenagers and Young Adults with Cancer (TYAC) pose a reminder that "intensive psychological approaches are not always appropriate, necessary, practical or wanted during cancer treatment" (Portsoy et al., 2016).

The Study

It was my postgraduate studies at the University of Cambridge that provided me with the opportunity to finally attend to the "bee in my bonnet," developed from professional observations that I had found both frustrating and motivating throughout my career: that it is essential that both the service and individual therapists within it must be flexible enough to reach each young person in the individual way that is required by that young person. In my mind, I held a catalogue of "missed opportunities." These were young people I had encountered, all with potential to build meaningful relationships with professionals, yet who were often left on the perimeters of therapeutic support. There appeared to exist a tension – a profound disconnect between what was being offered to young people – both by service providers and individuals and what was needed and desired by the young people themselves. It seemed a possibility that the essential conditions of engagement, particularly in relation to counselling and psychological support were lacking. So, I undertook a study investigating just what constitutes optimum conditions that enable young people encountering distress and adversity, to seek and sustain therapeutic contact. I did this in the most meaningful way I knew how – by talking to young people directly and accepting them as experts in their own psychological worlds. A framework of "Interpretative Phenomenological Analysis"

(Smith et al., 2009), underpinned by a humanistic and deeply reflexive philosophy, allowed me to gain insight of shared themes across the study group, whilst not losing focus on the value of everyone's unique experience.

I focused on a population where prolonged psychological anguish is prevalent. Where clinically significant levels of anxiety, depression and post-traumatic stress are commonplace (Kosir et al., 2018). These were young people living with and beyond cancer and I present more of the wisdom that they shared in the rest of this chapter.

Frankie

Frankie was 21 when diagnosed with acute myeloid leukemia, literally on the cusp of qualifying to work in the career of her dreams. From the offset of our conversation, I was in awe of her openness and self-knowledge. She shared with me the adverse childhood experiences (ACE) that had left her with entrenched relational distrust and a sense of being undeserving of help. Multiple clinical set-backs had reduced her chances of survival, triggering deep periods of depression, Frankie told me "I just couldn't see the light at the end of the tunnel anymore". Counselling felt particularly out of reach to her – she needed time to accept support and even more time to feel safe within it. A noted benefit of the hospital service was an openness to offer support at any point of treatment meaning that Frankie could begin sessions when she felt it was the right time. However, the adult, "talking based" approach felt intrusive, prescriptive and overly formal to her. The short session model meant the pace felt too fast and she felt she was encouraged to go too deep, too soon. A lack of creative materials gave her nowhere to hide – "it was basically just talking which for me isn't good". She soon disengaged.

Megan

Similarly, Megan was emerging into adulthood, in a loving relationship and enjoying her newly acquired independence when aged 24, she was diagnosed with bone cancer. By the time of our interview, Megan had undergone complex surgery, narrowly avoiding limb amputation and was awaiting further chemotherapy. She was softly spoken and incredibly eloquent – her language was poetic, bursting with metaphors that conjured up vivid and sometimes disturbing imagery to describe her experience. Megan had not accessed any formal counselling partly due to an untimely transition out of TYA and into adult oncology services when she turned 25. A flexible counselling offer was no longer available to her at the point she was feeling most in need. This had left her feeling overlooked and abandoned, provoking sadness and anxiety. Megan and Frankie's stories as they develop throughout the chapter will alert you to the limitations of words in therapy, the benefits of incorporating creative methods and perhaps above all else, being wary of applying adult models to young, still developing minds.

Lily

Determining whether young people are happily hidden or, albeit unconsciously, desperate to be found requires significant expertise. Too often, young people are left lost in their distress, rather than being helped to emerge from their defences through the building of relationships and creation of safe therapeutic spaces. Listening to Lily would cause me to frequently return to an observation made by Winnicott who stated: "It is a joy to be hidden, and disaster not to be found" (Winnicott, 1965/2018).

Lily, shell shocked by a diagnosis of Hodgkin's Lymphoma reflects this notion. Speaking about her diagnosis she told me: "It made me feel angry because I thought 'I am Lily. I should not have this, what the hell, this is not normal to have at 18', and I just kept dwelling on the fact that I was so young." I sensed with Lily that the interview was cathartic and that despite now being physically well, she is still making sense of an experience that shook her to the core. She sounded nervous but determined – this interview mattered to her, and she needed to be heard. Lodged into a dissociative cage, pinging between a state of flight and freeze, Lily needed someone to notice her suffering and see beyond her calm exterior, to notice and offer a hand to pull her out of the darkness. Being overlooked prolonged her distress until long after her treatment had ended. Lily told me: "If somebody tapped into what I was actually feeling I think they would get a glimpse of what I truly felt like and obviously it was not a great thing." Hearing how her pain had been overlooked, how she was never visited by counsellors tasked with reaching out to her, evoked in me a familiar stirring of anger and frustration. Her invisibility struck a chord. It was Lily more than any other who forced me into a deep space of reflexivity – to ensure I was remaining true to her story, that it was not being blurred with my own.

The Young People

Young people with cancer face psychological challenge to the extreme. Diagnosis leaves little choice but to begin a navigation of what is a flood of physical, social and emotional threat and change during what is already understood to be the most tumultuous period of the human life course – adolescence and young adulthood.

These are young people who have lived through the unthinkable, who for some remain uncertain what the future holds. Buddy, Penny, Rose, Frankie, Lily and Megan were all aged between 16 and 24; immersed in the innocence, adventure and self-discovery of youth when cancer crashed into their lives. Diagnosed with blood, bone and brain cancers, enduring chemotherapy, radiotherapy, transplants, surgery and so very much more, each has individual stories to tell, all are united in the absolute unfairness of being so very ill, so very young. With profound openness, eloquence and courage, they describe the emotional impact that the disease incurred and share what they felt they needed from the counselling service on offer via their treatment centre, in order to process, cope and move on with their lives.

The Hope

Over many months, I read and reread, listened, analysed and considered the meanings imbedded within each interview transcript. I was committed to gaining a unique understanding of each interview's experience, both individually and collectively. I hoped that through gaining understanding of how counselling services were perceived and experienced, I could share new learning with colleagues in the field of psychosocial support, not just for young people with cancer but beyond in a way that can inform practice – even if it's on the most micro of levels. I hope that by tuning in to the wisdom of these young people you may gain new understandings of how your approach can be adapted to ensure you are always within reach.

Can You Reach Me?

Understanding young people's help-seeking behaviours is an established area of research. "Self-stigma" and the need to "go it alone" frequently appear as explanations for the population's limited engagements in therapeutic support (Freake et al., 2007; Gulliver et al., 2010). Yet I questioned whether these were the only factors contributing to what was observed to be a paradoxical pattern within the TYAC support service in which my study was based. Here, many young people were known to be experiencing high levels of distress yet were infrequently engaging with the free and accessible counselling provision. Despite a service being available to specifically meet their emotional needs, young patients often sought alternative sources of psychosocial support through social workers, nurses, chaplains and youth workers. This suggested a curious and unique disconnect with the counselling on offer that I felt warranted being understood. What emerged was experiences of support that were both relational, environmental and intra-psychic. Narratives raised questions of just what enables the therapeutic relationship, how trauma is attended to and what approaches to therapy are welcomed rather than resisted.

Reaching Out in a Pandemic

The global pandemic posed a huge threat to my study taking place – I had many moments where I was close to defeat after what felt like a never-ending barrage of setbacks and delays. Constant revaluing of how my research design could be adapted to retain a connectedness to the young people I wanted to interview, through remote means, was exhausting – losing the study entirely was a painful and not unrealistic threat. My participants felt further out of reach by the day. It required tenacity, determination, flexibility and creativity to ensure the study happened. I realise now the process ran in parallel to what would be revealed in the findings of the research itself. These are the exact qualities needed to be adopted by professionals and by services to reach those waiting to be reached.

The whole process took place in my bedroom. Vicariously welcoming cancer back into my life felt non-negotiable. Having spent precious years myself working in a TYAC service, I knew that there were voices that needed to be heard, stories that had to be told. The experience was as painful at times as I knew it would be. It evoked memories of so many young people loved and lost, so much suffering and sadness witnessed.

As spring became summer, and summer became autumn, I remained in my bedroom, immersed in the thousands of words shared – drawn into these private worlds and breathing in air thick with guilt, fear, loss and anger, alongside positivity, hope and courage.

I was unexpectedly aware in telephone interviews of the powerful emotional sensations I was experiencing – a felt sense which reassured me that the connection I feared would be lost through distance, was present and real. At times, it was suffocating and by the end, relentless. I am certain the silence and isolation of lockdown research intensified this. I lacked the distractions, distance and relationships of working in the hospital. I was more present than I have perhaps ever been and as the interviewing drew to a close, I felt as if I might drown in the unshed tears of those I had listened to. A strategy employed to enable functioning in the world in the aftermath of their disease, or for some the existential threats still imminent, I imagined many had simply split off their overwhelming trauma. Profound loss and fear were largely expressed in an understated affect, recalled with calm reflection. In the stillness of lockdown, words felt heavier, more poignant. I can recollect my throat tightening and chest sinking when listening to their pain. Loneliness washed over me after the recording stopped. I would walk to clear my head, to try and ignore the feelings of anger, unfairness and powerlessness that crushed from within. Empty lockdown streets reflected my deep existential isolation and aloneness.

Most of the young people told me that speaking on the phone had helped them feel more at ease. A lack of gaze and physical closeness had welcomed a stream of consciousness and created a secure position from which to express their inner worlds. Many said they forgot, at times, I was even listening. Some found this was their first opportunity to create a chronological narrative of their cancer experience. I was amazed. Was the research process even in part mimicking enabling conditions of therapy? Even those most vehemently opposed to counselling spoke with such fluency and ease. Why, I wondered?

Themes Arising from the Interviews

Part of my research approach was to extrapolate themes that arose in the interviews as to why the counselling offered to the young people was or was not what they needed. I present a summarised version and analysis of some of these here.

Barriers From Within

Several internal inhibitors to therapeutic contact emerged in the narratives – yet none so much as guilt. Every single young person described guilt as the strongest emotional influence on how counselling was perceived and its role in propelling them to cope with their distress alone. Although guilt has a function, as posited by Klein (1939/1998) as critical for social regulation, it soon becomes maladaptive when it inflicts punishment on the self (Bastin et al., 2016). Certainly, feelings of guilt within the group were of the latter, fuelled by a sense of wasting professional time and convinced that others were more deserving. A common thread was in relation to loved ones, fearful of causing further worry on top of already existing anxiety relating to the cancer itself.

A cognitive dissonance was apparent throughout, whereby interviewees knew they were not to blame for their disease yet bore an overwhelming sense of responsibility: "Obviously it's not my fault but I do feel bad that I have put them [family] through all of that stuff of being ill" said Rose. Lily's presentation of guilt was rooted in distress despite having a curable diagnosis. She felt unworthy of help because "the aspect of dying from it was never a thing to me so I felt guilty". As described by Megan, this was compounded by feelings of being a burden: "In my brain why would I inflict any more pain on them?". "I did not like showing if I was upset or that it was not going to be alright because I knew that it would negatively affect everyone especially my parents".

For some, the sense of guilt appeared grounded in low self-worth. Frankie articulated this: "I always feel like I am wasting professional time and it makes me really anxious because I always feel like there is someone else that needs it more than I do". "I feel like it's never that serious or that there is always someone sicker than me or struggling more than me".

Hitting Rock Bottom

For many, only hitting "rock bottom" made counselling permissible. Lily said, "I had to push myself to the point where I was almost screaming for help because I don't think that I would have accepted it on my own". Frankie told me that "I just feel like I should be able to deal with it on my own because I should be strong enough to deal with it on my own" and Megan shared that "the whole asking for help thing was the last resort for me".

Service design, targeting early emergence and adopting preventive approaches to mental health are surely essential components of working with young people. In order to counteract the drive to "go it alone," an understanding of the developmental needs of the TYA age range is crucial. Particularly pertinent is recognising the need in young people to maintain agency and control. Considering how this can be attended to in service design and within the therapeutic relationship is essential.

Falling Forever

Rose had experienced a lack of containment in previous counselling relationships, leaving her with a sense that her emotions were harmful and contagious. Both Megan and Rose were terrified of psychologically unravelling. They did not trust that they could survive therapy.

Captured by Winnicott's theory of "primitive anxieties" and "falling forever" (Spelman, 2013), Rose feared she lacked sufficient strength to prevent ego disintegration:

> I feel like if I did really think in depth about it all and really digest it, like I said, I just think I would, I don't know, I just don't think that I could mentally recover from it, I just don't know how I would deal with it.

Her fears were reinforced by the lack of containment she experienced in therapy: "they [counsellors] would actually cry sometimes when I would talk about the stuff I went through. I felt bad and I felt that I was then counselling them, I felt bad that I had made them cry". Rose appeared to have introjected a sense that her feelings were dangerous, that she contaminated and overwhelmed anyone exposed to them, increasing her guilt. It is for the reader to interpret what the intention of the tearful therapist may have been – an expression of authenticity or empathy? This rupture scarred Rose's sense of self and has had long-lasting implications for her perception of therapy.

Agency and Control

Young people with cancer often reported to me a sense of feeling infantilised by well-meaning professionals and desperately anxious family members. Compas highlights that the lack of control, synonymous with serious illness, impacts directly on young people's capacity to apply active coping strategies (Compas et al., 2012). Rose's narrative was riddled with imposed powerlessness as she described the responses of both medical professionals and family as her mood deteriorated during treatment. No doubt well-intentioned efforts to encourage engagement in counselling in fact further reduced her agency and perpetuated her distress, eventually she succumbed. She told me that [counselling] "felt quite forced if I am being honest, like I had to do it. A lady always used to come in even though I said I didn't really want to have our sessions anymore". "They would say I was depressed but I said I wasn't depressed, then they said that's what a depressed person would say. I just didn't see how I would get out of that".

Megan also appeared to experience a deep fear of exploring her emotional world and connected this to feeling a loss of control. It is as if the "safe hands" of the doctors, medicines and treatment plans did not translate into psychological professions "dealing with inner emotions, I feel is more out of my control." It occurred to me that knowledge around physical health is much more openly shared. Whereas medics are encouraged to share their knowledge of disease, processes of treatments and plans for recovery, this is not always the case in psychotherapy. Redistributing psychological knowledge and unshrouding mysterious therapeutic processes is a change of practice I would certainly welcome.

One Size Fits All?

Penny impressed me with her ability to compress profound existential ideas and acute observations into simple, matter-of-fact statements. "There is no definite in any of it. Even if it's the same cancer its still different because how you take it is different". Later she returned to the theme of individualism: "everyone is different, and everyone needs to express themselves in their own way."

All the young people stressed the importance of retaining an individual identity. Every young person processed and coped with diagnosis, treatment and recovery in differently ways. Without an adaptive and individualised approach to psychological support, the therapeutic response to multifarious needs will risk being seriously inadequate. Although many therapists may opt to practice a singular modality, I am of the view that this is ill-fitting to work with this age group. I believe establishing a pluralistic offer should be central to the design of any service tasked with providing therapeutic support for young people.

Therapeutic offers that actively optimise choice and individuation not only work in parallel with young people's developmental processes but also account for their varied communication styles whilst actively promoting critical agency and control (Geldard et al., 2019). A pluralistic approach to therapy (Cooper & Dryden, 2016) is ideal for eliciting a young client's sense of agency and control in the process through its recognition that different people benefit from different therapeutic methods at different times. Pluralistic ideas create a fluidity and responsiveness that parallels the rapid evolving of "self," associated with adolescence. Rather than adopting assumptions of what clients need, collaborative dialogues are created providing fundamental opportunities for young clients to voice their needs and priorities and clearly state their communication and relational preferences.

Responding to Trauma

Unlike younger children, TYAs find themselves exposed to the full extent of the physical and psychological challenges posed by the disease leading to levels of trauma experienced uniquely by every patient. Providing therapy to people living in trauma and in its aftermath requires specialised training, skill and approach.

Interviews revealed counselling experiences, even from therapists based within TYAC services, had at times been retraumatising. This provoked in me ethical questions around safe practices in delivering counselling support to this unique population. Rose described her counselling sessions whilst undergoing treatment: "You're sitting in a room with someone and them just asking how you are, what has been going on, yeah just kind of relaying the whole situation which I hated". People will instinctively avoid the threat of traumatisation by resisting or disengaging from counselling (Denborough, 2014). High levels of disengagement within the study site service, along with the self-reports of participants may reflect that young people were perceiving a lack of safety within the counselling offered.

Portnoy et al. express concern for the narrative within oncology that troubling feelings should be encouraged to be expressed (Portnoy et al., 2016). Rose's experience reflected this, telling me: "I wanted to be distracted and sometimes they [clarified as referring to medics, counsellor and parents] didn't understand that, they thought talking about it would make things better but that's the opposite of what I wanted." For her, counselling eroded rather than improved her capacity to cope, overwhelming her with the thoughts and feelings she was instinctively trying to avoid. Yuen advocates for the deconstruction of a "no pain, no gain" discourse, instead promoting "less pain, more gain" approaches such as narrative therapy (Yuen, 2009). The creative arts therapies may be well positioned to enable this additional layer of psychological safety through their capacity to "reveal and conceal" traumatic material within the metaphor. Rose alluded to this when describing conversations with the hospital chaplain:

> With the Chaplain, I wasn't really directly talking about the situation I was in. We were just kind of speaking about things hypothetically, so it wasn't kind of real what we were talking about. I didn't like counselling because it was talking about me and my stuff – it made me overthink it.

The risk of "traumatisation" (White, 2005) increases when "single-storied" accounts of distressing experiences are encouraged to be retold. Rose recalled counselling as being problem saturated: "obviously with counselling you are just talking about hospital, hospital, hospital." Whilst experiencing long periods of clinical uncertainty, Rose lacked the safety of a metaphorical "riverbank" (Portnoy et al., 2016) from which to observe her experiences. She literally had no safe space when engaging in counselling sessions in a room on the cancer ward. I sensed a deep feeling of being trapped and prodded when Rose described counselling as "just kind of relaying the whole situation which I hated. It made me feel more anxious because it was present in my thoughts."

Being encouraged to accept counselling during active treatment likely also impacted on Frankie and Rose's negative experience of therapy. The constant presence of existential uncertainty was articulated by Rose: "I was aware of all possible worse scenarios" and then Frankie: "I was really scared of dying and being that ill and having that in the back of your head, every time you feel tired, I kept thinking "am I tired or am I actually really ill?"". "I kept telling everyone that it would be okay. Really deep down, I really did think that I was going to die in transplant". Lily was also bombarded with fears on top of gruelling, "horrid" side effects: "[the thought of] people knowing that I had cancer was so daunting and quite honestly petrifying to me". She felt in a state of "just pure shock, all of the negative emotions" that remained throughout her treatment and spiralling "down into a horrid dark hole." Risks of vicarious trauma are also a constant threat due to the hospital environment. Frankie would turn to counselling in the hope it would help her through a particularly "dark" period when she was told her bone marrow transplant had failed, significantly lowering her chance of survival: "she [the counsellor] would say "how are you feeling?" and I would say "I'm scared of dying" and she would say "why are you scared of dying" and it just didn't work for me...""

Essential to trauma work is creating safety and stabilisation – something that it is impossible to achieve whilst treatment is ongoing (Herman, 1992/1997; Havens, 1989). Megan reflected: "when you are in the thick of it, the last thing you want to be adding to the mix is my emotions. I wasn't ready to tackle my emotions". Appropriate training is required to recognise and maximise opportunities for processing, coping and integration when young people are in active treatment. Currently, the World Health Organization (2013) recommends that "Cognitive Behavioural Therapy (CBT)" and "Eye Movement Desensitisation and Reprogramming (EMDR)" are the only appropriate therapies for traumatised young people. Yet, despite a lack of empirical studies (Crenshaw, 2006), pioneers in the field of adult traumatology (Ogden, 2006; Van der Kolk, 2015) and child trauma therapy (Levine & Kline, 2006; Perry, 2017; Treisman, 2017) promote a range of creative and embodied approaches to trauma-based therapy.

With such high levels of trauma within this population, it is surprising that the support services embedded into the TYAC model can omit therapies shown to be safe and impactful both during and post traumatic experiences, whether it be CBT or Arts-based models that can "prevent more serious and prolonged emotional damage" (Carey, 2006). More concerning still is the fact that counsellors appear to be working in this field who can offer neither.

Beyond Words

Whilst play is largely accepted as the natural communication device of children, TYAs can often remain uncomfortably positioned within adult dyadic models of psychotherapy. Without the safety of the metaphor synonymous with the arts, didactic "talking only" approaches can quickly feel intolerable. I was warmed hearing Megan talk about a beading intervention she had engaged with whilst recovering from surgery. The irony though was striking. Megan was my oldest interviewee and yet she was recounting the powerful impact of an intervention designed for paediatric cancer patients. A process of bead threading based on narrative therapy principles had enabled her to create a meaningful and coherent narrative of her illness experience. She told me "the beads reinforce actually the events that you have overcome and gives validation back to those points because it is actually all the little things that sort of make it more than that." Megan had no choice but to leave her beads incomplete. When she returned to her principal hospital for post-surgery chemotherapy, this offer was limited to the paediatric ward. Perhaps deemed inappropriate for TYAC patients too old to play and create. The creative arts provide "a language for the ineffable" (Barone & Eisner, 2011). I can think of few things more "ineffable" than the existential threat of cancer.

A Unique Relationship

It is widely accepted that in therapy, "nothing happens without at least a thread of relationship" (Oaklander, 2007). For the remainder of this chapter, we will hear final thoughts from Buddy, Penny, Lily, Rose and Frankie, all of whom reiterate the absolute need to feel invested in, understood and accommodated within the therapeutic relationship.

What is also apparent is that the therapeutic relationships required by young people are unique and need to be approached differently to other age groups. My work has led me to feel certain that dynamic, creative therapeutic processes — where the boundaries of the therapeutic frame are elastic — are imperative to sustain engagement and create change. Young people can be notably "more restless and uncertain" (Geldard et al., 2019) about the counselling process than older adults and approaches need to be adapted in response.

Lily explained, "The person who was counselling me, I know it sounds so hippy but I did not really connect with." Frankie prematurely ended her counselling because "it was too structured and set out for me". By her scheduled sessions, she "would be so far past talking about how I felt so it was pointless". The approach felt too formulaic and scripted: "as soon as I realised it was like a traditional kind of therapy session of 'how are you feeling and how does that make you feel' kind of thing I think I realised it wasn't going to work for me".

Silence can be a valuable therapeutic tool, yet younger clients can perceive it as confusing and threatening if not managed sensitively. Rose described counselling sessions as being "quite silent and I didn't like that." Lily told me "I know counsellors are people who should sit there and listen to you, but he almost did too much of that and at a young age I think I found that uncomfortable." The "quiet listener" seems ill-fitted to work with young people. Instead what is needed are approaches that prevent boredom and reduce discomfort (Geldard et al., 2019). This can be achieved through incorporating fundamental components of spontaneity, creativity and humour.

Above all else, young people appeared to value the human element of the professional relationships they made. Buddy spoke incredibly fondly about his social worker:

> she was there as a person that I could talk to, now whether she was a counsellor or a social worker or not, it didn't really make much of a difference to me. As far as I knew she was there every single time I had my treatment, she was lovely to talk to.

Lily also shared the value of her relationship with her social worker, explaining

> it was not counselling I would say, but I spoke with her and she would help me sift through my emotions and by doing that and her leaving my house it felt like my negative emotions were leaving with her.

By listening to the participants, it seemed that where professional relationships were successful it was where they felt most "whole." Where the physical, the social, the psychological merged. I wondered if sometimes formal counselling just feels too fragmenting — too focused on the specific problem and not enough time spent understanding the person holistically. This might be particularly apt for young people who are so desperately trying to integrate both cancer and non-cancer identities. Ultimately it seemed the strongest relationships were formed by professionals who demonstrated genuine curiosity and interest, who were attentive. Not simply there to listen but also cheerlead, to motivate, to distract and to help young people remember who they are.

Final Thoughts

I am now more convinced than ever that the way adolescent and young adult well-being is approached, both in and outside of the therapy room, needs to change. Young people living with and beyond cancer are first and foremost young people. Each one is an individual, living through their own unique experience of this horrid disease whilst navigating a tumultuous developmental period of rapid growth – full of conflict, discovery and fun. Even cancer cannot halt this natural drive. Young people need to feel authentic and real. They want to explore and confirm their emerging identities through relationships, art, music, sport. They want to be listened to and understood. They want professionals to reach them in ways that reflects this.

This research and my own professional experience has confirmed my previously untested intuitive feeling that there are very few young people who are truly "unreachable." Like others writing in the field of adolescent psychotherapy (Fuller, 2014; Geldard et al., 2019), I believe most young people who are suffering are receptive to support and able to form strong working alliances with helping professionals when the conditions allow. When a space is created that offers safety; when professionals welcome in creativity, humour and humility; when practice is flexible and adaptive to the individual; when the relationship is truly at the centre, powerful connections can be made with even those most lost, traumatised, defended and distrustful.

Young people need *us* to be authentic and real. They need us to be human! Young people need us to be dynamic and flexible and creative and dare I say at times, fun. This study confirmed what my thousands of conversations with young people continue to illuminate: that therapeutic support is often too inflexible, too formal, too scripted and providing of far too few opportunities to express the emotional experience beyond words. I am advocating for a reconstituted framework that allows a more dynamic and pluralistic version of therapy that does not disregard traditional methods but acknowledges that times have changed, and practices now need to change too.

'Hard to Reach' has become a phrase ubiquitous with children and young people who are deemed by adults to be in need of, yet are resistant to support. To me, this language simply reinforces a myth that the "problem" of non-engagement is located within the young person whilst simultaneously denying them the agency to decide for themselves whether to access support or not. In doing that, alternative causes risk being overlooked. Perhaps therapeutic practice, approach, service offers and wider systems are what are actually "unreachable" and that the reasons for that go way beyond widely understood barriers such as access and self-stigma.

The phrase also implies that "professionals know best." Yet it is the individual, not the professional, who is the expert of a person's inner world.

Having immersed myself in the experiences of Buddy, Penny, Rose, Lily, Megan and Frankie, I sense that not one of them was ever truly unreachable. I find myself ruminating: "but what if counselling had looked different?" a faint hum of the "bee in my bonnet" still buzzing.

I hope that these stories have reached you. I hope you will tell others what you have heard. I hope together, we can strive to be within the reach of the many rather than the few.

★ Penny died in the early spring within 6 months of our interview. I will be forever grateful to her for so generously, thoughtfully, and openly sharing her experience of cancer. Penny will always symbolise to me the exceptional resilience of all young people who find themselves thrown into an ocean of uncertainty, navigating it in the best way they know how, with good days and with bad, often with humour and always with grace.

References

Barone, T., & Eisner, E. (2011). *Arts based research*. London: Sage.

Bastin, C., Harrison, B. J., Davey, C. G., Moll, J., & Whittle, S. (2016). Feelings of shame, embarrassment and guilt and their neural correlates: A systematic review. *Neuroscience & Biobehavioral Reviews, 71*, 455–471.

Carey, L. (2006). *Expressive and creative arts methods for trauma survivors*. Philadelphia, PA: Jessica Kingsley.

Compas, B., Jaser, S., Dunn, M., & Rodriguez, E. (2012). Coping with chronic illness in childhood and adolescence. *Annual Review of Clinical Psychology, 8*(1), 455–480. doi: 10.1146/annurev-clinpsy-032511-143108.

Cooper, M., & Dryden, W. (Eds) (2016). *The handbook of pluralistic counselling and psychotherapy*. London: Sage.

Crenshaw, D. (2006). Neuroscience and trauma treatment: Implications for creative arts therapists. In Carey, L. (Eds.), *Expressive and creative arts methods for trauma survivors* (pp. 21–39). Philadelphia, PA: Jessica Kingsley.

Denborough, D. (2014). *Retelling the stories of our lives: Everyday narrative therapy to draw inspiration and transform experience*. New York: W.W. Norton & Company.

Freake, H., Barley, V., & Kent, G. (2007). Adolescents' views of helping professionals: A review of the literature. *Journal of Adolescence, 30*, 639–653. doi: 10.1111/j.1467-9566.2007.01030.x.

Fuller, T. (2014). Working with the developmental tasks of adolescence in the secondary school years. In McLaughlin, C., & Holliday, C. (Eds.), *Therapy with children and young people integrative counselling in schools and other settings* (pp. 65–87). London: Sage.

Geldard, K., Geldard D., & Foo, R. (2019). *Counselling adolescents: The proactive approach for young people* (5th ed.). London: Sage.

Gulliver, A., Griffiths, K., & Christensen, H. (2010). Perceived barriers and facilitators to mental health help-seeking in young people: A systematic review. *BMC Psychiatry, 10*(1), 113. Retrieved from URL: https://bmcpsychiatry.biomedcentral.com/articles/10.1186/1471-244X-10-113

Havens, L. (1989). *A safe place. Laying the groundwork of psychotherapy.* London: Harvard University Press.

Herman, J. (1997). *Trauma and recovery.* New York: Basic Books.

Klein, M. (2002). *Love, guilt and reparation: and other works 1921–1945* (Vol. 1). New York: Simon and Schuster (Original work published 1975).

Kosir, U., Wiedemann, M., Wild, J., & Bowes, L. (2018). Psychiatric disorders among adolescent cancer survivors: A systematic review. *European Journal of Public Health*, 28 (Suppl4), 238–238. doi: 10.1093/eurpub/cky213.698.

Levine, P., & Kline, M. (2006). *Trauma through a child's eyes: Awakening the ordinary miracle of healing.* New York: North Atlantic Books.

Oaklander, V. (2007). *Hidden treasure: A map to the child's inner self.* London: Routledge.

Ogden, P. (2006). *Trauma and the body: A sensorimotor approach to psychotherapy.* New York: W. W. Norton & Company.

Perry B. D., & Dobson C. L. (2013). The neurosequential model of therapeutics. In J. D. Ford, & C. Courtois (Eds.), *Treating complex traumatic stress disorders in children and adolescents: Scientific foundations and therapeutic models* (pp. 249–260). New York: Guilford Press.

Portnoy, S., Girling, I., & Fredman, G. (2016). Supporting young people living with cancer to tell their stories in ways that make them stronger: The beads of life approach. *Clinical Child Psychology and Psychiatry*, 21(2), 255–267. doi: 10.1177/1359104515586467.

Smith, J., Flowers, P., & Larkin, M. (2009). *Interpretative phenomenological analysis: Theory, method and research.* London: Sage.

Spelman, M. B. (2013). *Winnicott's babies and Winnicott's patients* (1st ed.). London: Routledge.

Treisman, K. (2017). *A therapeutic treasure box for working with children and adolescents with developmental trauma.* London: Jessica Kingsley.

Van der Kolk, B. (2015). *The body keeps the score: Mind, brain and body in the transformation of trauma.* London: Penguin.

White, M. (2005). Children, trauma and subordinate storyline development. *International Journal of Narrative Therapy & Community Work*, 10–22. Retrieved from URL: https://dulwichcentre.com.au/product/children-trauma-and-subordinatestorylinedevelopment michaelwhite/#:~:text=In%20this%20paper%2C%20Michael%20White%20emphasises %20the%20importance,to%20give%20voice%20to%20their%20experiences%20of%20 trauma

Winnicott, D. W. (2007/1965). Communicating and not communicating leading to a study of certain opposites. *The maturational processes and the facilitating environment.* London: Karnac Books; Hogarth, 1965.

World Health Organization. (2013). *Guidelines for the management of conditions specifically related to stress.* Retrieved from URL: https://www.who.int/mental_health/emergencies/stress_guidelines/en/

Yuen, A. (2009). Less pain, more gain: Explorations of responses versus effects when working with the consequences of trauma. *Explorations: An E-Journal of Narrative Practice*, 1, 6–16. Retrieved from URL: http://www.dulwichcentre.com.au/explorations2009-1-angel-yuen.pdf

Zebrack, B., Kwak, M., Salsman, J., Cousino, M., Meeske, K., Aguilar, C., … & Cole, S. (2015). The relationship between posttraumatic stress and posttraumatic growth among adolescent and young adult (AYA) cancer patients. *Psycho-Oncology*, 24(2), 162–168.

Index

For Product Safety Concerns and Information please contact our EU
representative GPSR@taylorandfrancis.com Taylor & Francis Verlag GmbH,
Kaufingerstraße 24, 80331 München, Germany

Printed and bound by CPI Group (UK) Ltd, Croydon, CR0 4YY

08/06/2025

01897002-0012